About the Authors

Clara Vitorino teaches Spanish at the Catholic University in Lisbon, and has also worked as a translator. She has a Masters Degree in Modern French Literature and is currently completing a PhD degree on 17th century Portuguese and Spanish Literature.

AmeriConsulta, Lda. is a Lisbon-based company that provides educational, translating and editing services to clients worldwide. It's owned and managed by Paula Fassman, Stephanie Gettelfinger, and Audrey Un – Americans who have lived in Portugal for a number of years.

From the Authors

Our sincerest thanks go to Paulo Fassman Correia and Wendy Graça for the unselfish loan of their superior translating skills, Inês Vitorino for providing advice on transliteration problems and Claudio Silva, António Pascoal, Kyle Oliveira and Dionísio Martínez for their customarily unselfish moral support. Gems all.

From the Publisher

Patrick Marris illustrated and laid out both the book and cover. Natasha Velleley produced the map, Vicki Webb edited, and Karin Vidstrup Monk proofread.

D0250080

CONTENTS

6 Contents

PORTUGAL

Viana do Castelo
MINHO
Braga
DOURO
Porto

Bragança
TRÁS-OS-MONTES
Vila Real

Zamora

BEIRA ALTA

0 30 60 km

Aveiro
BEIRA LITORAL
Viseu
Guarda

Salamanca

Coimbra

BEIRA BAIXA

Leiria
Castelo Branco

ESTREMADURA

PORTUGAL

SPAIN

Santarém
RIBATEJO
Portalegre

LISBON
ALTO ALENTEJO
Badajoz

Setúbal
Évora

Beja
BAIXO ALENTEJO

ATLANTIC OCEAN

ALGARVE
Faro

STRAIT OF GIBRALTAR

Atlantic Ocean
France
Andorra Italy
Spain
Portugal
Mediterranean Sea
Morocco Algeria Tunisia

INTRODUCTION

Portuguese is a Romance language, which means it evolved from the Latin that was spoken by Roman settlers. Yet Portuguese, as we know it today, has also adopted a number of features from other languages it has come in contact with throughout the ages.

When the Romans invaded the part of the Iberian Peninsula that is now modern-day Portugal, they found a people who spoke a language that linguists conjecture was a variety of Celtic. Although the nature of that language is unknown today, it left recognisable traces, one of which is the word *ainda*, 'still' or 'yet'. However, the greatest influence on Portuguese, after Latin, was left by the Arabs who invaded Iberia in 711 AD and remained on the Peninsula until the 13th century. The Arabs contributed a host of words to the Portuguese lexicon, including *alcatifa*, 'carpet', *alcatrão*, 'tar' and *albornoz*, 'burnouse' (a hooded cloak).

Today, Portuguese is the official language of Portugal, Brazil and five African nations: Cape Verde, São Tomé and Principe, Guinea-Bissau, Angola and Mozambique. Portuguese is also commonly spoken in Asia in Macau and East Timor.

As former Portuguese colonies, all of these territories were once part of a vast empire that began in the 15th century, when the Portuguese began their maritime quest for a sea route to India. The search led the Portuguese to explore a vast expanse of coastal Africa, making them the first to round the treacherous Cape of Storms, which was later triumphantly redubbed by King João II as the Cape of Good Hope. The quest also led them to Brazil in 1500, which was, as the other territories, subsequently colonised.

While Brazil achieved independence in the 19th century, Portugal's former African colonies as well as the Indian territory of Goa and some of its Asian holdings were only decolonised in the second half of the 20th century. Macau, the last vestige of Portugal's once-sprawling empire, was returned to China at the end of 1999.

INTRODUCTION

This colourful era of navigation, exploration and colonisation, the heyday of Portugal's colonial power, is known as the *Descobrimentos*, 'the Discoveries'. Although it's been somewhat tarnished by the injustices and excesses usually associated with colonialism, it is the era the Portuguese are most proud of, and the period in history they consider their 'finest hour'.

Portuguese is spoken by nearly 200 million people worldwide, making it the third most spoken European language after English and Spanish. Brazil accounts for the majority, with 166 million speakers, while Portugal's 10 million inhabitants and the Portuguese-speaking nations in Africa make up the rest.

There are marked distinctions between European and Brazilian Portuguese. Aside from the immediately detectable difference in pronunciation (see page 18 for examples), there are also differences in vocabulary, spelling and grammar. Attempts have been made at standardising spelling, but the Portuguese and the Brazilians haven't been able to come up with a mutually acceptable agreement that would standardise Portuguese spelling throughout the world.

This book uses Portuguese as it's spoken in Portugal. Despite the differences between European and Brazilian Portuguese, nearly all of the phrases can be understood by Portuguese speakers throughout the world.

Worldwide, the importance of Portuguese promises to grow. Brazil is a founding member of Mercosur (or *Mercosul* in Portuguese), the organisation created to set up a free trade zone in South America. Portugal is a member of the European Union, Mercosur's largest foreign trade partner. Both countries hope that, as a result, Portuguese will soon be able to take its place as a major language of the international marketplace. Yet, even without the prospect of an economic boost, the Portuguese language shows signs of rapid expansion. Forecasts predict that the number of Portuguese speakers will reach 300 million by the year 2025.

The literature of this centuries-old world language has shone in several epochs throughout the course of history. In the 12th and 13th centuries, it predominated as the primary language of poetry in the whole of the Iberian Peninsula. It was the idiom used in the *Cantigas*, popular lyric poems, which were a favourite with the troubadours. Yet it was in the 16th century that Portugal's

INTRODUCTION

greatest work was penned – the *Lusíadas* by Luís de Camões. An epic poem of stunning breadth and grandeur, the *Lusíadas* celebrates Portugal's glory days of maritime discovery. It's considered by Portuguese speakers everywhere to be the most outstanding and enduring work in the Portuguese language.

Noteworthy Portuguese writers in later years have been novelists Eça de Queiroz and Camilo Castelo Branco in the 19th century, and in the 20th century, Fernando Pessoa, who is considered to be one of the most significant voices in contemporary world poetry. Currently, the novel is enjoying an upsurge, with writers such as José Cardoso Pires, António Lobo Antunes and José Saramago. Winner of the 1998 Nobel Prize for Literature, the first ever to be awarded for a work in the Portuguese language, Saramago is one of Portugal's most widely translated and best-selling authors.

As with any other people, the Portuguese are generally proud of their linguistic, historical and cultural heritage and thoroughly enjoy discussing their country's traditions, language and geography with any foreigner who shows even the slightest interest. However, with a history of over 800 years as a sovereign nation, which is one of the oldest in Europe, they're particularly sensitive to being confused with neighbouring Spain. And although most Portuguese understand Spanish, and can even speak a bit of it, they instantly warm to any person who makes even the clumsiest attempt to speak Portuguese.

The vocabulary and grammatical structure of European Portuguese will seem familiar to travellers who've studied other Romance languages – namely, Spanish, Italian and French. And in its written

INTRODUCTION

form, the language seems to be fairly decipherable to those with a good command of other Romance languages. The pronunciation, however, is much more complex, and often makes first contact with the language a frustrating experience for those expecting to be aided by their knowledge of Spanish or Italian. There's a tendency to reduce vowel sounds, which makes the language sound like a series of consonants in which 'zh' and 'sh' mysteriously seem to predominate. There are also a number of nasalised vowels and diphthongs. These two features in particular can make pronouncing and understanding the spoken word a challenge for the foreign visitor.

Plunging in, as always, is the most effective tactic for the timorous speaker. We suggest following the advice of one of Portugal's most beloved proverbs, which cautions *Quem não arrisca, não petisca* which, loosely translated, means, 'No risk, no reward'. Or more literally, for the survival-conscious traveller, 'He who doesn't take a risk, just doesn't get a meal'.

ARTHUR OR MARTHA?

In this book, the masculine form of a word appears first. The alternative feminine ending is separated by a slash.

lawyer	uhdvoogahdoo/uh	*advogado/a*

This indicates that the masculine form is *advogado*, while the feminine form is *advogada* (see Grammar, page 25, for an explanation of nouns and gender).
In cases where masculine and feminine forms follow a different pattern, both forms appear in full, separated by a slash.

farmer	uhgreekooltor/	*agricultor/*
	uhgreekooltoruh	*agricultora*

INTRODUCTION

ABBREVIATIONS USED IN THIS BOOK

adj	adjective
coll	colloquial
f	feminine
inf	informal
imp	imperfect (see Grammar page 33)
m	masculine
sg	singular
pl	plural
pol	polite

HOW TO USE THIS PHRASEBOOK
You Can Speak Another Language

It's true – anyone can speak another language. Don't worry if you haven't studied languages before, or that you studied a language at school for years and can't remember any of it. It doesn't even matter if you failed English grammar. After all, that's never affected your ability to speak English! And this is the key to picking up a language in another country. You don't need to sit down and memorise endless grammatical details and you don't need to memorise long lists of vocabulary. You just need to start speaking. Once you start, you'll be amazed how many prompts you'll get to help you build on those first words. You'll hear people speaking, pick up sounds from TV, catch a word or two that you think you know from the local radio, see something on a billboard – all these things help to build your understanding.

Plunge In

There's just one thing you need to start speaking another language – courage. Your biggest hurdle is overcoming the fear of saying aloud what may seem to you to be just a bunch of sounds.

The best way to start overcoming your fear is to memorise a few key words. These are the words you know you'll be saying again and again, like 'hello', 'thank you' and 'how much?'. Here's an important hint though – right from the beginning, learn at least one phrase that will be useful but not essential. Such as 'good morning' or 'good afternoon', 'see you later' or even a conversational piece like 'lovely day, isn't it?' or 'it's cold today' (people everywhere love to talk about the weather). Having this extra phrase (just start with one, if you like, and learn to say it really well) will enable you to move away from the basics, and when you get a reply and a smile, it'll also boost your confidence. You'll find that people you speak to will like it too, as they'll understand that at least you've tried to learn more of the language than just the usual essential words.

Ways to Remember

There are several ways to learn a language. Most people find they learn from a variety of these, although people usually have a preferred way to remember. Some like to see the written word and remember the sound from what they see. Some like to just hear it spoken in context (if this is you, try talking to yourself in Portuguese, but do it in the car or somewhere private, to give yourself confidence, and so others don't wonder about your sanity!). Others, especially the more mathematically inclined, like to analyse the grammar of a language, and piece together words according to grammar rules. The very visually inclined like to associate the written word and even sounds with some visual stimulus, such as illustrations, TV and general things they see in the street. As you learn, you'll discover what works best for you – be aware of what made you really remember a particular word, and if it sticks in your mind, keep using that method.

Kicking Off

Chances are you'll want to learn some of the language before you go. The first thing to do is to memorise those essential phrases and words. Check out the basics (page 45) ... and don't forget that extra phrase (see Plunge In!). Try the sections on making conversation or greeting people for a phrase you'd like to use.

Write some of these words down on a separate piece of paper and stick them up around the place. On the fridge, by the bed, on your computer, as a bookmark – somewhere where you'll see them often. Try putting some words in context – the 'How much is it?' note, for instance, could go in your wallet.

Building the Picture

We include a chapter on grammar in our books for two reasons.

Firstly, some people have an aptitude for grammar and find understanding it a key tool to their learning. If you're such a person, then the grammar chapter will help you build a picture of the language, as it works through all the basics.

The second reason for the grammar chapter is that it gives answers to questions you might raise as you hear or memorise some key phrases. You may find a particular word is always used when there is a question – check out the grammar heading on questions and it should explain why. This way you don't have to read the grammar chapter from start to finish, nor do you need to memorise a grammatical point. It will simply present itself to you in the course of your learning. Key grammatical points are repeated throughout the book.

Any Questions?

Try to learn the main question words (see page 39). As you read through different situations, you'll see these words used in the example sentences, and this will help you remember them. So if you want to hire a bicycle, turn to the Bicycles section in Getting Around (use the Contents or Index pages to find it quickly). You've already tried to memorise the word for 'where' and you'll see the word for 'bicycle'. When you come across the sentence 'Where can I hire a bicycle?', you'll recognise the key words and this will help you remember the whole phrase. If there's no category for your need, try the dictionary (the question words are repeated there too, with examples), and memorise the phrases 'Please write

INTRODUCTION

it down' and 'How do you say ...?' (see page 58).

I've Got a Flat Tyre

Doesn't seem like the phrase you're going to need? Well in fact, it could be very useful. As are all the phrases in this book, provided you have the courage to mix and match them. We have given specific examples within each section. But the key words remain the same even when the situation changes. So while you may not be planning on any cycling during your trip, the first part of the phrase 'I've got ...' could refer to anything else, and there are plenty of words in the dictionary that, we hope, will fit your needs. So whether it's 'a ticket', 'a visa' or 'a condom', you'll be able to put the words together to convey your meaning.

Finally

Don't be concerned if you feel you can't memorise words. On the inside front and back covers are the most essential words and phrases. You could also try tagging a few pages for other key phrases, or use the notes pages to write your own reminders.

PRONUNCIATION

Portuguese has the most complex system of pronunciation of all the Romance languages. Many letters have alternative pronunciations, depending on their position in a word or phrase. Because it has many muted vowels and 'sh' and 'zh' sounds, one startled tourist was said to have remarked that it sounded like 'a drunken Frenchman trying to speak Spanish.' However, most often visitors say that it sounds Slavic.

In spite of its complexity, the pronunciation of Portuguese is quite regular and most sounds aren't difficult for English speakers to produce, although the nasal sounds require a bit of practice.

Three of the accent marks can be keys to better pronunciation. The acute accent (´) and the grave accent (`) signify that a vowel is open, and are pronounced with your mouth opened a little more. The circumflex (^) signals a closed vowel, made with the mouth a bit more closed.

TRANSLITERATION SYSTEM

To help you understand the relationship between the letters and their corresponding sounds, a simple phonetic transliteration has been given throughout this book. Since Portuguese has several letters with special markings not found in English, the transliteration should help you become comfortable speaking Portuguese. All transliterations are given in green.

At times you'll see up to three identical vowels in a row in the transliterations in this book. A hyphen is used to separate these vowels to indicate when a new syllable begins.

| alcoholic | ahlkoo-ohleekoo | *alcoólico* |

When identical consonants appear together, a hyphen indicates that they have different sounds.

| language | ling-gwuh | *língua* |

PRONUNCIATION

BRAZILIAN PORTUGUESE

The variety of vowel sounds in European Portuguese distinguishes it from Brazilian Portuguese, which has fewer vowel sounds and predominantly open vowels, making them easier to recognise.

When 'e' appears at the end of a word, it's nearly inaudible in European Portuguese, but pronounced as 'ee' after the letters 't' or 'd' in Brazil.

	Brazil	Portugal	
excellent	eshelengtshee	shelengt	*excelente*

In Brazil, the 'o' is usually pronounced as it looks – as in 'hot', while in Portugal, the unstressed 'o' takes on an 'oo' sound.

	Brazil	Portugal	
desert	dezerto	dzehrtoo	*deserto*

When it comes to consonants, there are many striking differences between European and Brazilian Portuguese. In Brazil, when 'd' is followed by an 'i' – as in *dividir*, 'to divide' – or is at the end of a word followed by an 'e' – as in *liberdade*, 'liberty' – the 'd' is pronounced as if it were an English 'j'. A 't' followed by an 'i' as in *tia*, 'aunt', or by an 'e' at the end of a word as in *sabonete*, 'soap', is pronounced as the 'ch' in 'chair'.

A final 'l' often has a muted 'u' sound. When 's' appears at the end of a phrase or before *p, t, c(k)* or *f*, it's much less likely to be pronounced as 'sh' in Brazil as it is in Portugal.

Stress also differs markedly between the two countries. Like English, European Portuguese is a stress-timed language, where certain words or syllables in a phrase are given more stress, while others practically disappear.

Brazilian Portuguese is syllable-timed, which is more like Spanish. This partly accounts for the difference in the overall sound of the two versions. In Portugal, when someone says:

Como é que se diz ...?
  komoo ali kê se deesh ...?
  How do you say ...?

you may only hear something like 'k'meks deesh?'.

PRONUNCIATION

VOWELS

To the visitor, Portuguese can sound like a long succession of consonants with no vowels except a conspicuous nasalised *ão* sound at the end of certain words. You can be sure, though, that there *are* vowels and that most of them have more than one pronunciation.

Portuguese letters are given on the left, while transliterations are given in green on the right.

a (stressed, open)	ah	as the 'a' in 'father'
a (stressed, closed; unstressed)	uh	as the 'u' in 'cut'
e (stressed, open)	eh	as the 'e' in 'bet'
e (stressed, closed)	e	as the 'e' in 'berry'
e (unstressed)		barely perceptible in speech, and not represented in the transliterations
i	ee	as the 'ee' in 'see'
o (stressed, open)	oh	as the 'o' in 'hot'
o (stressed, closed)	o	as the 'o' in 'port'
o (unstressed)	oo	as the 'oo' in 'too'
u	oo	as the 'oo' in 'too'

PRONUNCIATION

Diphthongs

Sometimes two vowel sounds are combined in the same syllable.

ai	ai	as the 'y' in 'fly'
au	ow	as the 'ow' in 'now'
ei	ay	as the 'ay' in 'day'
eu	e-w	as the 'e' in 'bet' + the 'oo' in 'too'
oi	oy	as the 'oy' in 'boy', but shorter
ua	wa	as the 'w' in 'what' + the 'a' in 'far'
ue	we	as the 'whe' in 'when'
uo	wo	as the 'wo' in 'wobble'
ui	wi	as the word 'we'

Nasal Vowels

When a vowel is followed by *n* or *m*, or is marked with a tilde (~), the vowel is nasal. Imagining an 'ng' at the end of the syllable, as in the word 'sing', can help you make this nasal sound. Remember, though, that the 'g' isn't actually pronounced.

M & N's

At the end of a word or syllable, the consonants *m* and *n* often cause a preceding vowel to become nasalised.

ã/an	ang	as the 'an' in 'fan' + 'ng'
em/en	eng	as the 'e' in 'bet' + 'ng'
im/in	ing	as the 'ee' in 'see' + 'ng'
õ/om/on	ong	as the 'o' in 'bone' + 'ng'
um/un	oong	as the 'oo' in 'too' + 'ng'

Nasal Diphthongs

Almost all transliterations of diphthongs include a 'w' or 'y', depending on the sound. A very common word, *muito*, 'much/very', is pronounced as a nasal diphthong, even though the letter combination 'ui' isn't normally nasalised.

ão	õw	as the 'oun' in 'ounce'
am	õw	like ão, but unstressed
ãe/em/en	ãy	at the end of a word, as the 'i' in 'wine' + 'ng'
õe	õy	as the 'oy' in 'boy' + 'ng'

CONSONANTS

The pronunciation of many consonants is the same as in English, but there are a few you should learn.

In some regions of Portugal, when r appears at the start of a word it's slightly rolled, while rr is rolled more strongly.

c	k	as the 'k' in 'kite' before *a*, *o* and *u*; as the 's' in 'sin' before *e* and *i*
ç	s	as the 'c' in 'celery'. This letter's known as 'c-cedilha'.
ch	sh	as the 'sh' in 'ship'
g	g	as the 'g' in 'game' before *a*, *o*, and *u*
	zh	as the 's' in 'pleasure' before *e* and *i*
h		always silent
j	zh	as the 's' in 'pleasure'
lh	ly	as the 'li' in 'million'
nh	ny	as the 'ny' in 'canyon'
qu	k	as the 'k' in 'kite' before *e* or *i*
	kw	as the 'qu' in 'quit' before *a* or *o*
r	rr	at the beginning of a word or when written as *rr*, this is a very guttural, raspy sound;
	r	elsewhere, as the 'tt' in 'butter' when pronounced quickly
s	s	as the 's' in 'sin' at the beginning of a word or when written as *ss*
	sh	as the 'sh' in 'ship' at the end of a phrase or before *p*, *t*, *c(k)*, or *f*
	z	between vowels, as the 'z' in 'zebra'
	zh	as the 's' in 'pleasure' before *b*, *d*, *g*, *m*, *n* or *r x*
	z	after *e*, when followed by any other vowel, as the 'z' in 'zebra';
	sh	elsewhere, as the 'sh' in 'ship'
z	zh	as the 's' in 'pleasure' at the end of a word or phrase
	z	as the 'z' in 'zebra' between two vowels

PRONUNCIATION

PRONUNCIATION

In a few Portuguese words, such as *próxima*, the consonant *x* sounds like the 'x' in 'axe', and is represented in the transliterations as ks.

In still fewer words, it sounds like the 's' in 'sin', and is represented as s.

STRESS

Stress falls on a syllable which contains a vowel marked with an acute accent (´) or a circumflex (ˆ). The grave accent (`) shows a contraction of two *a*'s (see Grammar page 43) – it doesn't show stress.

	Saturday	*sah*buhdoo	*sá*bado
	shampoo	shang*po*	cham*pô*
but ...			
	that one	ah*kel*	à*que*le

ABBREVIATIONS

Av	Avenida	Avenue
BI	Bilhete de Identidade	National Identity Card
Dr/Dra	Doutor/Doutora	Doctor
Lda	Limitada	Limited
Lx	Lisboa	Lisbon
Pr	Praça	Square/Plaza
PS	post scriptum	PS (postscript)
R	rua	Street
r/c	rés-do-chão	ground floor
RTP	Radiotelevisão Portuguesa	Portuguese National Television
Sr/Sra	Senhor/Senhora	Mr/Mrs or Ms
Tel	telefone	Telephone

If a word contains both an acute accent (´) and a tilde (~), stress falls on the vowel with the accent. Otherwise, the vowel with the tilde is stressed.

| attic | sohtõw | sótão |

Words with no accent, that end in *m*, *s* or the vowels *a*, *e* or *o*, are stressed on the second-last syllable.

man	ohmãy	*ho*mem
pastries	boloosh	*bo*los
phone call	tlefoo*ne*muh	telefo*ne*ma

When a word ends in two vowels which have no accent marks, stress falls on the syllable containing the second-last vowel.

| cold | freeoo | *fri*o |
| he/she left | puhr*tee*oo | par*ti*u |

When a word ends in three vowels which have no accent marks, the first two vowels form a diphthong – a vowel sound made up of two vowels – and stress falls on that syllable.

| beach | *prai*uh | *prai*a |
| idea | ee*da*yuh | i*dei*a |

Words ending in *i*, *im*, *l*, *r*, *z*, *u* or *um* are always stressed on the last syllable.

| to sleep | door*meer* | dor*mir* |
| poster | kuhr*tahsh* | car*taz* |

PRONUNCIATION

DID YOU KNOW ...

Portuguese and the language spoken in Galicia in Spain belong to the same language group. Known as *galaico-* or *galego-português*, the language evolved from Latin Vulgate and was once the predominant idiom throughout the whole western strip of the Iberian Peninsula.

Although it has largely been subsumed by Castilian Spanish, the *galego* language is still spoken in many Galician households and is being jointly promoted by Galician and Portuguese authorities eager to revive their common linguistic heritage.

GRAMMAR

This chapter is designed to give an idea of how Portuguese phrases are built, and provide the basic rules to constructing sentences.

WORD ORDER

Portuguese word order is fairly flexible but in general, the same subject-verb-object word order used in English is followed.

António is at the airport. O António está no aeroporto.
(lit: the António he-is in-the airport)

NOUNS
Gender

Portuguese has two gender forms: the masculine and the feminine. It's usually easy to tell the gender of a word by looking at its ending. Words ending in-o are nearly always masculine, and words ending in-a nearly always feminine.

uncle	tio	aunt	tia

Plurals

Plurals are usually formed by adding -s to a noun that ends in a vowel, and -es to a noun that ends in a consonant.

house	casa	houses	casas
boy	rapaz	boys	rapazes

ARTICLES

In Portuguese, the articles 'a/an/the' reflect both gender and number. Articles are also used before a person's name and before possessive pronouns.

Antonio	O António	(lit: the António)
my house	a minha casa	(lit: the my house)
my shoes	os meus sapatos	(lit: the my shoes)

Feminine			
a house	uma casa	some houses	umas casas
the house	a casa	the houses	as casas

Masculine			
a plane	um avião	some planes	uns aviões
the plane	o avião	the planes	os aviões

ADJECTIVES & ADVERBS
Adjectives

Generally, adjectives follow the same rules that apply to nouns. They have the same types of endings and change, as nouns do, in gender and number. They nearly always follow the noun they modify and must agree with it in gender and number.

She's a clever girl.	É uma rapariga esperta.
	(lit: she-is a girl clever)
The beaches are clean.	As praias são limpas.
	(lit: the beaches they-are clean)

Most adjectives ending in -e take the same form when used with both masculine and feminine nouns.

a tolerant man	um homem tolerante
a tolerant woman	uma mulher tolerante

Adverbs

Simple adverbs are formed by adding -mente to the feminine singular form of the adjective.

clear	clara	clearly	claramente
slow	lenta	slowly	lentamente

Intensifiers

The ending a -íssimo/os/a/as can be added to intensify an adjective or adverb to imply *very* or *extremely*.

GRAMMAR

| The museum is very, very interesting. | O museu é interessantíssimo. (lit: the museum it-is very-interesting) |

Comparatives

as ... as	more ... than
tão ... como	mais ... do que

| as quickly as | tão rapidamente como |
| taller than | mais alto do que (lit: more tall than) |

| She runs as quickly as he does. | Ela corre tão rapidamente como ele. (lit: she she-runs as quickly as he) |

Superlatives

the most ...	
o/os/a/as noun(s) mais (adjective)	
(lit: the ... more ...)	

| the richest man | o homem mais rico (lit: the man more rich) |
| They're the cheapest shirts. | São as camisas mais baratas. (lit: they-are the shirts more cheap) |

PRONOUNS
Subject Pronouns

In Portuguese, subject pronouns aren't used nearly as much as in English, since the way the verb is conjugated – along with the context of the sentence – will usually tell you who or what the subject is. The subject pronoun is used, however, for emphasis or when there is ambiguity.

SUBJECT PRONOUNS

I	eu	we	nós
you (inf)	tu	they (m; m+f)	eles
you (pol)	você	they (f)	elas
he/it	ele		
she/it	ela		

Direct & Indirect Object Pronouns

The direct object indicates what or who the verb refers to, as in 'he hit **me**', while the indirect object refers to the recipient, as in 'he gave the present to **me**'.

	Direct Object	Indirect Object
me	me	me
you (inf)	te	te
you (pol)	o/a	lhe
him/her/it	o/a	lhe
us	nos	nos
them	os/as	lhes

Notice that objects are separated from the verb with a hyphen.

I saw them yesterday.   Vi-os ontem.
                                           (lit: I-saw–them yesterday)

Prepositional Pronouns

Prepositional pronouns are the form of the pronoun used after a preposition.

me	mim	for me	para mim
you	ti	without you	sem ti
him/her/you	ele/ela/você	with her	com ela
you (m, pol)	o senhor	for you	para o senhor
you (f, pol)	a senhora	for you	para o senhora
us	nós	of/from us	de nós
them (m; m+f)	eles/elas	by/for them	por eles/elas

Certain objects also change if they follow the preposition com, 'with':

with me	comigo	with us	connosco
with you (inf)	contigo	with you (pl)	consigo
with you (pol)	consigo		

When the direct objects o, a, os and as are coupled with an indirect object, the two objects are often contracted.

He sold it to me.	Vendeu-ma. (me + a)
	(lit: he-sold–me-it)

DIMINUTIVES

The diminutive is widely used in Portuguese, and can give a number of nuances to nouns, proper nouns, adjectives, adverbs and adverbials. Depending on context, diminutives can convey affection, small size, irony or condescension. Less often, they're used to convey disdain.

When a word ends in an unstressed -o or -a, the ending is replaced by -inho, -inha, -inhos or -inhas.

dedo	finger	dedinho
bonita	pretty	bonitinha

With words ending in a consonant or an accented vowel, -zinho, -zinha, -zinhos or -zinhas is added to the end of the word.

mãe	mother	mãezinha
café	coffee	cafézinho
animal	animal	animalzinho
Adeus!	Bye!	Adeuzinho!

GRAMMAR

POSSESSION
Possessive Pronouns & Adjectives

Possessive pronouns are identical in form to possessive adjectives. Note that in Portugal the possessive adjective is almost *always* preceded by the definite article, while in Brazil it's virtually *never* preceded by the definite article.

Singular	(m)	(f)
my/mine	o meu	a minha
your/yours (inf)	o teu	a tua
your/yours (pol)	o seu	a sua
his/her/hers/its	o seu	a sua
our/ours	o nosso	a nossa
their/theirs	o seu; deles	a sua; delas

Plural	(m)	(f)
my/mine	os meus	as minhas
your/yours (inf)	os teus	as tuas
your/yours (pol)	os seus	as suas
his/her/hers/its	os seus	as suas
our/ours	os nossos	as nossas
their/theirs	os seus; deles	as suas; delas

Your (pol) address.   A sua morada.
                       (lit: the your address)

VERBS

Portuguese regular verbs usually fall into three distinct categories, based on the ending of the verb.

-ar	falar	to speak
-er	comer	to eat
-ir	abrir	to open

By removing these endings, you're left with what's called a *stem*, which, in the cases of the verbs mentioned above, would be fal-, com-, abr-. To conjugate and change the tenses of the verbs in these three categories, standard endings are added to the stems.

GRAMMAR

Present Tense

1) The **present tense** is used for actions or states that exist habitually or at the time you're speaking.

	-ar	-er	-ir
I	falo	como	abro
you (inf)	falas	comes	abres
you (pol)	fala	come	abre
he/she/it	fala	come	abre
we	falamos	comemos	abrimos
you (pl); they	falam	comem	abrem

I speak English. Falo inglês.
  (lit. I-speak English)

KEY VERBS

to be able (can)	poder; ser capaz de	to know (something)	saber
to agree	concordar	to like	gostar
to be	ser/estar	to make	fazer
to bring	trazer	to meet	encontrar-se com
to come	vir		
to cost	custar	to need	precisar de
to depart (leave)	partir	to prefer	preferir
to do	fazer	to return	voltar
to go	ir	to say	dizer
to have	ter	to see	ver
to know (someone)	conhecer	to stay	ficar
		to take	tomar
		to understand	entender
		to want	querer

GRAMMAR

In Portuguese, the present tense is also often used when we'd use the future tense or the present perfect tense in English.

I'll phone you tomorrow.
　Telefono-te amanhã.
　(lit: I-telephone–you tomorrow)

She has lived in Lisbon a long time.
　Ela mora em Lisboa há muito tempo.
　(lit: she she-lives in Lisbon there-is much time)

2) The **present continuous** is used to express an action or state occurring at the very moment you're speaking, which is expressed in English as 'am speaking' or 'are doing'. In Portuguese, the present continuous is formed by using a conjugated form of the verb estar, 'to be', together with the preposition a plus an infinitive.

PRESENT CONTINUOUS
estar + a + infinitive

It's raining.　　　　　　Está a chover.
　　　　　　　　　　　　(lit: it-is to to-rain)

Past Tense

1) The **preterite** refers to an action or state that had a clearly marked beginning and end in the recent or distant past. It's used virtually the same way we use the simple past tense in English.

	-ar	-er	-ir
I	falei	comi	abri
you (fam)	falaste	comeste	abriste
you (pol)	falou	comeu	abriu
he/she/it	falou	comeu	abriu
we	falámos	comemos	abrimos
you (pl); they	falaram	comeram	abriram

They spoke to me yesterday.   Falaram comigo ontem.
(lit: they-spoke with-me
yesterday)

2) The **imperfect** is used for actions or states that were repeated or continued for an indefinite period of time in the past. This is often expressed in English by the expression 'used to …'.

	-ar	-er	-ir
I	falava	comia	abria
you	falavas	comias	abrias
you (pol)	falava	comia	abria
he/she/it	falava	comia	abria
we	falávamos	comíamos	abríamos
you (pl); they	falavam	comiam	abriam

He used to talk a lot in class.   Falava muito nas aulas.
(lit: he-talk-IMP much
in-the classes)

The imperfect is also used as a polite way of expressing a request or desire, much as we would use the modals 'could' or 'would' in English.

Could you bring me a   Trazia-me uma
sandwich, please?   sandes, faz favor?
(lit: bring-IMP–me a
sandwich, do favour)

Future Tense

Although Portuguese has a simple future tense, it's practically never used in conversation. The future is usually expressed by using the present tense of the verb ir, 'to go', plus the infinitive of the main verb. In English, this is expressed as 'going to ...'.

ir 'to go' (Present Tense)			
I	vou	he/she/it	vai
you (inf)	vais	we	vamos
you (pol)	vai	you (pl); they	vão

He's going to buy the tickets. Ele vai comprar os bilhetes.
(lit: he he-goes
to-buy the tickets)

Subjunctive Tense

The subjunctive is often used, usually in the present and imperfect. The subjunctive conveys – among other states – desire, possibility, opinion and doubt. It often appears after the verb querer, 'to want', and is frequently used when giving commands.

	-ar	-er	-ir
I	fale	coma	abra
you (sg, inf)	fales	comas	abras
you (sg, pol)	fale	coma	abra
he/she/it	fale	coma	abra
we	falemos	comamos	abramos
you (pl); they	falem	comam	abram

They want us to   Querem que
speak Portuguese.   falemos português.
(lit: they-want that
we-speak Portuguese)

KEY VERBS
Conjugated

ser (to be)

past participle (ter) sido

	present	simple past	imperfect past	future
I	sou	fui	era	serei
you	és	foste	eras	serás
he/she/it	é	foi	era	será
we	somos	fomos	éramos	seremos
you/they	são	foram	eram	serão

estar (to be)

past participle (ter) estado

	present	simple past	imperfect past	future
I	estou	estive	estava	estarei
you	estás	estiveste	estavas	estarás
he/she/it	está	esteve	estava	estará
we	estamos	estivemos	estávamos	estaremos
you/they	estão	estiveram	estavam	estarão

poder (to be able)

past participle (ter) podido

	present	simple past	imperfect past	future
I	posso	pude	podia	poderei
you	podes	pudeste	podias	poderás
he/she/it	pode	pôde	podia	poderá
we	podemos	pudemos	podíamos	poderemos
you/they	podem	puderam	podiam	poderão

ir (to go)

past participle (ter) ido

	present	simple past	imperfect past	future
I	vou	fui	ia	irei
you	vais	foste	ias	irás
he/she/it	vai	foi	ia	irá
we	vamos	fomos	íamos	iremos
you/they	vão	foram	iam	irão

ter (to have)

past participle (ter) tido

	present	simple past	imperfect past	future
I	tenho	tive	tinha	terei
you	tens	tiveste	tinhas	terás
he/she/it	tem	teve	tinha	terá
we	temos	tivemos	tínhamos	teremos
you/they	têm	tiveram	tinham	terão

GRAMMAR

TO BE
The verb 'to be' can take two forms in Portuguese: ser or estar.

Ser
Ser is used when speaking about permanent characteristics. It's also used when talking about time, dates, permanent location origin, marital status and professions.

> **TO BE**
>
> Many expressions that use the verb 'to be' in English are expressed in Portuguese with the verb ter, 'to have' (see page 37).

SER			
I am	sou	we are	somos
you (sg, inf) are	és	you (pl)	são
you (sg, pol) are	é	they are	são
he/she/it is	é		

They are tall.   São altos.
                        (lit: they-are tall)

Estar
The verb estar is used for characteristics or states that are temporary. It's also the form of the verb 'to be' that's used when talking about the weather, the whereabouts of someone or something, or states of mind and feelings you're having at the moment.

ESTAR			
I am	estou	we are	estamos
you are (sg, inf)	estás	you (pl) are	estão
you are (sg, pol)	está	they are	estão
he/she/it is	está		

It's cold.   Está frio.
                    (lit: it-is cold)

GRAMMAR

TO HAVE

There are two forms of 'have' in Portuguese: haver and ter. The verb haver is most commonly used as the auxiliary to the main verb in compound tenses. However, when used in the third person singular, it means 'there is' or 'there are'.

There is fruit in the market.　　Há fruta no mercado.
　　　　　　　　　　　　　　(lit: there-is fruit at-the-market)

There are no more seats.　　　Não há mais lugares.
　　　　　　　　　　　　　　(lit: no there-are more seats)

FALSE FRIENDS

The word	looks like it means ...	but really means ...
actual	actual	current
aniversário	anniversary	birthday
argumento	argument	plot; story line
assaltar	assault	to rob
assistir	to assist	to attend
cigarros	cigars	cigarettes
constipação	constipation	a cold
diário	diary	daily
discussão	discussion	argument
educado	educated	polite
em frente	in front of	across the street
gabinete	cabinet	office
jornal	journal	newspaper
largo	large	wide
livraria	library	bookshop
móveis	movies	furniture
ordinário	ordinary	crass/vulgar
pretender	to pretend	to intend/plan
puxe	push	pull
realizar	to realise	to carry out
sensível	sensible	sensitive
tentar	to attempt	to try
vulgar	vulgar	ordinary/common

GRAMMAR

Ter, 'to have', usually indicates possession.

I have	tenho	we have	temos
you have (sg, inf)	tens	you (pl) have	têm
you (sg, pol)	tem	they have	têm
he/she/it has	tem		

I have a flight at eight o'clock.   Tenho um voo às oito.
(lit: I-have a flight at eight)

A lot of English expressions that use the verb 'to be' are expressed in Portuguese with the verb ter, 'to have' (see pages 54 and 56 in Meeting People).

QUESTIONS

As with English, you can often tell a sentence is a question because of a rise in the speaker's intonation. To create yes/no questions in Portuguese, use the simple declarative form of a sentence and raise the intonation at the end.

Do you (inf) like the food?   Gostas da comida?
(lit: you-(inf)-like of-the food?)

The answer to a yes/no question in Portuguese is usually not just 'yes', sim, or 'no', não, but the conjugated form of the verb used in the question.

Are you taking a picture?   Está a tirar uma fotografia?
(lit: you-(pol)-are to to-take a photograph?)

I am (not).   (Não) estou. (lit: (no) I-am)

Question Words

When there's a question word such as onde, 'where' or quando, 'when' the subject appears after the verb.

How much does   Quanto custa este postal?
this postcard cost?   (lit: how-much it-costs
                        this postcard?)

However, it's very common to insert the phrase é que , 'is it that',
between the question word and the rest of the sentence. Although
you'll hear most Portuguese people using it to form questions in
more formal situations, the é que phrase is by no means obliga-
tory and a question is considered correct without it.

When does the plane arrive?   Quando (é que) chega o avião?
                              (lit: when (it-is that) it-arrives
                              the plane?)

Question Words	Palavras Interrogativas
Where	Onde?
(From) where?	Donde; De onde?
When?	Quando?
What?	O quê?
How?	Como?
Who(m)?	Quem?
Which/What?	Qual (sg)/Quais (pl)?
Why?	Porque (é que)?
How much?	Quanto?
How many?	Quanto/a/os/us?

NEGATIVES

Generally, the negative in Portuguese is formed simply by putting
não, 'no', before the main verb:

I don't want to walk any more.   Não quero andar mais.
                                 (lit: no I-want to-walk more)

As with other Latin-based languages, the double negative isn't only acceptable, but correct.

| I can't see anything. | Não vejo nada. |
| | (lit: no I-see nothing) |

NEGATIVE WORDS			
no	não	nobody	ninguém
none (sg)	nenhum/a (m/f)	not	não
none (pl)	nenhuns (m) /	nothing	nada
	nenhumas (f)	neither	nem
never	nunca	nor	nem

MODALS
Must/Have To/Need To

Need or obligation is expressed by the verb ter, 'to have', followed by que or de plus the infinitive. You'll also often hear the verb precisar, 'to need', followed by de plus the main verb in the infinitive.

I have/need to buy a	Preciso de comprar uma
souvenir for my cousin.	recordação para a minha prima.
	(lit: I-have/need-to of to-buy a
	souvenir for the my cousin)

Can/To Be Able

The verb poder, 'to be able', is used to express both 'can' and 'be able'. It's also used for asking permission.

I can eat all kinds of food.	Posso comer todo o
	género de comida.
	(lit: I-can to-eat all the
	type of food)
May I sit down?	Posso sentar-me?
	(lit: I-can to-sit-down—me?)

GRAMMAR

THE THREE P'S

In spoken Portuguese, you'll often hear three expressions that often mystify the beginning language learner.

pode ser

(lit: can be) pronounced as *potser*. This expression stands in for *sim* as a more non-committal way of saying 'yes'.

Quer outra bebida?
Do you want another drink?

Pode ser.
Yes (but I'm not wildly enthusiastic and I'm sort of doing you a favour and being polite by accepting. Or, now that you mention it, it sounds like a good idea).

pois (pois)

(lit: well) pronounced *poish*. This is what most catches the traveller's ear and means everything from 'uh-huh' to 'yes, you're right', to 'I'm still listening attentively though you've been rambling on for half an hour'. With the appropriate ironic intonation, it can also mean 'in a pig's eye!'

pá

an empty interjection that can crop up in every sentence. It's used to emphasise what the speaker's saying, and often to give the speaker time to think, much as 'um' or 'ah' does in English. It's almost exclusively used by men and, when over-used, gives a feeling of 'tough guy talk' to what the speaker is saying.

Eh pá, ó João, pá. Onde vais, pá?
(lit: hey pá, the João, pá to-where you-go, pá)
    Hey, João. Where are you goin'?

To Like

The verb gostar, 'to like', is followed by de and a noun or the main verb in its infinitive form when talking about a certain thing or activity.

I like to travel.   Gosto de viajar.
                                     (lit: I-like of to-travel)

PREPOSITIONS

Though most prepositions don't change in form, there are four that always contract with the article in spoken Portuguese. These four prepositions are:

de	of/from	em	in/on
por	by/for	a	to

1) When the preposition de, 'of/from', contracts with an article, the e is dropped.

de + o = do   de + a = da
de + os = dos   de + as = das

It's not far from the beaches.   Não é longe das (de+as) praias.
                                    (lit: no it-is far from-the beaches)

De also contracts with the indefinite articles um, uma, uns and umas

    de + um = dum

2) When the preposition em, 'in/on', is combined with an article, it becomes n.

em + o = no	em + os = nos
em + a = na	em + as = nas

There are flowers in the rooms.

Há flores nos (em+os) quartos. (lit: there are flowers in-the rooms)

Em also contracts with the indefinite articles um, uma, uns and umas

    em + uns = nuns

3) When combined with a definite article, por, 'by', changes to pel.

por + o = pelo	por + os = pelos
por + a = pela	por + as = pelas

It was made by the girls.

Foi feito pelas (por+as) meninas. (lit: it-was made by-the girls)

4) When combined with a definite article, or the demonstrative aquele/a, aqueles/aquelas, the preposition a, 'to/at', has the following forms:

a + o = ao	a + os = aos
a + a = à	a + as = às

I went to the cinema.

Fui ao cinema. (lit: I-went to-the cinema)

The demonstratives este, esse and aquele also undergo these changes.

```
de + este    = deste       em + este    = neste
de + esse    = desse       em + esse    = nesse
de + aquele  = daquele     em + aquele  = naquele
```

Remember that the preposition com, 'with', also has several contracted forms (see page 29).

Prepositions			
at	a	on	em
between	entre	over	por cima de
by	por	to	a/para
for	para	until	até
from	de	under	debaixo de
in	em	with	com
of	de	without	sem

GRAMMAR

MEETING PEOPLE

CONHECER PESSOAS

In a first encounter, no matter what the age of the people involved, the Portuguese shake hands and address each other using the polite forms of both pronouns (see page 28) and verbs (see page 30).

After greeting, acquaintances will usually ask 'How are you?', expecting a quick response like 'fine, thanks'.

YOU SHOULD KNOW

DEVE SABER

These are the essential expressions for greeting, apologising, getting someone's attention or saying 'thank you'.

Hello/Hi.	ohlah!	*Olá!*
Goodbye.	uhde-wsh!/tshow!	*Adeus!/Ciao!*
Yes.	sing	*Sim.*
No.	nõw	*Não.*
Please.	(se) fahsh fuhvor	*(Se) faz favor.*
Thank you.	obreegahdoo/uh	*Obrigado/a.*

Many thanks.
    mwingtoo ohbreegahdoo/uh   *Muito obrigado/a.*
You're welcome.
    de nahduh; nõw tãy de ke   *De nada; Não tem de quê.*
Excuse me. (to interrupt someone)
    dshkoolp   *Desculpe.*
Excuse me. (if you want
to get past someone)
    kong/dahm lisengsuh   *Com/Dá-me licença.*
Would you mind?
    nõw se ingpohrtuh?   *Não se importa?*

GREETINGS & GOODBYES

CUMPRIMENTOS E DESPEDIDAS

Portuguese greetings vary, depending on the time of day.

Good morning. (before noon)	bong deeuh	*Bom dia.*
Good afternoon. (until about 7 pm)	bouh tahrd	*Boa tarde.*
Good evening. (after about 7 or 8 pm)	bouh noyt	*Boa noite.*

See you later.	uhteh lohgoo!	*Até logo!*
See you in a while.	uhteh zhah!	*Até já!*
See you sometime.	uhteh kwalkehr deeuh!	*Até qualquer dia!*
See you soon.	uhteh brehv!	*Até breve!*
How are you?	komoo shtah?	*Como está?*
Fine, thanks.	bãy obreegahdoo/uh	*Bem, obrigado/a.*
Could be worse.	vais angdangdoo	*Vai-se andando.*
So-so.	uhsing uhsing	*Assim, assim.*

CIVILITIES

BOAS MANEIRAS

Thank you (very much).
  (mwingtoo) obreegahdoo/uh
  (Muito) obrigado/a.
You're welcome.
  de nahduh/nõw tãy de ke
  De nada/Não tem de quê.
I'm (very) sorry. (pol)
  pehsoo (imengsuh)
  dshkoolpuh
  Peço (imensa) desculpa.

COMING THROUGH

To ask someone to move aside or let you pass in front of them, use the expression *Com licença* (lit: with your permission).

Excuse me. (pol)	dshkoolp	*Desculpe.*
May I?	pohsoo?	*Posso?*
Do you mind?	ingpohrtuhs	*Importa-se?*

FORMS OF ADDRESS

FORMAS DE SE DIRIGIR A ALGUÉM

The third person singular form of the verb is commonly used when speaking with people of the same age and social status. An even more courteous and formal way of addressing someone is to

MEETING PEOPLE

use the expression *o senhor* or *a senhora*, without using any name or surname after it. The verb that follows is in the third person singular.

You're very kind.   uh snyoruh eh mwingtoo uhmahvehl
                     A senhora é muito amável.
                     (lit: the lady is very kind)

The equivalent of Mr, Mrs, Ms or Miss consists of adding the person's academic title if you know it. The title *Doutor/Doutora*, 'Doctor', isn't limited to physicians or those with a PhD, but can be used for anyone who has a university degree. You can also add the person's professional title, such as *Senhor/Senhora Engenheiro/a* (lit: Mr/Mrs Engineer). For women, you can use the expression *Dona* if you don't know the person's title or if they don't have one.

Você, 'you', is used when you don't have a very close relationship with people of the same social status, such as work colleagues. But it can also be used as a sign of hierarchical seniority, such as between a boss and employee. Often, it's used by a speaker to distance themself from another person, and may be interpreted to mean a lack of respect. It's best to avoid this form of address altogether because of the risk of offending someone.

Children are addressed using the pronoun *tu*, 'you', and this is how they address one another. *Tu* is also often used among close friends or among students.

Mrs/Ms/Miss (plus given name)	uh snyoruh donuh	*A senhora dona*
Madam (without adding given name or surname)	meenyuh snyoruh	*Minha senhora*
Sir (plus surname)	oo snyor	*O senhor*
Dr	oo snyor dotor; uh snyoruh dotoruh	*O senhor doutor; A senhora doutora*
Dr (plus given name)	oo dotor; uh dotoruh	*O doutor; A doutora*
Miss (usually used in shops)	uh mneenuh	*A menina*

YOU MAY HEAR ...

The colloquial terms:

| me-w | *meu* (m) |
| meenyuh | *minha* (f) |

both meaning something like 'man', are common, especially among teenagers.

The expression pah, *pá*, has a similar meaning (see also page 41), but is used by people of all ages, especially when expressing some feeling, as in the sentence:

oh pah vãy koomeegoo ow seenemuh nõw suhzhuhsh shahtoo!
Oh pá, vem comigo ao cinema, não sejas chato!

Come on don't be a bore, come with me to the movies!

BODY LANGUAGE   LINGUAGEM CORPORAL

When greeting each other, Portuguese men and women in professional situations will usually shake hands. Young people, women, and friends of the opposite sex often kiss each other first on the left cheek, then on the right, while men may greet with a hug.

The Portuguese are fairly expressive physically. During a conversation, people will often move close to one another and touch.

FIRST ENCOUNTERS   PRIMEIROS ENCONTROS

How are you? (pol/inf)
  komoo shtah/shtahsh?   *Como está/estás?*

Fine. And you? (pol)
  bãy obreegahdoo,
  ee oo snyor/uh snyoruh?   *Bem, obrigado.*
                                        E o senhor/a senhora?

Fine. And you? (inf)
  toodoo bãy, ee too?   *Tudo bem. E tu?*

What's your name? (pol)
  komoo se shuhmuh?   *Como se chama?*

My name's ...
   shuhmoom ...   *Chamo-me ...*
I'd like to introduce you to ... (pol)
   kreeuh uhprzengtahrly ...   *Queria apresentar-lhe ...*
I'm pleased to meet you. (pol)
   mwingtoo goshtoo; mwingtoo   *Muito gosto; Muito*
   pruhzer ãy koonyseloo/luh   *prazer em conhecê-lo/la.*

MAKING CONVERSATION   FAZER CONVERSA

The Portuguese are by nature friendly and accommodating. As in many countries, it's common to talk about health and the weather, and you may be asked about your country.

Do you live here?
   veev uhkee/mohruh uhkee?   *Vive aqui/Mora aqui?*
Where are you going?
   puhruh ongd vai?   *Para onde vai?*
What are you doing?
   oo ke shtah uh fuhzer?   *O que está a fazer?*
What do you think (about ...)?
   oo ke pengsuh (sobr ...)?   *O que pensa (sobre ...)?*
Can I take a photo of you?
   pohsoo teerahrly   *Posso tirar-lhe*
   oomuh footoogruhfeeuh?   *uma fotografia?*
What's this called?
   komoo se shuhmuh eeshtoo?   *Como se chama isto?*
Beautiful, isn't it!
   shpehtuhkoolahr nõw eh?   *Espectacular, não é?*
We love it here.
   uhdooruhmoosh eeshtoo!   *Adoramos isto!*
Are you waiting too?
   tangbãy shtah ah shpehruh?   *Também está à espera?*
That's strange!
   ke shtruhnyoo/shkzeetoo!   *Que estranho/esquisito!*
That's funny! (amusing)
   ke eng-gruhsahdoo!   *Que engraçado!*
Are you here on holiday?
   shtah uhkee de fehreeuhsh?   *Está aqui de férias?*

MEETING PEOPLE

I'm here ...   shto uhkee ...   *Estou aqui ...*
   for a holiday   de fehreeuhs   *de férias*
   on business   ãy ngohsiwsh   *em negócios*
   to study   puhruh shtoodahr   *para estudar*

How long are you here for?
   poor kwangtoo tengpoo   *Por quanto tempo*
   vai feekahr?   *vai ficar?*
I'm/We're here for ... weeks/days.
   vo/vuhmoosh feekahr   *Vou/Vamos ficar*
   ... smuhnuhsh/deeuhs   *... semanas/dias.*
Do you like it here?
   shtah uh gooshtahr deeshtoo?   *Está a gostar disto?*

USEFUL PHRASES   ## FRASES ÚTEIS

Sure.   klahroo; kong sertezuh   *Claro; Com certeza.*
Just a minute.   eh soh oong moomengtoo   *É só um momento.*
It's OK.   toodoo bãy   *Tudo bem.*

It's (not) important.
   (nõw) eh ingpoortangt   *(Não) é importante.*
Don't worry about it.
   nõw fahzh mahl   *Não faz mal.*
It's (not) possible.
   (nõw) eh pooseevehl   *(Não) é possível.*
Careful!; Watch out!
   kwidahdoo!   *Cuidado!*
Just a second!
   eh soh oong moomengteenyoo!   *É só um momentinho!*

That's enough!   sheguh!   *Chega!*
Look!   ohly/rrpahr!   *Olhe/Repare!*
Listen (to this)! oysuh (eeshtoo)!   *Oiça (isto)!*
I'm ready.   shto prongtoo/uh   *Estou pronto/a.*
Are you ready?   shtah prongtoo/uh?   *Está pronto/a?*
Wait!   shpehruh!   *Espera!*
Good luck!   bouh sohrt!   *Boa sorte!*

MEETING PEOPLE

NATIONALITIES   NACIONALIDADES

Unfortunately, we can't list all countries here. However, you'll find that many names of countries, continents and cities in Portuguese are similar to those in English. Remember, though, that even if a word looks like the English equivalent, it will have a Portuguese pronunciation. If your country isn't listed here, try pointing on the map.

Where are you from?	de ongd eh?	*De onde é?*
I'm from ...	so ...	*Sou ...*
Australia	duh owshtrahleeuh	*da Austrália*
Belgium	duh behlzheekuh	*da Bélgica*
Canada	doo kuhnuhdah	*do Canadá*
China	duh sheenuh	*da China*
Czech Republic	duh rrehpoobleekuh shehkuh	*da República Checa*
Denmark	duh deenuhmahrkuh	*da Dinamarca*
England	duh ing-gluhtehrruh	*da Inglaterra*
Europe	duh e-wrohpuh	*da Europa*
Germany	duh uhlmuhnyuh	*da Alemanha*
India	duh ingdeeuh	*da Índia*
Ireland	duh eerlangduh	*da Irlanda*
Lebanon	doo leebuhnoo	*do Líbano*
the Netherlands	duh olangduh	*da Holanda*
New Zealand	duh nohvuh zlangdyuh	*da Nova Zelândia*
Scotland	duh shkohsyuh	*da Escócia*
South America	duh uhmehreekuh doo sool	*da América do Sul*
Spain	de shpuhnyuh	*de Espanha*
Sweden	duh swesyuh	*da Suécia*
Switzerland	duh swisuh	*da Suiça*
the US	dooz shtahdooz ooneedoosh	*dos Estados Unidos*
Wales	doo puheezh de gahlesh	*do País de Gales*

I come from the/a ...	vuhnyoo de ...	*Venho de ...*
I live in the/a ...	veevoo	*Vivo ...*
city	nuh seedahd	*na cidade*
countryside	noo kangpoo	*no campo*
mountains	nuh mongtuhnyuh	*na montanha*
seaside	ah bayruh mahr	*à beira-mar*
suburbs of ...	noosh	*nos*
	uhrredohresh de ...	*arredores de ...*
town	noomuh veeluh	*numa vila*
village	noomuh ahldayuh	*numa aldeia*

CULTURAL DIFFERENCES

DIFERENÇAS CULTURAIS

How do you do this in your (sg/pl) country?
komoo se fahz eestoo noo se-w/vohsoo puheesh?

Como se faz isto no seu/vosso país?

Is this a local or national custom?
ehshtuh eh oomuh truhdeesõw lookahl o nuhsiwnahl?

Esta é uma tradição local ou nacional?

I don't want to offend you (sg/pl).
nõw kreeuh ofengdeloo/ ofengdervoosh

Não queria ofendê-lo/ ofender-vos.

I'm sorry, it's not the custom in my country.
deshkoolp, nõw eh kooshtoom noo me-w puheesh

Desculpe, não é costume no meu país.

I'm not accustomed to this.
nõw shto uhbeetwadoo/uh uh eeshtoo

Não estou habituado/a a isto.

I don't mind watching, but I'd prefer not to participate.
nõw me ingpohrtoo de feelkahr uh ver, muhsh prefreeuh nõw puhrteeseepahr

Não me importo de ficar a ver, mas preferia não participar.

AGE   IDADE

Age is expressed using the verb ter, 'to have'.

How old are you (pol)?
   kwangtoosh uhnoosh tãy?   *Quantos anos tem?*
I'm ... years old.
   tuhnyoo ... uhnoosh   *Tenho ... anos.*

(See Numbers & Amounts, page 239, for your age.)

RELIGION   RELIGIÃO

Before using any of the following phrases, take into consideration that Portuguese people don't often speak about religion and rarely ask someone about their religious beliefs.

What's your religion?
   kwal eh uh twuh rrleezheeõw?   *Qual é a tua religião?*

I'm…	so…	*Sou ...*
Buddhist	boodeeshtuh	*budista*
Catholic	kuhtohleekoo/uh	*católico/a*
Christian	kreeshtõw/kreeshtang	*cristão/cristã*
Hindu	ingdoo	*hindu*
Jewish	zhoode-w/zhoodeeuh	*judeu/judia*
Muslim	moosoolmuhnoo/uh	*muçulmano/a*

I'm Catholic, but not practising.
   so kuhtohleekoo/uh muhzh   *Sou católico/a, mas*
   nõw so pruhteekangt   *não sou praticante.*
I believe in destiny/fate.
   uhkrdeetoo noo deshteenoo   *Acredito no destino.*
I'm not religious.
   nõw so rrleezheeozoo/   *Não sou religioso/a.*
   rrleezheeozoouh
I'm agnostic.
   so uhgnohshteekoo/uh   *Sou agnóstico/a.*
I'm an atheist.
   so uhte-w/uhtayuh   *Sou ateu/ateia.*

OCCUPATIONS

What work do you do?	oo ke fahsh?

OCUPAÇÕES

O que faz?

I'm a/an ...	so ...	*Sou ...*
actor	ahtor/ahtreesh	*actor/actriz*
architect	uhrkeetehtoo/uh	*arquitecto/a*
artist	uhrteeshtuh	*artista*
bricklayer	pdrayroo	*pedreiro*
businessperson (m/f)	ŏong ohmãy; oomuh moolyehr de ngohsiwsh	*um homem; uma mulher de negócios*
designer	dzenyuhdor/ dzenyuhdoruh	*desenhador/ desenhadora*
doctor	mehdeekoo/uh	*médico/a*
electrician	eelehtreeseeshtuh	*electricista*
engineer	engzhnyayroo/uh	*engenheiro/a*
farmer	uhgreekooltor/ uhgreekooltoruh	*agricultor/ agricultora*
journalist	zhoornuhleeshtuh	*jornalista*
lawyer	uhdvoogahdoo/uh	*advogado/a*
mechanic	mkuhneekoo/uh	*mecânico/a*
nurse	engfermayroo/uh	*enfermeiro/a*
office worker	engprgahdoo/uh de shkreetohriw	*empregado/a de escritório*
plumber	kuhnuhleezuhdor/ kuhnuhleezuhdoruh	*canalizador/ canalizadora*
sales assistant	vengddor/ vengddoruh	*vendedor/ vendedora*
scientist	see-engteeshtuh	*cientista*
secretary	skretahriw/skretahryuh	*secretário/a*
student	shtoodangt	*estudante*
teacher	proofsor/uh	*professor/a*
translator	truhdootor/uh	*tradutor/a*
waiter	engprgahdoo/uh de mezuh	*empregado/a de mesa*
writer	shkreetor/uh	*escritor/a*

I have my own business.		
tuhnyoo uh myeenyuh prohpryuh feermuh		*Tenho minha própria firma.*
I'm unemployed.		
shto dzengprgahdoo/uh		*Estou desempregado/a.*
I'm retired.		
so rrfoormahdoo/uh		*Sou reformado/a.*
What are you studying?		
oo ke shtooduhsh?		*O que estudas?*

I'm studying ...	shto uh shtoodahr ...	*Estou a estudar ...*
art	ahrt	*arte*
economics	eekohnoomeeuh	*economia*
management	zheshtõw	*gestão*
engineering	engzhenyuhreeuh	*engenharia*
humanities	letruhsh	*letras*
languages	ling-gwuhs	*línguas*
law	deeraytoo	*direito*
medicine	mdseenuh	*medicina*
Portuguese	poortoogesh	*português*
science	see-engsyuhs	*ciências*

FEELINGS   SENTIMENTOS

When talking about feelings in Portuguese, the verb ter, 'to have', is often used with a noun where English uses 'be' with an adjective.

I'm ...	tuhnyoo ...	*Tenho ...* (lit: I have ...)
Are you ...?	tãy ...?	*Tem ...?*
		(lit: Do you have ...?)
afraid	medoo	*medo* (lit: fear)
cold	freeoo	*frio*
hot	kuhlor	*calor*
hungry	fohm	*fome*
in a hurry	prehsuh	*pressa*
right	rruhzõw	*razão*
sorry (regret)	penuh	*pena*
thirsty	sed	*sede*

I'm ...	shto kong ...	*Estou com ...*
		(lit: I'm with ...)
keen to ...	vongtahd de ...	*vontade de ...*
sleepy	sonoo	*sono*

I'm ...	shto ...?	*Estou ...*
Are you ...?	shtah ...?	*Está ...?*
angry	zang-gahdo/a	*zangado/a*
annoyed (inf)	shuhteeahdoo/uh	*chateado/a*
happy	fleesh	*feliz*
sad	treeslt	*triste*
tired	kangsahdoo/uh	*cansado/a*
upset (inf)	shuhteeahdoo/uh	*chateado/a*
well	bay	*bem*
worried	preeokoopahdoo/uh	*preocupado/a*

I feel great. (inf/pol)		
shto nuh muhyor;		*Estou na maior;*
shto ohteemoo/uh		*Estou óptimo/a.*
I'm feeling down.		
shto ay baisho		*Estou em baixo.*
I'm sorry (condolence).		
singtoo mwingtoo;		*Sinto muito;*
oozh me-wsh sengtimengtoosh		*Os meus sentimentos.*
I'm grateful.		
mwingtoo uhgruhdseedoo/uh		*Muito agradecido/a.*

BREAKING THE LANGUAGE BARRIER
ULTRAPASSANDO A BARREIRA DA LÍNGUA

Do you speak English?
fahluh ing-glesh? — *Fala inglês?*

Yes, I do.
fahloo — *Falo.*

No, I don't.
nōw (nōw fahloo) — *Não (não falo).*

Does anyone speak English?
ah ahlgāy ke fahl ing-glesh? — *Há alguém que fale inglês?*

I speak a little.
e-w faloo oong pokoo — *Eu falo um pouco.*

Do you understand?
shtah uh persber? — *Está a perceber?*

I (don't) understand.
(nōw) perseboo — *(Não) percebo.*

Could you speak more slowly?
poodeeuh fuhlahr maizh dvuhgahr? — *Podia falar mais devagar?*

Could you repeat that?
pohd rrpteer eesoo? — *Pode repetir isso?*

Please write it down.
shkrevuh, se fash fuhvor — *Escreva, se faz favor.*

How do you say ...?
komoo eh ke se deesh ...? — *Como é que se diz ...?*

What does ... mean?
oo ke seegneefeekuh ...? — *O que significa ...?*

GETTING AROUND

DESLOCAR-SE

It's fairly easy to get around Portugal by bus or train. Four-and seven-day tourist passes can be used for both bus and underground services.

FINDING YOUR WAY

À PROCURA DO CAMINHO

Excuse me, can you help me?
deshkoolp, poodeeuh uhzhoodahrm?

Desculpe, podia ajudar-me?

I'm looking for ...
ohtu uh prohkooruh duh ...

Estou à procura da ...

Where's the ...?	ongd eh uh ...?	*Onde é a ...?*
bus stop	puhrahzhãy doo owtohkahrroo	*paragem do autocarro*
road to ...	shtrahduh puhruh ...	*estrada para ...*
... station	shtuhsõw ...	*estação ...*
train	de kongboyoosh	*de comboios*
underground	doo mehtroo	*do metro*
taxi stand	prahsuh de tahkseesh	*praça de táxis*

Where does this ... go?
puhruh ongd vai esht ...?

Para onde vai este ...?

What time does the ... arrive/leave?	uh ke ohruhsh sheguh/pahrt oo ...?	*A que horas chega/parte o ...?*
boat	bahrkoo	*barco*
bus	owtohkahrroo	*autocarro*
plane	uhveeõw	*avião*
train	kongboyoo	*comboio*
underground	mehtroo	*metro*

GETTING AROUND

How do we get to ...?
komoo eh ke se vai puhruh ...?   *Como é que se vai para ...?*
Is it far from/near here?
eh longzh/pehrtoo duhkee?   *É longe/perto daqui?*
Can we walk there?
pohd se eer uh peh?   *Pode-se ir a pé?*
Can you show me (on the map)?
pohd mooshtrahrm   *Pode mostrar-me*
(noo mahpuh)?   *(no mapa)?*
Are there other means of getting there?
ah ahlgoomuh otruh muhnayruh   *Há alguma outra maneira*
de shgahr lah?   *de chegar lá?*

DIRECTIONS   INDICAÇÕES

Turn (at the) ...   veer   *Vire ...*
  left   ah shkerduh   *à esquerda*
  right   ah deeraytuh   *à direita*
  intersection   noo kroozuhmengtoo *no cruzamento*
  roundabout   nuh rrootoongduh   *na rotunda*
  traffic lights   noo smahfooroo   *no semáforo*
  next corner   nuh prohseemuh   *na próxima*
                       shkeenuh   *esquina*

Straight ahead.
  vah ãy frengt   *Vá em frente.*
In the next block.
  noo prohseemoo kwuhrtayrõw   *No próximo quarteirão.*
It's very near/far.
  eh mwingtoo pehrtoo/longzh   *É muito perto/longe.*

in front of   deeangt de;   *diante de;*
                      ãy frengt de   *em frente de*
behind   uhtrahzh de   *atrás de*
far   longzh   *longe*
near   pehrtoo   *perto*
opposite   doo otroo lahdoo;   *do outro lado;*
                      ãy frengt doo/duh   *em frente do/da*

here	uhkee	*aqui*
there	uhlee	*ali*
north	uh nohrt	*a norte*
south	uh sool	*u sul*
east	uh chsht	*a este*
west	uh ohehsht	*a oeste*

ADDRESSES   MORADAS

A Portuguese address usually looks something like this:

> Exmº Sr. António Martins
> R. Damasceno Monteiro, 5, 1º Dtº
> 1900-047 LISBOA

This means that (the Honorable Mr) António Martins lives at
number 5 Damasceno Monteiro Street (*R.* or *Rua* means 'street'),
on the first floor, apartment on the right (*Dtº* is short for *direita*,
meaning 'right'). The postal code in this case is 1900-047 (all
postcodes in Portugal have seven numbers). Towns and cities are
usually written in capital letters.

BUYING TICKETS   COMPRAR BILHETES

Excuse me, where's the ticket office?
   deshkoolp, ongd eh
   uh beelytayruh?
Desculpe, onde é
a bilheteira?

We want to go to ...
   kreeuhmoosh eer puhruh ...
Queríamos ir para ...

How much is it?
   kwangtoo eh?
Quanto é?

Do I need to book?
   eh preseezoo fuhzer oomuh
   rrzehrvuh?
É preciso fazer uma
reserva?

I'd like to book a seat to ...
   kreeuh rzervahr oong
   loogahr puhruh ...
Queria reservar um
lugar para ...

GETTING AROUND

Can I get a stand-by ticket?
pohd porm nuh   *Pode pôr-me na*
leeshtuh de shpehruh   *lista de espera?*

I'd like (a) ...	kreeuh ...	*Queria ...*
(one-way) ticket	oong beelyet (de eeduh)	*um bilhete (de ida)*
return ticket	oong beelyet de eeduh ee vohltuh	*um bilhete de ida e volta*
two tickets	doysh beelyetsh	*dois bilhetes*
a/an ... fare	oong beelyet kong deshkongtoo puhruh ...	*um bilhete com desconto para ...*
senior	tersayruh eedahd	*terceira idade*
student	shtoodangtsh	*estudantes*
youth	zhohvāysh	*jovens*
... ticket	beelyet ...	*bilhete ...*
daily	deeahriw	*diário*
weekly	smuhnahl	*semanal*
10-trip	de dehsh viahzhāysh	*de dez viagens*
1st class	āy preemayruh klahs	*em primeira classe*
2nd class	āy sgoongduh klahs	*em segunda e classe*

Where can I pick the ticket up?
ongd pohsoo lvangtahr   *Onde posso levantar*
oo beelyet?   *o bilhete?*
Have you got change?
tāy trokoo?   *Tem troco?*
departure
puhrteeduh   *partida*

destination
  desteenoo
(non)smoking section
  loogahrsh puhruh
  (nōw) foomuhdors
ticket vending machine
  vengduh owtoomahteekuh
  de beelyetsh

destino

lugares para
(não) fumadores

venda automática
de bilhetes

AT CUSTOMS

I have nothing to declare.
  nōw tuhnyoo nahduh
I want to declare ...
  tuhnyoo uh dkluhrahr ...
Do I have to declare this?
  tuhnyoo ke dkluhrahr eeshtoo?
This is all my luggage.
  chshtuh eh toduh uh
  meenyuh buhgahzhāy
I didn't know I had to declare it.
  nōw suhbeeuh ke teenyuh
  ke dekluhrahr eeshtoo

Can I call my ...?   pohsoo tlefoonahr ...
  consulate   ow me-w
                   kongsoolahdoo
  embassy   ah meenyuh
                   engbaishahduh

NA ALFÂNDEGA

Não tenho nada

Tenho a declarar ...

Tenho que declarar isto?

Esta é toda a
minha bagagem.

Não sabia que
tinha que declarar isto.

Posso telefonar ...
  ao meu
  consulado
  à minha
  embaixada

GETTING AROUND

AIR   TRANSPORTES AÉREOS

Flights within Portugal are relatively expensive. The main domestic carrier, Portugália, gives a 50 per cent discount to anyone holding an under-26 card.

Is there a flight to ...?
    ah ahlgoong vo-oo puhruh ...?   *Há algum voo para ...?*
When's the next flight to ...?
    kwangdoo eh oo
    prohseemoo vo-oo puhruh ...?   *Quando é o próximo voo*
                                          para ...?

What's the flight number?
    kwahl eh oo noomroo doo vo-oo?   *Qual é o número do voo?*
Do I need a visa for ...?
    preseezoo de oong   *Preciso de um*
    veeshtoo puhruh ...?   *visto para ...?*
How much does a kilo of
excess baggage cost?
    kwangtoo eh ke kooshtuh   *Quanto é que custa*
    oong keeloo uh maish   *um kilo a mais*
    nuh buhgahzhãy?   *na bagagem?*
What time do I have to
check in at the airport?
    uh ke ohruhsh tuhnyoo ke   *A que horas tenho que*
    fuhzer oo tshehk een noo   *fazer o 'check in' no*
    uhehroportoo?   *aeroporto?*

SIGNS	
ALFÂNDEGA	CUSTOMS
ARTIGOS LIVRES DE IMPOSTOS	DUTY-FREE
IMIGRAÇÃO	IMMIGRATION CONTROL
CIDADÃOS DA UE	EUROPEAN UNION CITIZENS
PASSAPORTES	PASSPORT CONTROL

Where's the baggage claim?
 ongd eh ke se lvangtuh
 uh buhgahzhãy?

Onde é que se levanta
u bagagem?

Where's the lost and found?
 ongd feekuh uh sehksõw de
 perdeedoosh ee uhshahdoosh?

Onde fica a secção de
perdidos e achados?

My baggage ...	uh meenyuh buhgahzhãy ...	*A minha bagagem ...*
didn't arrive	now shgo	*não chegou*
is lost	perde-ws	*perdeu-se*
airport tax	tahshuh doo uhahrohportoo	*taxa do aeroporto*
arrivals	shegahduhsh	*chegadas*
baggage claim	rrkolyuh de buhgahzhãysh	*recolha de bagagens*
boarding card	kuhrtõw de engbahrk	*cartão de embarque*
changeover	trangshfrengsyuh	*transferência*
check in	tshehk een	*check in*
departures	puhrteeduhsh	*partidas*
... flights	vo-oosh ...	*vôos ...*
domestic	doomehshteekoosh	*domésticos*
international	ingternuhsiwnaish	*internacionais*
gate number	pohrtuh noomroo	*porta número*
passport	pahsuhpohrt	*passaporte*
residence permit	kuhrtõw de rrzeedengsyuh	*cartão de residência*
stopover	shkahluh	*escala*
visa	veeshtoo	*visto*

BUS   AUTOCARRO

City buses are called *autocarros*. Intercity buses are called *camionetes*
and may or may not provide an express service. The only cities
that have metropolitan bus systems are Lisbon, Oporto and
Coimbra. Monthly bus passes and special one- and three-day un-
limited-travel bus tickets are available.

GETTING AROUND

Where's the bus stop?
   ongd feekuh/eh uh puhrahzhãy   *Onde fica/é a paragem*
   doo owtohkahrroo   *do autocarro?*

Where do I get the bus for ...?
   ongd eh ke pohsoo uhpuhnyahr   *Onde é que posso apanhar*
   oo owtohkahrroo puhruh ...?   *o autocarro para ...?*

Which bus goes to ...?
   kwal eh oo owtohkahrroo/uh   *Qual é o autocarro/a*
   kahmiwneht ke vai puhruh ...?   *camionete que vai para ...?*

Does this bus go to ...?
   esht owtohkahrroo/ehstuh   *Este autocarro/esta*
   kuhmioneht vai puhruh ...?   *camionete vai para ...?*

How often do buses come?
   de kwangtoo ãy kwangtoo   *De quanto em quanto*
   tengpoo vãyãy ooz   *tempo vêm os*
   owtohkahrroosh?   *autocarros?*

POCKET PILLAGERS

Watch your wallet and handbag – pick-pocketing is common on
public transport.

Don't bother me!	nõw me ingkoomohd!	Não me incomode!
Help!	sookorroo	Socorro!
Thief!	oong luhdrõw!	Um ladrão!
Watch out!	uhtengsõw!	Atenção!

What time's	uh ke ohruhsh sai oo	*A que horas sai o*
the ... bus?	... owtohkahrroo?	*... autocarro?*
next	prohseemoo	*próximo*
first	preemayroo	*primeiro*
last	oolteemoo	*último*

Could you let me know when we get to ...?
  poodreeuh uhveezahrm
  kwangdoo shgahrmoosh uh ...?   *Poderia avisar-me
                                       quando chegarmos a ...?*

TRAIN   COMBOIO

Aside from the commuter trains that serve the Cascais and Sintra lines, Portugal has a complete network of regional and intercity trains. The intercity trains, called *inter-cidades*, are the fastest and most direct way of getting to some of Portugal's major cities. Lisbon and Oporto both have underground subway systems.

What station is this?
  ke shtuhsōw eh chshtuh?   *Que estação é esta?*

How many more stops is it to ...?
  fahltow kwangtulish
  puhrahzhāysh puhruh ...   *Faltam quantas
                                       paragens para ...*

Does this train stop at ...?
  esht kongboyoo pahruh āy ...?   *Este comboio para em ...?*

How long will it be delayed?
  kwal eh oo uhtrahzoo?   *Qual é o atraso?*

Is that seat taken?
  esht loogahr shtah okoopahdoo?   *Este lugar está ocupado?*

Which line goes to ...?
  kwal ch uh leenyuh puhruh ...?   *Qual é a linha para ...?*

What's the next station?
  kwal eh uh prohseemuh shtuhsōw?   *Qual é a próxima estação?*

Do I have to change lines to get to ...?
  tuhnyoo de moodahr de leenyuh
  puhruh shgahr uh ...?   *Tenho de mudar de linha
                                       para chegar a ...?*

The train is ...	oo kongboyoo shtah ...	*O comboio está ...*
delayed	uhtruhzahdoo	*atrasado*
cancelled	foy kangslahdoo	*foi cancelado*
conductor	rrveezor	*revisor*
reserved seats	loogahrsh rrzervahdoosh	*lugares reservados*

GETTING AROUND

THEY MAY SAY ...

O seu bilhete, por favor?
  oo se-w beelyet, poor fuhvor?
  Your ticket, please.
O comboio parte no cais número ...
  oo kongboyoo pahrt noo kaish noomroo ...
  The train leaves from platform ...
Está cheio.
  shtah shayoo
  It's full.

TAXI   TÁXI

Taxis can be hailed anywhere on the street. It's customary to tip
the driver five to 10 per cent of the fare. Taxi fares within the city
limits of larger cities are charged according to the meter. Outside
city limits, the fare is charged per kilometre.

Is this taxi free?	shtah leevr?	*Está livre?*
Please take	ehvm puhruh ..., se	*Leve-me para ...,*
me to (the) ...	fahsh fuhvor	*faz favor.*
airport	oo uhehrohportoo	*o aeroporto*
this address	ehshtuh moorahduh	*esta morada*
... station	uh shtuhsõw de ...	*a estação de ...*
bus	owtohkahrroosh	*autocarros*
coach	kahmiwnehtsh	*camionetes*
train	kongboyoosh	*comboios*

How much does it
cost to go to ...?
  kwangto eh ke kooshtuh eer uh ...?   *Quanto é que custa ir a ...?*
Do we pay extra for luggage?
  pahguhs maish peluh buhgahzhãy?   *Paga-se mais pela bagagem?*
Can you take (five) passengers?
  pohd lvahr (singkoo) psouhsh?   *Pode levar (cinco) pessoas?*

Instructions Instruções

Continue!	kongteenooe!	*Continue!*

The next street to the left/right.
  nuh prohseemuh roouh veer
  ah shkerduh/ah deeraytuh

*Na próxima rua vire
à esquerda/direita.*

Please slow down.
  poor fuhvor, vah maizhdvuhgahr!

Por favor, vá mais devagar!

Please wait here.
  shpehr, se fash fuhvor

Espere, se faz favor.

Stop here!
  pahr ulikee!

Pare aqui!

Stop at the corner.
  pahr nuh shkeenuh

Pare na esquina.

SIGNS

TÁXIS (T)	TAXI RANK

BOAT BARCO

A drive across the 25th of April Bridge will take you to the south side of the Tagus. Another more relaxing and scenic way to make the trip is on a trans-Tagus ferry.

Where does the ferry leave from?
  de ongd eh ke sai/
  pahrt oo bahrkoo?

*De onde é que sai/
parte o barco?*

Where does the ferry dock?
  oo bahrkoo sheguh/pahruh
  āy ke shtuhsōw?

*O barco chega/pára
em que estação?*

What time does the ferry leave/arrive?
  uh ke ohruhsh pahrt/
  sheguh oo bahrkoo?

*A que horas parte/
chega o barco?*

How much is it if I bring my car?
  kwangtoo kooshtuh oo beelyct
  doomuh psouh kong kahrroo?

*Quanto custa o bilhete
duma pessoa com carro?*

GETTING AROUND

CAR   CARRO

Major improvements have been made over the last decade to
Portugal's roads. But be forewarned about Portuguese drivers –
they love to drive fast and overtake others in unexpected places.
Parking space is scarce in most major cities, although metered
parking and paid underground parking do exist in some major
city centres.

Where can I rent a car?
   ongd pohsoo uhloogahr   *Onde posso alugar*
   oong kahrroo?   *um carro?*
How much is it daily/weekly?
   kwangtoo kooshtuh poor   *Quanto custa por*
   deeuh/poor smuhnuh?   *dia/por semana?*

Does that include ...? noo presoo shtah ...? *No preço está ...?*
   insurance   ingklooeedoo   *incluído*
                   oo sgooroo   *o seguro*
   mileage   ingklooeeduh   *incluída*
                   uhkeeloomtrahzhãy? *aquilometragem?*

Where's the next petrol station?
   ongd feekuh uh prohseemuh   *Onde fica a próxima*
   bongbuh de guhzooleenuh?   *bomba de gasolina?*
Please fill the tank.
   shayoo, poor fuhvor; uhteshtahr *Cheio, por favor; Atestar.*
I'd like (three) thousand escudos
worth of petrol/diesel.
   kreeuh (tresh) kongtoosh de   *Queria (três) contos de*
   guhzooleenuh/gahzohliw   *gasolina/gasóleo.*
Can I park here?
   pohsoo shtuhsiwnahr uhkee? *Posso estacionar aqui?*

Please check the ...   poor fuhvor,   *Por favor,*
                  vreefeek oo ...   *verifique o ...*
   oil   neevehl doo ohliw   *nível do óleo*
   tyre pressure   ahr doosh pne-wsh *ar dos pneus*
   water   neevehl duh ahgwuh *nível da água*

Does this road lead to ...?
  ehshtuh shtrahduh vai uhteh ...? *Esta estrada vai até ...?*

air	ahr	*ar*
battery	buhtreeuh	*bateria*
brakes	truhvoysh	*travões*
clutch	engbrialızhāy	*embriagem*
driving licence	kahrtuh de	*carta de*
	kongdoosōw	*condução*
engine	mootor	*motor*
garage	ohfeeseenuh	*oficina*
highway	owtohshtrahduh	*auto-estrada*
indicator	peeshkuhsh	*piscas*
lights	fuhroysh	*faróis*
leaded	guhzooleenuh kong	*gasolina com*
	shoongboo	*chumbo*
regular	guhzooleenuh	*gasolina*
	sāy shoongboo	*sem chumbo*
oil	ohliw	*óleo*
motorway	owtohshtrahduh	*auto-estrada*
national highway	shtrahduh nuhsiwnahl	*estrada nacional*

GETTING AROUND

puncture	pne-w foorahdoo/ fooroo	*pneu furado/ furo*
radiator	rruhdyuhdor	*radiador*
(main) road	shtrahduh (pringseepahl)	*estrada (principal)*
roadmap	mahpuh de shtrahduhsh	*mapa de estradas*
seatbelt	singtoo de sgoorangsuh	*cinto de segurança*
self-service	sehlf-suhrvees	*self-service*
speed limit	leemeet de vlooseedahd	*limite de velocidade*
tyres	pne-wsh	*pneus*
windscreen	pahruhbreezuhsh	*parabrisas*

Car Problems   Problemas de Carros

We need a mechanic.

preseezuhmoosh doong mkuhneekoo	*Precisamos dum mecânico.*

What make is it?

de ke mahrkuh eh?	*De que marca é?*

The car broke down at ...

oo karroo uhvuhreeos áy ...	*O carro avariou-se em ...*

The battery is flat.

uh buhtreeuh deshkuhrregos	*A bateria descarregou-se.*

The radiator is leaking.

oo rruhdyuhdor táy oomuh fooguh	*O radiador tem uma fuga.*

I have a flat tyre.

tuhnyoo oong pne-w foorahdoo	*Tenho um pneu furado.*

It's overheating.

shtah uh uhkehser dmaish	*Está a aquecer demais.*

It's not working.

nõw shtah uh truhbuhlyahr	*Não está a trabalhar.*

I've lost my car keys.

perdee uhsh shahvsh doo kahrroo	*Perdi as chaves do carro.*

I've run out of petrol.

feekay sãy guhzooleenuh	*Fiquei sem gasolina.*

TRAFFIC SIGNS

CEDA A VEZ	GIVE WAY
DESVIO	DETOUR
NÃO ULTRAPASSAR	DO NOT OVERTAKE
OBRAS	ROAD WORK
PEÕES	PEDESTRIAN CROSSING
PERIGO!	CAUTION!
PROIBIDO ESTACIONAR	NO PARKING
REDUZA A VELOCIDADE	
(CRIANÇAS)!	SLOW DOWN (CHILDREN)!
SAÍDA	EXIT
STOP	STOP
SENTIDO PROIBIDO	NO ENTRY
SENTIDO ÚNICO	ONE WAY
TRÂNSITO LOCAL	LOCAL TRAFFIC ONLY
PARQUE DE	CAR PARK
ESTACIONAMENTO (P)	

BICYCLE   BICICLETA

Because of heavy traffic and often hilly terrain, riding a bicycle isn't a common way of getting around in big cities. However, on country roads, cycling is popular as a sport and for leisure, and sometimes as a means of transportation in small towns and villages.

Is it within cycling distance?
kongsehgs lah shgahr
de beeseeklehtuh?

*Consegue-se lá chegar
de bicicleta?*

Where can I find secondhand
bikes for sale?
ongd eh ke pohsoo engkongtrahr   *Onde é que posso encontrar*
beeseeklehtuhsh ãy sgoongduh   *bicicletas em segunda*
mõw ah vengduh?   *mão à venda?*

Where can I hire a bicycle?
ongd eh ke pohsoo uhloogahr   *Onde é que posso alugar*
oomuh beeseeklehtuh?   *uma bicicleta?*

I've got a flat tyre.
tuhnyoo un pne-w foorahdoo   *Tenho um pneu furado.*

How much is it for an/the ...?	kwangto eh ke kooshtuh ...?	Quanto é que custa ...?
hour	oomuh ohruh	uma hora
morning	oomuh muhnyang	uma manhã
afternoon	oomuh tahrd	uma tarde
day	oong deeuh	um dia
brakes	truhvōysh	travões
to cycle	angdahr de beeseeklehtuh	andar de bicicleta
gear stick	moodangsuhsh	mudanças
handlebars	geeuhdor	guiador
helmet	kuhpuhset	capacete
inner tube	kuhmuhruh	câmara
lights	loozesh	luzes
mountain bike	beeseeklehtuh de mongtuhnyuh	bicicleta de montanha
padlock	kuhdyahdoo	cadeado
pump	bongbuh	bomba
puncture	fooroo	furo
racing bike	beeseeklehtuh de koorreeduh	bicicleta de corrida
saddle	sling	selim
tandem	tangdem	tandem
wheel	rrohduh	roda

(See pages 136 and 195 for more cycling terms.)

In cities, travellers can find hotels for all budgets, ranging from one to five stars. In larger cities, international chains can be found. *Pensões*, 'pensions' and *residenciais*, 'guesthouses', offer a room and breakfast without the wide range of services offered at large hotels but at a lower price. Motels are fairly rare in Portugal.

You can also stay at one of the state-run *pousadas*. These are luxury hotels in buildings that have been restored or especially built in keeping with the architectural style of the surrounding area. Many are in historic castles, monasteries or palaces, and can be found all over the country.

Another option is *turismo de habitação*, 'bed & breakfast', which can be found in both city and country areas. This is where private homes of historical or architectural interest are refurbished by the owners, usually with government backing, to offer guest accommodation. *Turismo rural* is similar, but in this case the guest can participate in activities such as fishing, hunting, horse riding or even farm chores. Both *turismo de habitação* and *turismo rural* have different price levels based on how luxurious they are.

All three types of accommodation are usually decorated in the style characteristic of the region, and local specialities are included on the menu.

FINDING ACCOMMODATION

À PROCURA DE ALOJAMENTO

I'm looking for a ...	shto ah prohkooruh de ...	*Estou à procura de ...*
bed & breakfast	tooreezhmoo de uhbeetuhsõw	*turismo de habitação*
camping ground	oong pahrk de kangpeezhmoo	*um parque de campismo*
guesthouse	oomuh pengsõw/ rrzeedengsyahl/ rrzeedengseeuh	*uma pensão/ residencial/ residência*

ACCOMMODATION

hotel	oong otehl	*um hotel*
luxury hotel	oomuh pozahduh	*uma pousada*
motel	oong motehl	*um motel*
youth hostel	oomuh pozahduh duh zhoovengtood	*uma pousada da juventude*

Where's the ...?	ongd feekuh/eh ...?	*Onde fica/é ...?*
best hotel	oo mlyohr otehl	*o melhor hotel*
cheapest hotel	oo otehl maizh buhrahtoo	*o hotel mais barato*

Where's the ... hotel?
  ongd feekuh oo otehl ...? *Onde fica o hotel ...?*
What's the address?
  kwal eh uh moorahduh? *Qual é a morada?*
Could you write down
the address, please?
  poodreeuh shkrever uh *Poderia escrever a morada,*
  moorahduh, poor fuhvor? *por favor?*

BOOKING AHEAD   FAZER RESERVAS

I'd like to book a room, please.
  kreeuh rrzervahr oong *Queria reservar um quarto,*
  kwartoo, poor fuhvor *por favor.*
Do you have any rooms available?
  tãy ahlgoong kwarto leevr? *Tem algum quarto livre?*
For (three) nights.
  puhruh (trezh) noytsh *Para (três) noites.*

How much per/for ...?	kwangtoo kooshtuh ...?	*Quanto custa ...?*
person	poor psouh	*por pessoa*
two people	puhruh dwuhsh psouhsh	*para duas pessoas*
night	poor oomuh noyt	*por uma noite*
week	poor oomuh smuhnuh	*por uma semana*

My name is ...
   oo me-w nom eh ...   *O meu nome é ...*
We'll be arriving at ...
   vuhmoosh shgahr ahsh ...   *Vamos chegar às ...*

(For times, see Time & Dates, page 233.)

CHECKING IN

CHEGADA

I have a reservation
under the name of ...
   feezh oomuh rrsehrvuh   *Fiz uma reserva*
   ay nom de ...   *em nome de ...*
Do you have any
rooms available?
   tay ahlgoong kwartoo   *Tem algum quarto*
   deeshpooneevehl?   *disponível?*

Do you have a ...?	tay ahlgoong kwartoo ...?	*Tem algum quarto ...?*
single room	ingdeeveedwal	*individual*
room with two beds	dooploo	*duplo*
room with a double bed	kong kuhmuh de kuhsahl	*com cama de casal*

I'd like to share a room.
   kreeuh purteelyahı   *Queria partilhar*
   oong kwartoo   *um quarto.*

We want a room with a ...	kreeumoozh oong kwartoo kong ...	*Queríamos um quarto com ...*
bathroom	kahzuh de buhnyoo	*casa de banho*
shower	doosh	*duche*
TV	teve	*TV*
window	zhuhnehluh	*janela*
view of the ...	veeshtuh puhruh ...	*vista para ...*
mountains	uh mongtuhnyuh	*a montanha*
sea	oo mahr	*o mar*

Can I see it?
  pohsoo veloo? — *Posso vê-lo?*

Are there any others?
  tãy maish kwartoosh deeshpooneevaysh? — *Tem mais quartos disponíveis?*

Where's the bathroom?
  ongd eh uh kahzuh de buhnyoo? — *Onde é a casa de banho?*

Is there hot water all day?
  ah ahgwuh kengt todoo oo deeuh? — *Há água quente todo o dia?*

Is there a discount for children/students?
  ah ahlgoong dshkongtoo puhruh kreeangsuhsh/shtoodangtesh? — *Há algum desconto para crianças/estudantes?*

It's fine. I'll take it.
  mwingtoo bãy feekoo kong el — *Muito bem. Fico com ele.*

Do I have to pay a deposit?
  eh prseezoo puhgahr kowsõw? — *É preciso pagar caução?*

Can I pay by credit card?
  pohsoo puhgahr kong kuhrtõw de krehdeetoo? — *Posso pagar com cartão de crédito?*

I'll be staying (one/two/three) nights.
  vo feekahr (oomuh/dwuhsh/tresh) noytsh — *Vou ficar (uma/duas/três) noites.*

I'm not sure yet how long I'll be staying.
  uhingduh nõw say kwangtoo tengpoo feekoo — *Ainda não sei quanto tempo fico.*

REQUESTS & QUERIES / PEDIDOS E PERGUNTAS

Do you have a safe?
  tãy oong kohfr? — *Tem um cofre?*

Is there somewhere to wash clothes?
  ah ahlgoong seetiw puhruh luhvahr uh ropuh? — *Há algum sítio para lavar a roupa?*

Can we use the telephone?
pohsoo oozahr oo tlfohn? · *Posso usar o telefone?*

Can I use the kitchen?
tãy servengteeuh de koozeenyuh? · *Tem serventia de cozinha?*

Do you have room service?
tay serveesoo de kwartoosh? · *Tem serviço de quartos?*

Does the room have a private bath?
tãy kahzuh de buhnyo
preevuhteevuh? · *Tem casa de banho privativa?*

I need another ...	preseezahvuh de otroo/uh ...	*Precisava de outro/a ...*
blanket	koobertor	*cobertor* (m)
pillow	ahlmoofahduh	*almofada* (f)
towel	twalyuh	*toalha* (f)

Can I change money in this ...?	pohsoo trookahr deenyayroo ...?	*Posso trocar dinheiro ...?*
hotel	nesht otehl	*neste hotel*
pension	nehshtuh pengsõw	*nesta pensão*

You can clean the room now.
zhah pohd lingpahr oo kwartoo · *Já pode limpar o quarto.*

I locked myself out.
fshay uh pohrtuh ee shkehsee-m
duhsh shahvzh dengtroo · *Fechei a porta e esqueci-me das chaves dentro.*

Do I have to leave the key
at the reception desk?
tulunyoo ke dayshahr uh
shahv nuh rrsehpsõw? · *Tenho que deixar a chave na recepção?*

Are there any messages for me?
ah ahlgoong rrkahdoo
puhruh ming? · *Há algum recado para mim?*

The key to room (211), please.
uh shahv doo kwartoo
se fahsh fuhvor · *A chave do quarto ..., se faz favor.*

Would you wake me at
(7) o'clock, please.
   poor fuhvor uhkohrd-me   *Por favor, acorde-me*
   ahzh (seht)   *às (sete).*

COMPLAINTS   RECLAMAÇÕES
By law, all hotels, pensions and camping grounds have a com-
plaints book where guests can write any complaints they have.
The authorities check these periodically.

It's too cold/hot.
   eh mwingtoo freeoo/kengt   *É muito frio/quente.*
It's too noisy.
   eh mwingtoo buhroolyengtoo   *É muito barulhento.*
Can I change rooms?
   pohsoo moodahr puhruh   *Posso mudar para*
   otroo kwartoo?   *outro quarto?*
I can't open/close the window.
   nõw kongseegoo uhbreer/   *Não consigo abrir/*
   fshahr uh zhuhnehluh   *fechar a janela.*

This ... isn't clean. esht/ehshtuh ...   *Este/esta ...*
                nõw shtah lingpoo/uh *não está limpo/a.*
  blanket   koobertor   *cobertor* (m)
  pillow   ahlmoofahduh   *almofada* (f)
  pillow case   fronyuh   *fronha* (f)
  sheet   lengsohl   *lençol* (m)

Please change ... poor fuhvor, moode ... *Por favor, mude ...*
  it   oo/uh   *o/a*
  them   oosh/uhsh   *os/as*

CHECKING OUT   SAÍDA
Can I pay by travellers cheque?
   pohssoo puhgahr kong   *Posso pagar com*
   trehvuhlers shehk?   *travellers cheque?*
Could I have the bill please?
   kreeuh uh kongtuh poor fuhvor *Queria a conta por favor.*

There's a mistake in the bill.
    ah oong eng-guhnoo nuh kongtuh *Há um engano na conta.*
Could I have a receipt?
    puhsahvuh-m oomuh fahtooruh? *Passava-me uma factura?*

LONGER STAYS   ESTADIAS MAISLONGAS

I've come about the advertisement
for a room to rent.
    veenyuh poor kowzuh doo   *Vinha por causa do*
    uhnoongseeoo doo kwartoo ke   *anúncio do quarto que*
    tãyãy puhruh uhloogahr   *têm para alugar.*
Do you have a flat for rent?
    tãy ahlgoong angdahr   *Tem algum andar*
    puhruh uhloogahr?   *para alugar?*
Is use of the kitchen included?
    tãy servengteeuh   *Tem serventia*
    dě koozeenyuh?   *de cozinha?*
Does it have a private bathroom?
    uh kahzuh de buhnyoo   *A casa de banho*
    eh preevahduh?   *é privada?*
How many rooms?
    de kwangtuhzh   *De quantas*
    uhswuhlyahduhsh?   *assoalhadas?*

How much   kwangtoo kehr poor ...?   *Quanto quer por ...?*
is it per ...?
    month   mesh   *mês*
    week   smuhnuh   *semana*
    day   deeuh   *dia*

ACCOMMODATION

SIGNS

HOTEL (H)	HOTEL
PARQUE DE CAMPISMO	CAMPING SITE
PENSÃO (P)	PENSION
POUSADA DA JUVENTUDE	YOUTH HOSTEL
RESIDENCIAL (R)	GUESTHOUSE

ACCOMMODATION

I'm looking for a flat/room to rent …	shto ah prohkooruh doong angdahr/ kwartoo puhruh uhloogahr …	*Estou à procura de um andar/ quarto para alugar …*
in the city centre	noo sengtroo duh seedad	*no centro da cidade*
in the country	noo kangpoo	*no campo*
in a village	noomuh ahldayuh	*numa aldeia*
near a beach	pehrtoo doomuh praiuh	*perto duma praia*
near public transport	noong seetiw kong bongsh trangshpohrtesh	*num sítio com bons transportes*

May I see it?
  pohssoo ve-loo?   *Posso vê-lo?*
I only want to rent it for (one) month.
  soh kreeuh uhloogahr   *Só queria alugar*
  poor (ong) mesh   *por (um) mês.*

USEFUL WORDS

PALAVRAS ÚTEIS

air-conditioning	oo ahr kongdeesiwnahdoo	*o ar condicionado*
bar of soap	oo suhboonete	*o sabonete*
bottle of water	uh guhrrahfuh dahgwuh	*a garrafa de água*
clean	lingpoo/uh	*limpo/a*
face cloth	uh twalyuh de roshtoo	*a toalha de rosto*
key	uh shahv	*a chave*
lamp	oo kangdeeayroo	*o candeeiro*
lock	uh fshuhdooruh	*a fechadura*
toilet	uh suhneetuh	*a sanita*
toilet paper	oo puhpehl eezhyehneekoo	*o papel higiénico*
towel	uh twalyuh	*a toalha*
water (cold/hot)	uh ahgwuh (freeuh/kengt)	*a água (fria/quente)*

PAPERWORK

name	nom
address	moorahduh
date of birth	dahtuh de
	nuhs-seemengtoo
place of birth	loogahr de
	nuhs-seemengtoo/
	nuhtooruhleedahd
age	eedahd
sex	sehksoo
nationality	nuhsiwnuhleedahd
religion	rrleezheeõw
profession/work	proofeesõw/
	truhbahlyoo
reason for travel	mooteevoo
	duh veeahzhãy

DOCUMENTOS

nome
morada
data de
nascimento
lugar del
nascimento/
naturalidade
idade
sexo
nacionalidade
religião
profissão/
trabalho
motivo da viagem

ACCOMMODATION

THEY MAY SAY ...

Lamento, mas estamos cheios.
luhmengtoo muhsh shtuhmoosh shayoosh
   Sorry, we're full.

Tem o seu ...? tãy oo se-w ...? I need to see your ...
   bilhete de beelyet   identity card
   identidade dee edeng-
              teedahd
   passaporte pahsuhpohrt   passport

Há um telefone público ...
ah oong tlfõhn poobleekoo ...
   There's a public phone ...

   no corredor
   noo koorrdor
   in the corridor

   ao pé da recepção
   aw peh duh rrsehpsõw
   next to the reception desk

ACCOMMODATION

marital status	shtahdoo seeveel	*estado civil*
single	soltayroo/uh	*solteiro/a*
married	kuhzahdoo/uh	*casado/a*
divorced	deevoorseeahdoo/uh	*divorciado/a*
widow/widower	veeoovoo/uh	*viúvo/a*
identification	eedengteefeekuhsõw	*identificação*
passport number	noomroo doo pahsuhpohrt	*número do passaporte*
identity	noomroo doo	*número do*
card number	beelyet deedengteedahd	*bilhete de identidade*
date of issue	dahtuh deemeesõw	*data de emissão*
expiry date	vahleedoo uhteh	*valido até ...*
visa	veeshtoo	*visto*
baptismal certificate	serteedõw de bahtizhmoo	*certidão de baptismo*
driving licence	kahrtuh de kongdoosõw	*carta de condução*
immigration	eemeegruhsõw	*imigração*
purpose of visit	feenuhleedahd duh veezeetuh	*finalidade da visita*
holiday	fehryuhsh	*férias*
business	ngohsiwsh	*negócios*
visiting relatives	veezeetuh uh fuhmeeleeahrsh/uh puhrengtsh	*visita a familiares/a parentes*
visiting the homeland	veezeetuh ah tehrruh nuhtahl	*visita à terra natal*

LOOKING FOR ...   ## À PROCURA ...

Where's a/the ...?	ongd eh ...?	*Onde é ...?*
(nearest) bank	oo bangkoo (maish prohseemoo)	*o banco (mais próximo)*
city/town centre	oo sengtroo duh seedahd/veeluh	*o centro da cidade/vila*
consulate	oo kongsoolahdoo	*o consulado*
embassy	uh engbaishahdhuh	*a embaixada*
market	oo merkahdoo	*o mercado*
museum	oo moose-w	*o museu*
(nearest) post office	oo koorrayoo (maish prohseemoosh)	*o correio (mais próximo)*
public telephone	tlefohn poobleekoo	*telefone público*
public toilet	oomuh kahzuh de buhnyoo poobleekuh	*uma casa de banho pública*
police	uh pooleesyuh	*a polícia*
tourist office	oo poshtoo de tooreezhmoo	*o posto de turismo*
underground	oo mehtroo	*o metro*

AT THE BANK   NO BANCO

Portugal's currency is the *escudo*, which is further divided into 100 *centavos*. Coins come in 1, 5, 10, 20, 50, 100 and 200 escudo denominations. However, there are very few one *escudo* coins in circulation, and shopkeepers and even banks will round to the nearest 5 *escudos*. Notes come in 1,000$00, 2,000$00, 5,000$00 and 10,000$00 escudo denominations. (Prices are usually denoted with a $ sign between escudos and centavos, so that 25 *escudos*, 50 centavos is written as 25$50.)

If you have an internationally recognised automatic teller machine (ATM) card, cash can be obtained at ATMs 24 hours a day. Still, it's a good idea to check that your ATM system is available in Portugal. If not, you can exchange money at any bank. However, banks have a fairly high service charge.

Banks typically open at 8.30 am and close at 3 pm, and don't close for lunch.

Can I use my credit card to
withdraw money?
   pohsoo lvangtahr deenyayroo
   kong oo me-w kuhrtōw
   de krehdeetoo?

*Posso levantar dinheiro
com o meu cartão
de crédito?*

Can I exchange money here?
   pohsoo trookahr
   deenyayroo uhkee?

*Posso trocar
dinheiro aqui?*

Please write it down.
   poor fuhvor shkrevuh-oo

Por favor, escreva-o.

Can I have smaller notes?
   tãy nohtuhzh maish pkenuhsh?

Tem notas mais pequenas?

The ATM swallowed my card.
   oo moolteebangkoo kome-w
   oo me-w kuhrtōw

*O Multibanco comeu
o meu cartão.*

I want to exchange (a) …	kreeuh trookahr …	*Queria trocar …*
cash	deenyayroo	*dinheiro*
cheque	oong shehk	*um cheque*
travellers cheque	oong trehvuhluhrs shehk	*um travellers' cheque*

What time does the bank open?
   uh ke ohruhzh eh ke
   ahbr oo bangkoo?

*A que horas é que
abre o banco?*

Where can I cash a travellers cheque?
   ongd eh ke pohsoo trookahr
   oong trehvuhluhrs shehk?

*Onde é que posso trocar
um travellers cheque?*

What's the exchange rate?
   kwal eh uh tahshuh de kangbiw?

Qual é a taxa de câmbio?

Can I transfer money here
from my bank?
   pohsoo trangshfererer deenyayroo
   doo me-w bangkoo puhruh uhkee?

*Posso transferir dinheiro
do meu banco para aqui?*

Can I transfer money to
another country?
   pohsoo fuhzer oomuh
   trangshferengsyuh eelehtrohneekuh
   puhruh oo shtrangzhayroo?

*Posso fazer uma
transferência electrónica
para o estrangeiro?*

How long will it take to arrive?
  kwangtoo tengpoo lehvuh?   *Quanto tempo leva?*

Automatic Teller Machine	oo moolteebangkoo	*o multibanco*
bank notes	uhzh nohtuhsh (de bangkoo)	*as notas (de banco)*
coins	uzh mwehduhsh	*as moedas*
credit card	oo kuhrtõw de krehdeetoo	*o cartão de crédito*
exchange	oo kangbiw	*o câmbio*
identification	uh eedengteefeekuhsõw	*a identificação*
loose change	oosh trohkoosh	*os trocos*
signature	uh uhseenuhtooruh	*a assinatura*

SIGNS

ABERTO	OPEN
CASA DE BANHO	TOILETS
CENTRO	CITY CENTRE
COMER	EATING
CORREIO (CTT)	POST OFFICE
ENCERRADO	CLOSED
ENTRADA	ENTRANCE
ENTRADA PROIBIDA	NO ENTRY
FARMÁCIA (F)	CHEMIST
FECHADO	CLOSED
FOTOGRAFAR	TAKING PHOTOGRAPHS
FUMAR	SMOKING
HOMENS	MEN'S TOILETS
INFORMAÇÃO	INFORMATION
PONTO DE ENCONTRO	MEETING POINT
PROIBIDO ...	... PROHIBITED
QUENTE/FRIO	HOT/COLD
SAÍDA (DE EMERGÊNCIA)	(EMERGENCY) EXIT
SENHORAS	WOMEN'S TOILETS
TURISMO (I)	TOURIST INFORMATION
USAR O FLASH	USING FLASH

AT THE POST OFFICE   NOS CORREIOS

Portugal's postal service is fast and efficient. If you don't make it to the post office in time, you can buy stamps at stamp vending machines around the city. The post office at the airport in Lisbon is open 24 hours a day for regular and express mail services.

I want to buy (an) ...	kreeuh kongprahr ...	*Queria comprar ...*
envelope	oong engvlohp	*um envelope*
postcards	pooshtaish	*postais*
stamps	seloosh	*selos*

I want to send a ...	kreeuh engveeahr ...	*Queria enviar ...*
fax	oong fahks	*um fax*
letter	oomuh kahrtuh	*uma carta*
parcel	oomuh	*uma*
	engkoomengduh	*encomenda*
telegram	oong tlegruhmuh	*um telegrama*

How much does it cost to
send this to ...?

kwangtoo eh ke kooshtuh   *Quanto é que custa*
engveeahr eeshtoo puhruh ...?   *enviar isto para ...?*

Please send it by ... mail.	poor fuhvor engvee-e eeshtoo ...	*Por favor, envie isto ...*
air	veeuh uhehreeuh	*via aérea*
express	ehksprehs mayl	*express mail*
fast	koorrayoo uhzool	*correio azul*
registered	koorrayoo rrzheeshtahdoo	*correio registado*
regular	koorrayoo nohrmahl	*correio normal*
surface	veeuh trrehshtre/ muhreeteemuh	*via terrestre/ marítima*

Please send it registered with a
return receipt.

poor fuhvor engvee-e eeshtoo   *Por favor, envie isto*
koorrayoo rrzheeshtahdoo   *correio registado*
kong uhveezoo de rrsehpsõw   *com aviso de recepção.*

mailbox	oo mahrkoo doo korrayoo	o marco do correio
padded envelope	oo engvlohp ahlmoofuhdahdoo	o envelope almofadado
parcel	oo engbroolyoo	o embrulho
pen	uh kuhnetuh/ shfchrohgrahfeekuh	a caneta/ esferográfica
postcode	oo kohdeegoo pooshtahl	o código postal
postal money order	oo vahl pooshtahl	o vale postal
receiver	deshteenuhtahriw	destinatário
sender	rremtengt	remetente

TELECOMMUNICATIONS

TELECOMUNICAÇÕES

Please connect me to
directory assistance.

   leeg-m ahz ingfoormuhsōyshs,
poor fuhvor

*Ligue-me às informações,
por favor.*

Could I please use the telephone?

   pohsoo oozahr oo tlefohn
se fahsh fuhvor?

*Posso usar o telefone,
se faz favor?*

How much does a (three)
minute call cost?

   kwangto eh ke kooshtuh
oomuh shuhmahduh de
(trezh) meenootoosh?

*Quanto é que custa
uma chamada de
(três) minutos?*

| I want to call ... | kreeuh tlefoonahr ... | Queria telefonar ... |
| The number is ... | oo noomroo eh ... | O número é ... |

I want to make a(n) ... call.	kreeuh fuhzer oomuh shuhmahduh ...	Queria fazer uma chamada ...
international	ingternuhsiwnahl	internacional
local	lookahl	local
long distance (within Portugal)	nuhsiwnahl	nacional
regional	ingtehroorbuhnuh	interurbana

I want to make a reverse-charge
(collect) call.
   kreeuh fuhzer oomuh   *Queria fazer uma*
   shuhmahduh uh puhgahr   *chamada a pagar*
   no deshteenoo   *no destino.*

What's the area code for ...?
   kwal eh oo ingdeekuhteevoo   *Qual é o indicativo*
   puhruh ...?   *para ...?*

It's engaged.
   shtah okoopahdoo   *Está ocupado.*

I've been cut off.
   uh shuhmahduh kuheeoo   *A chamada caiu.*

to call	leegahr	*ligar*
dial	muhrkahr oozh noomroosh	*marcar os números*
mobile phone	oo tehlehmohvehl	*o telemóvel*
operator	oo opruhdor/uh opruhdoruh	*o operador/a operadora*
phone book	uh lishtuh tlefohneekuh	*a lista telefónica*
phone box	uh kahbeen tlefohneekuh	*a cabine telefónica*
phonecard	oo kuhrtõw de tlefohn	*o cartão de telefone*
telephone	oo tlefohn	*o telefone*
telephone number	oo noomroo de tlefohn	*o número de telefone*
urgent	oorzhengt	*urgente*

Making a Call Fazer um Telefonema

Hello, is ... there?	shtah sing? shtah ...?	*Está sim? Está ...?*
Hello. (answering call)	shtah sing	*Está sim.*
May I speak to ...?	pohsoo fuhlahr kong ...?	*Posso falar com ...?*
It's	eh ...	*É ...*
Yes, s/he's here.	sing shtah	*Sim, está.*

Who's calling?
 kãy fahluh poor fuhvor? *Quem fala, por favor?*
One moment, please.
 oong moomengtoo, poor fuhvor *Um momento, por favor.*
I'm sorry, s/he's not here.
 deshkoolp muhzh nõw shtah *Desculpe, mas não está.*
What time will s/he be back?
 uh ke ohruhsh vohltuh? *A que horas volta?*
Can I leave a message?
 pohsoo dayshahr oong rrkahdoo? *Posso deixar um recado?*
Please tell him/her I called.
 poor fuhvor deeguh-ly *Por favor, diga-lhe*
 ke deloonay *que telefonei.*
I'll call back later.
 vohltoo uh tlefoonahr *Volto a telefonar*
 maish tahrd *mais tarde.*

The Internet A Internet

Where can I get Internet access?
 ongd ch ke pohsoo fuhzer *Onde é que posso fazer*
 oomuh leeguhsõw ah ingtehrneht? *uma ligação à Internet?*
I want to get Internet access.
 prseezoo de uhseder *Preciso de aceder*
 ah ingtehrneht *à Internet.*
I need to check my email.
 prseezoo de ver oo me-w eemayl *Preciso de ver o meu email.*

SIGHTSEEING   FAZER TURISMO

Where's the tourist office?
 ongd eh oo poshtoo *Onde é o posto*
 de tooreezhmoo? *de turismo?*
Do you have a local map?
 tãy oong mahpuh lookahl? *Tem um mapa local?*

AROUND TOWN

What are the best things
to see around here?
  kwaish sōw uhsh
  pringseepaiz uhtrahksōysh?

*Quais são as
principais atracções?*

What time does it open/close?
  uh ke ohruhzh eh
  ke ahbr/fuhshuh?

*A que horas é
que abre/fecha?*

What's that building?	oo ke eh uhkel eedfeesiw	O que é aquele edifício?
What's this monument?	oo keh eh esht moonoomengtoo?	O que é este monumento?
Is it very old?	eh mwingtoo angteegoo?	E muito antigo?
What century is it from?	de ke sehkoonloo eh?	De que século é?
Can we take photographs?	poodemoosh teerahr footoogruhfeeuhsh?	Podemos tirar fotografias?
Could you take a photograph of me?	poodeeuh teerahr-m oomuh footoogruhfeeuh?	Podia tirar-me uma fotografia?
Is there an entrance fee?	eh nsesahriw puhgahr uh engtrahduh?	É necessário pagar a entrada?

Is there a discount for …?	ah ahlgoong deshkongtoo puhruh …?	Há algum desconto para …?
children	kreeangsuhsh	crianças
seniors	uh tersayruh eedahd	a terceira idade
students	shtoodangtsh	estudantes

I'd like to see the …	gooshtahvuh de ver …	Gostava de ver …
castle	oo kuhshtehloo	o castelo
church	uh eegrezhuh	a igreja
cathedral	uh kuhtdrahl	a catedral
cinema	oo seenemuh	o cinema
concert	oo kongsertoo	o concerto
convent	oo kongvengtoo	o convento
monastery	oo mooshtayroo	o mosteiro
museum	oo moose-w	o museu
park	oo zluhrding	o jardim
statue	uh shtahtwuh	a estátua
university	uh ooneeverseedahd	a universidade

AROUND TOWN

ON THE STREETS

PELAS RUAS

What's this?
  oo keh eeshtoo?

O que é isto?

What's happening?
  oo keh ke se pahsuh?

O que é que se passa?

What happened?
  oo keh ke uhkongtse-w?

O que é que aconteceu?

How much is it?
  kwangtoo eh?

Quanto é?

Can I have one please?
  kreeuh oong/oomuh
  se fahsh fuhvor

Queria um/uma,
se faz favor.

beggar	oo/uh mengdeegoo/uh	*o/a mendigo/a*
block	oo kwuhrtayrõw	*o quarteirão*
crowded	kong mwingtuh zhengt	*com muita gente*
demonstration	uh muhneefshtuhsõw	*a manifestação*
festival	oo fshteevahl	*o festival*
kiosk	oo keeohshk	*o quiosque*
litter bin	uh puhplayruh	*a papeleira*
neighborhood	oo bairroo	*o bairro*
parade (with pomp & ceremony)	oo deshfeel	*o desfile*
procession	uh prooseesõw	*a procissão*
rubbish bin	oo kongtentor doo leeshoo	*o contentor do lixo*
street	uh rrwuh	*a rua*
street artist	oo/uh uhrteeshtuh de rwuh	*o/a artista de rua*

In smaller towns and villages, a night out usually consists of a visit to the local café after dinner and an evening stroll. Visitors are always surprised at the fact that even the smallest town will have at least one or two cafés on every block.

Nightlife in the big cities is more diverse. An outing in the evening could include either eating out at a restaurant and/or a movie. Bar-hopping and pub and club crawling is popular with the younger set, and many places come alive after midnight in major cities like Lisbon and Oporto.

WHERE TO GO   ONDE IR

What's there to do in the evening?
ke uhkteeveedahdzh ah ah noyt?   *Que actividades há à noite?*

I'd like to go to a/the …	tuhnyoo vongtahd deer …	*Tenho vontade de ir …*
bar	uh oong bahr	*a um bar*
café	uh oong kuhfeh	*a um café*
cinema	ow seenemuh	*ao cinema*
club	uh oomuh deeshkootehkuh	*a uma discoteca*
concert	uh oong kongsertoo	*a um concerto*
opera	ah ohpruh	*à opera*
restaurant	uh oong rreshtowrangt	*a um restaurante*
theatre	ow teeahtroo	*ao teatro*

I feel like …	uhptehsm …	Apetece-me …
going dancing	eer dangsahr	ir dançar
going for a drive	puhsyahr de kahrroo	passear de carro
going out	eer puhseeahr	ir passear
going back	vohltahr puhruh	voltar para
to the hotel	oo ohtehl	o hotel
relaxing	rrlahshahr	relaxar
resting	deshkangsahr	descansar
taking a walk	angdahr uh peh	andar a pé

INVITATIONS   CONVITES

Do you (inf) want to go out tonight?
  kehrsh suheer ehshtuh noyt?   *Queres sair esta noite?*

Are you (inf)	tāysh pluhnoosh	Tens planos
doing anything …?	puhruh …?	para …?
tonight	ehshtuh noyt	esta noite
this weekend	esht fing de smuhnuh	este fim de semana

Do you (inf) feel like getting
something to eat?
  kehrsh koomer kwalkehr koysuh?   *Queres comer qualquer coisa?*

We're going to the cinema.
Would you (pol) like to come?
  vuhmoozh ow seenemuh.   *Vamos ao cinema.*
  vāy kongnoshkoo?   *Vem connosco?*

Do you (inf) want to come with us?
  kehrsh veer kongnoshkoo?   *Queres vir connosco?*

It's on me.
  eh poor meenyuh kongtuh!   *É por minha conta!*

Responding to Invites   Resposta a Convites

I'd love to!; Sure!
  klahroo (ke sing)!   *Claro (que sim)!*

It's very kind of you, but I can't go.
  eh mwingtoo uhmahvehl duh   *É muito amável da*
  swuh pahrt muhzh nōw   *sua parte, mas não*
  me eh pooseevehl eer   *me é possível ir.*

I can't. I have other plans.
  nõw pohsoo, zhah tuhnyoo   *Não posso, já tenho*
  oong engkontroo muhrkahdoo   *um encontro marcado.*

What if we went ...?   ee se fosemoozh ...?   *E se fôssemos ...?*
  tomorrow   ahmuhnyang   *amanhã*
  next week   puhruh uh   *para a*
    smuhnuh ke vãy   *semana que vem*

ARRANGING TO MEET / COMBINAR ENCONTROS

Where shall we meet?
  ongd eh ke nooz   *Onde é que nos*
  engkongtruhmoosh?   *encontramos?*
What time should we make it for?
  uh ke ohruhzh eh ke   *A que horas é que*
  muhrkuhmoosh?   *marcamos?*
Let's meet (in the city) at (6 pm).
  engkongtruhmoonoozh nuh   *Encontramo-nos na*
  (baishuh) ahzh (dzoytoo ohruhsh)   *(Baixa) às (18 horas).*
I'll pick you up at ...
  vo booshkahrt ahsh ...   *Vou buscar te às ...*
I'll try to make it, but I don't know if I'll get there in time.
  vo tengtahr eer ... muhzh nõw   *Vou tentar ir ... mas não*
  say se shegoo uh tengpoo   *sei se chego a tempo.*
OK. See you later.
  shtah bãy uhteh lohgoo!   *Está bem. Até logo!*

NIGHTCLUBS & BARS / CLUBES NOCTURNOS E BARES

Where are the bars and clubs in this city?
  ongd eh ke ah bahrzh ee   *Onde é que há bares e*
  deeshkootehkuhzh   *discotecas*
  nehshtuh seedahd?   *nesta cidade?*

GOING OUT

Where's the best place to go clubbing in (Lisbon)?	
kwal eh uh zonuh duhzh deeshkootehkuhzh āy (leezhbouh)?	*Qual é a zona das discotecas em (Lisboa)?*
How much is it to get in?	
kwangtoo kooshtuh uh engtrahduh?	*Quanto custa a entrada?*
I don't know how to dance!	
nōw say dangsahr!	*Não sei dançar!*
Let's dance.	
vuhmoozh dangsah	*Vamos dançar.*
Dance with me!	
dangsuh koomeegoo!	*Dança comigo!*
Come on! Don't be such a pain!	
angduh lah! nōw sayzhuhzh shahtoo/uh!	*Anda lá! Não sejas chato/a!*
Let's go to a bar where the music isn't so loud.	
vuhmoosh puhruh oong bahr kong moozeekuh maish kahlmuh	*Vamos para um bar com música mais calma.*
Let's have a drink!	
vuhmoosh toomahr oong kohpoo!	*Vamos tomar um copo!*
I had a great time!	
deeverteem eemengsoo!	*Diverti-me imenso!*
We'll have to do it again!	
temoozh de rrpteer uh dohz!	*Temos de repetir a dose!*

DATING & ROMANCE   SAIR E ROMANCE

Although the Portuguese are, in general, charming and very flirtatious, men and women of nearly all age groups will balk at an aggressive sexual overture. The Portuguese prize charm and romance over the blatant 'come-on', and still tend to be somewhat conservative in their lifestyles and vocabulary.

Choose your words carefully when referring to love-making – certain words are normally only freely used within committed relationships.

GOING OUT

The Date A Saída

Do you feel like
going out ...?

uhptehst
suheer ...?

Apetece-te sair ...?

   tonight

ehshtuh noyt

esta noite

   tomorrow?

ahmuhnyang

amanhã

Do you feel like having a drink?

   uhptehst toomahr ahlgoomuh
koyzuh?

*Apetece-te tomar
alguma coisa?*

OK.

shtah bãy

Está bem.

I'd love to.

gooshtahvuh eemengsoo!

Gostava imenso!

Thanks, but I really don't feel like it!

   obreegahdoo/uh muhzh
nõw me uhptehs nahduh!

*Obrigado/a, mas
não me apetece nada!*

CLASSIC PICK-UP LINES

Can I have a light, please?

   tãy loom poor fuhvor?   *Tem lume, por favor?*

May I sit here?

   pohsoo sengtahrm uhkee?   *Posso sentar-me aqui?*

Shall we go out for a bit of air?

   vuhmoozh uhpuhnyahr
oonh pokoo dahr?   *Vamos apanhar
um pouco de ar?*

Would you like me to
take you home?

   kehrsh ke tuhkongpuhny
uh kahzuh?   *Queres que te acompanhe
a casa?*

Do you have a
boyfriend/girlfriend?

   tãyzh nuhmoorahdoo/uh?   *Tens namorado/a?*

Can I call you tomorrow?

   pohsoo tlefoonahrt
(ahmuhnyang)?   *Posso telefonar-te
(amanhã)?*

Do you come here often?

   vãysh kah mwingtuhsh
vezsh?   *Vens cá muitas vezes?*

GOING OUT

Where would you like to go now?
    uhongd eh ke kehrzh
    eer uhgohruh?
         Aonde é que queres
         ir agora?
Will you take me home, please?
    lehvuhzhm uh kahzuh?
         Levas-me a casa?

CLASSIC REJECTIONS

No thanks, I'm busy.
    nõw obreegahdoo
    tuhnyoo mwingtoo truhbahlyoo
         Não obrigado.
         Tenho muito trabalho.
I don't have time.
    nõw tuhnyo tengpoo
         Não tenho tempo.
I'm here with my ...
    shto uhkee kong ...
         Estou aqui com ...

boyfriend	oo me-w nuhmoorahdoo	*o meu* *namorado*
girlfriend	uh meenyuh nuhmoorahduh	*a minha* *namorada*

Sorry, I'm not interested.
    dshkoolp muhzh nõw
    shto ingtresahdoo/uh
         Desculpe, mas não
         estou interessado/a.
You're not my type.
    vose nõw fahzh oo
    me-w teepoo
         Você não faz o
         meu tipo.
I'm married.
    so kuhzahdoo/uh
         Sou casado/a.
I have a boyfriend/girlfriend.
    tuhnyoo nuhmoorahdoo/uh
         Tenho namorado/a.
Sorry, I can't.
    dshkoolp muhsh nõw pohsoo
         Desculpe, mas não posso.
Look. Just leave me alone.
    ohly. fahsh fuhvor de me
    dayshahr ãy pahzh
         Olhe. Faz favor de me
         deixar em paz.
Get lost!
    dzuhpuhresuh duhkee!
         Desapareça daqui!
Beat it!
    vai boozheeahr; vai
    dahr oomuh vohltuh!
         Vai bugiar; Vai
         dar uma volta!

Would you like to
come in for a drink?
  kehrsh engtrahr ee toomahr   *Queres entrar e tomar*
  oomuh bebeeduh?   *uma bebida?*

When can we see each other again?
  kwangdoo eh ke suheemoozh   *Quando é que saímos*
  otruh vesh?   *outra vez?*

Will I see you tomorrow?
  vemoonoozh ahmuhnyang?   *Vemo-nos amanhã?*

OK. Call me and we'll set up a time.
  shtah bãy leeguhm puhruh   *Está bem. Liga-me para*
  kongbeenahrmoozh uh ohruh   *combinarmos a hora.*

Making Love Fazer Amor

I want you.	dzuhzhoot	*Desejo-te.*
Kiss me.	bayzhuhm	*Beija-me.*
I (don't) like that.	(nõw) gohshtoo deesoo	*(Não) gosto disso.*
Please stop.	pahruh poor fuhvor!	*Pára, por favor!*
Faster!	maizh dprehsuh!	*Mais depressa!*
Slower!	maizh dvuhgahr!	*Mais devagar!*
Harder!	maish forsuh!	*Mais força!*
Softer!	maish swav!	*Mais suave!*

Would you like to come in?
  kehrzh engtrahr?   *Queres entrar?*

I want to make love to you.
  kehroo fuhzer uhmor kongteegoo   *Quero fazer amor contigo.*

Let's go to bed.
  vuhmoosh puhruh oo   *Vamos para o*
  kwartoo/uh kuhmuh   *quarto/a cama.*

I think we should stop.
  ahshoo ke dvereeuhmoosh puhrahr   *Acho que deveríamos parar.*

Oh, baby don't stop.
  nõw pahrzh uhmor!   *Não pares, amor!*

You can touch me (here).
  pohdsh tookahrm (uhkee)   *Podes tocar-me (aqui).*

GOING OUT

INTIMATE BODY

body	oo korpoo	o corpo
breasts	oosh sayoosh	os seios
bottom/bum	oo rrahboo	o rabo
eyes	ooz ohlyoosh	os olhos
hair	oo kuhbeloo	o cabelo
hands	uhzh mõwsh	as mãos
lips	oosh lahbiwsh	os lábios
mouth	uh bokuh	a boca
penis	oo pehneesh	o pénis
skin	uh pehl	a pele
tongue	uh ling-gwuh	a língua

I think we should use a condom.
   ahshoo ke dveeuhmoosh   *Acho que devíamos*
   oozahr przervuhteevoo   *usar preservativo.*
Do you have a condom?
   tãyzh oong przervuhteevoo?   *Tens um preservativo?*
I only have safe sex.
   soh pruhteekoo sehkso sgooroo   *Só pratico sexo seguro.*

Afterwards Depois
So, was it good for you?
   engtõw gooshtahsht?   *Então, gostaste?*
It was great.
   foy ohteemoo   *Foi óptimo.*
Would you like a cigarette?
   kehrzh oong seegahrroo?   *Queres um cigarro?*
Can I stay the night?
   pohsoo feekahr oo   *Posso ficar o*
   rehshtoo duh noyt?   *resto da noite?*
It's better if you don't.
   eh mlyohr nõw   *É melhor não.*

GOING OUT

Love Amor

I'm in love with you.
shto uhpaishoonahdoo/uh
poor tee

*Estou apaixonado/a
por ti.*

I love you!
uhmoot!

Amo-te!

Do you love me?
uhmuhahm?

Amas-me?

Do you like me?
gohshtuhzh de ming?

Gostas de mim?

I'd like to see you again.
gooshtahvuh de voltahr uh vert

Gostava de voltar a ver-te.

Why don't we live together?
poork nōw veevemoosh
zhoongtoosh?

*Porque não
vivemos juntos?*

INTIMATE PORTUGUESE

celibate	sleebuhtahriw/yuh	celibatário/a
embrace	oo uhbrahsoo	o abraço
erection	uh eerehksōw	a erecção
diaphragm	oo deeuhfrahgmuh	o diafragma
kiss	oo bayzhoo	o beijo
lover	oo/uh uhmangt	o/a amante
making love	fuhzer uhmor	fazer amor
to masturbate	muhshtoorbahrs	masturbar-se
orgasm	oo ohrgahzhmoo	o orgasmo
the Pill	uh peelooluh	a pílula
... sex	oo sehksoo ...	o sexo ...
anal	uhnahl	anal
oral	orahl	oral
safe	sgooroo	seguro
virgin	veerzhãy	virgem

Why don't you move in with me?
    poork eh ke nōw te   *Porque é que não te*
    mooduhsh puhruh oo me-w   *mudas para o meu*
    uhpuhrtuhmengtoo?   *apartamento?*
Will you marry me?
    kehrsh kuhzahr koomeegoo?   *Queres casar-te comigo?*

Leaving & Breaking Up Partir e Separar-se

I have to go.
    tuhnyoo de meer engbohruh   *Tenho de me ir embora.*
I'm going to miss you.
    vo ter suhwdahdsh twuhsh   *Vou ter saudades tuas.*
I don't want to lose touch.
    gooshtahvuh ke nōw   *Gostava que não*
    perdesemoozh oo kongtahktoo *perdêssemos o contacto.*
I don't think we get along very well.
    ahshoo ke nōw noozh   *Acho que não nos*
    duhmoosh bāy   *damos bem.*
I think we're (not) made for each other.
    ahshoo ke (nōw) shtuhmoosh   *Acho que (não) estamos*
    faytoozh oong puhruh oo otroo *feitos um para o outro.*
Let's just be friends, OK?
    feekuhmoosh   *Ficamos*
    uhmeegoosh shtah bāy?   *amigos, está bem?*

FAMILY   FAMÍLIA

QUESTIONS   ## PERGUNTAS

Are you married?
   eh kuhzahdoo/uh?   *É casado/a?*
Do you have any children?
   tãy teelyoosh?   *Tem filhos?*
Do you live with your family?
   veev kong uh swuh fuhmeelyuh?   *Vive com a sua família?*
Do you get along well
with your family?
   dahs bãy kong uh   *Dá-se bem com a*
   swuh fuhmeelyuh?   *sua família?*
How many siblings do you have?
   kwangtooz eermõwsh tãy?   *Quantos irmãos tem?*

Is your ... here?   ... shtah uhkee?   *... está aqui?*
   husband   oo se-w muhreedoo   *O seu marido*
   wife   uh swuh moolyehr   *A sua mulher*

REPLIES   ## RESPOSTAS

I'm ...   so ...   *Sou ...*
   single   soltayroo/uh   *solteiro/a*
   married   kuhzahdoo/uh   *casado/a*
   a widower/widow   veeoovoo/uh   *viuvo/a*
   divorced   deevoorseeahdoo/uh   *divorciado/a*

We live together but we're not married.
   veevemoozh zhoongtoosh   *Vivemos juntos,*
   muhzh nõw somoosh kuhzahdoosh   *mas não somos casados.*
I'm involved with someone.
   shto kongproomteedoo/uh   *Estou comprometido/a.*
I live with my partner (companion).
   veevoo kong oo me-w   *Vivo com o meu*
   kongpuhnyayroo/uh   *companheiro/a*
   meenyuh kongpuhnyayruh   *minha companheira.*

FAMILY

I don't have any children.
nõw tuhnyoo feelyoosh

Não tenho filhos.

I/we have a boy and a girl.
tuhnyoo/temooz
oong kuhzuhleenyoo

*Tenho/temos
um casalinho.*

I live ...
  by myself
  with my family

veevoo ...
sohzeenyoo/uh
kong uh meenyuh
fuhmeelyuh

*Vivo ...
sozinho/a
com a minha
família*

FAMILY MEMBERS   MEMBROS DA FAMÍLIA

aunt	teeuh	*tia*
baby	behbeh	*bebé*
brother	eermõw	*irmão*
children	feelyoosh/kreeangsuhsh	*filhos/crianças*
cousin	preemoo/preemuh	*primo/prima*
daughter	feelyuh	*filha*
family	fuhmeelyuh	*família*
father	pai	*pai*
father-in-law	sogroo/sohgruh	*sogro/sogra*
grandfather	oo uhvo	*o avô*
grandmother	uh uhvoh	*a avó*
half-brother	mayoo eermõw	*meio irmão*
half-sister	mayuh eermang	*meia irmã*
husband	muhreedoo	*marido*
mother	mãy	*mãe*
mother-in-law	sogroo/sohgruh	*sogro/sogra*
niece	soobreenyuh	*sobrinha*
nephew	soobreenyoo	*sobrinho*
sister	eermang	*irmã*
son	feelyoo	*filho*
stepfather	puhdrahshtoo	*padrasto*
stepmother	muhdrahshtuh	*madrasta*
stepson/stepdaughter	engtyahdoo/uh	*enteado/a*
uncle	teeoo	*tio*
wife	moolyehr	*mulher*

TALKING WITH PARENTS   A FALAR COM PAIS

How many children do you have?
  kwangtoosh feelyoosh tãy?   *Quantos filhos tem?*

We don't have any children.
  nõw temoosh feelyoosh   *Não temos filhos.*

How old are they?
  ke cedahd tãyãy?   *Que idade têm?*

FAMILY

I have (a) ...	tuhnyoo oong/oomuh ...	*Tenho um/uma ...*
daughter	feelyuh	*filha*
son	feelyoo	*filho*
(two) children	(doysh) feelyoosh	*(dois) filhos*

How old is your ...?	kwangtoosh uhnoosh tem...?	*Quantos anos tãy ...?*
son	o seu filho	*oo se-w feelyoo?*
daughter	a sua filha	*uh swuh feelyuh?*

(See Numbers & Amounts, page 239, for ages.)

What do your children do?
  ke fahzãy oosh se-wsh feelyoosh?   *Que fazem os seus filhos?*

Where do your children live?
  ongd veevãy oosh se-wsh feelyoosh?   *Onde vivem os seus filhos?*

Are your children still in school?
  oosh se-wsh feelyooz
  uhingduh angdõw nuh shkohluh?   *Os seus filhos
  ainda andam na escola?*

What does your	oo ke eh ke	*O que é que*
... study?	... shtooduh?	*... estuda?*
son	oo se-w feelyoo	*o seu filho*
daughter	uh swuh feelyuh	*a sua filha*

When's the baby due?
  puhruh kwandoo eh oo behbeh?   *Para quando é o bebé?*

What are you going to name him/her?
  komoo eh ke se vai shuhmahr?   *Como é que se vai chamar?*

FAMILY

Is this your first child?
    eh oo preemayroo feelyoo?   *É o primeiro filho?*

What's the baby's name?
    komoo eh ke se   *Como é que se*
    shuhmuh oo behbeh?   *chama o bebé?*

Is it a boy or a girl?
    eh mneenoo o mneenuh?   *É menino ou menina?*

Does s/he behave well?
    pohrtuhs bāy?   *Porta-se bem?*

Does s/he let you get a night's sleep?
    dayshuhvoosh doormeer ah noyt?   *Deixa-vos dormir à noite?*

S/he looks just	puhrehses mwingtoo	*Parece-se*
like his/her ...	kong ...	*muito com ...*
father	oo pai	*o pai*
mother	uh māy	*a mãe*

I can't believe it! You look so young.
    nōw uhkrdeetoo. muhsh   *Não acredito! Mas*
    puhrehs tōw zhohvāy!   *parece tão jovem!*

TALKING WITH CHILDREN
A FALAR COM CRIANÇAS

An adult will usually use the informal *tu* form of a verb with children. And young children, unaware of linguistic nuances, nearly always use the *tu* form with everybody.

What's your name?
    komoo eh ke te shuhmuhsh?   *Como é que te chamas?*

How old are you?
    ke eedahd tāysh?   *Que idade tens?*

When's your birthday?
    kwangdoo eh oo deeuh   *Quando é o dia*
    doosh te-wsh uhnoosh?   *dos teus anos?*

Do you have any brothers or sisters?
    tāyz eermōwsh?   *Tens irmãos?*

Do you have any pets?
    tāyz ahlgoong uhneemahl   *Tens algum animal*
    de shteemuhsōw?   *de estimação?*

Do you go to school/kindergarten?
   zhah vaiz ah shkohluh/ow
   ingfangtahrıw?

Já vais à escola/ao
infantário?

Do you like school?
   gohshtuhzh duh shkohluh?

Gostas da escola?

Do you play sports?
   fahzsh ahlgoong deshportoo?

Fazes algum desporto?

FAMILY

FAMILY

What's your favourite game?
  kwahl eh oo te-w zhogoo
  prefreedoo?

*Qual é o teu jogo
preferido?*

What do you do after school?
  oo ke eh ke kooshtoomuhsh
  fuhzer dpoyzh duhz owluhs?

*O que é que costumas
fazer depois das aulas?*

Are you learning English?
  shtahs uh uhprengder
  uh fuhlahr ing-glesh?

*Estás a aprender
a falar inglês?*

It's my language.
  eh uh meenyuh ling-gwuh

É a minha língua.

I'm from far away.
  vuhnyoo de mwingtoo longzh

Venho de muito longe.

Do you want to play with me?
  kehrsh bringkahr koomeegoo?

Queres brincar comigo?

What do you want to play?
  uh ke eh ke
  vuhmoosh bringkahr?

*A que é que
vamos brincar?*

How do you play that game?
  komoo eh ke se zhohguh?

Como é que se joga?

(See also Pets on page 201.)

INTERESTS   INTERESSES

COMMON INTERESTS INTERESSES COMUNS

What do you (pol) do in your spare time?
oo ke eh ke fazh noosh
se-wsh tengpoosh leevrsh?

O que é que faz nos
seus tempos livres?

I (don't) like ...	(nõw) gohshtoo de	(Não) gosto de ...
Do you (pol) like ...?	gohshtuh de ...?	Gosta de ...?
art	ahrt	arte
cooking	koozeenyahr	cozinhar
dancing	dangsahr	dançar
draw	dzenyahr	desenhar
film	seenemuh	cinema
gardening	zhurdeenahzãy	jardinagem
going out	suheer	sair
going to the beach	eer ah praluh	ir à praia
music	moozeekuh	música
painting	pingtahr	pintar
photography	fuhzer	fazer
	footoogruhfeeuh	fotografia
pottery	sruhmeekuh	cerâmica
reading books	ler	ler
sew	koozer	coser
the theatre	tyahtroo	teatro
travelling	veeuhzhahr	viajar
writing	shkrever	escrever

STAYING IN TOUCH FICAR EM CONTACTO

Today's my last day here.
ozh eh oo me-w oolteemoo
deeuh uhkee

Hoje é o meu último
dia aqui.

Let's exchange addresses.
trookuhmoozh moorahduhsh?

Trocamos moradas?

Do you have paper and a pen/pencil?
tãy puhpehl ee kuhnetuh/lahpeesh?

Têm papel e caneta/lápis?

Here's my card with all my numbers.
 tăy uhkee oo me-w kuhrtõw
 kong todoozh ozh me-wsh
 kongtahktoosh

*Tem aqui o meu cartão,
com todos os meus
contactos.*

What's your address?
And your phone number?
 kwal eh uh swuh moorahduh?
 ee oo se-w noomroo de tlefohn?

*Qual é a sua morada? E
o seu número de telefone?*

If you're ever passing through ...
you must stop by and visit.
 se ahlgoomuh vezh puhsahr
 poor ... tãy de noosh veezeetahr

*Se alguma vez passar
por ... tem de nos visitar.*

You always have a place to stay in ...
 tăy oomuh kahzuh sengpr
 ow se-w deeshpor ãy ...

*Tem uma casa sempre
ao seu dispor em ...*

Do you have email?
 tăy koorrayoo eelehtrohneekoo?

Tem correio electrónico?

When I get the pictures developed,
I'll send them to you (inf).
 kwangdoo rrvlahr uhsh
 footoogruhfeeuhz engveeootuhsh

*Quando revelar as
fotografias envio-tas.*

Don't forget to write!
 nõw te shkesuhzh de
 me shkrever!

*Não te esqueças de
me escrever!*

It was great meeting you (pol).
 gooshtay mwingtoo
 de oo/uh koonyser

*Gostei muito
de o/a conhecer.*

Writing Letters Escrever Cartas

Once you get back home, you may want to drop a line to people
you've met. Here are a few lines to help you.

Dear ... (pol) *Caro/a ...*
Dear ... (inf) *Querido/a ...*

I'm sorry it's taken me so long to write to you (sg/pl).
 Desculpa ter demorado tanto a escrever-te/vos.

It was great meeting you (sg/pl).
Gostei muito de te/vos conhecer.
Thank you (inf/pol) so much for your hospitality.
Muito obrigado pela tua/sua hospitalidade.

I miss you (sg/pl).	*Tenho saudades tuas/vossas.*
I had a fantastic time in …	*Diverti-me imenso em …*
My favourite place was …	*O sítio de que mais gostei foi …*
I hope to visit … again.	*Espero voltar a visitar …*
Say 'hi' to … and … for me.	*Dá cumprimentos meus a … e a …*
I'd love to see you (sg/pl) again.	*Adoraua tornar a ver-te/vos.*
Write soon!	*Escreve me depressa!*
My (new) address is …	*O meu (novo) endereço é …*
With love/kisses,	*Beijinhos,*
Affectionately,	*Um grande abraço,*
Regards,	*Cumprimentos,*
Best regards, (pol)	*Com os melhores cumprimentos,*

INTERESTS

MUSIC   MÚSICA

There are three types of traditional Portuguese music that still
have widespread appeal. These are *ranchos*, *tunas* and *fado*.

Ranchos are amateur troupes that play, sing and often dance to
tunes characteristic of the region the *rancho* comes from. Usually
the songs, dances and costumes as well as the props have been
reconstructed and researched with the help of local ethnographers
or anthropologists. *Ranchos* from all over the country travel, mainly
during summer, performing at fairs, festivals and concerts.

Tunas are musical ensembles made up of university students
and alumni who wear the student's black cape, dotted with
colourful badges. *Tuna* groups specialise in singing *fado* tunes from
the town of Coimbra and other traditional Portuguese songs.
They're usually accompanied by the Portuguese guitar, a 12-stringed
instrument that sounds something like a mandolin.

Fado is Portugal's most well-known and best-loved musical genre. Though *Fado* is sung throughout the country, Lisbon and Coimbra *fado* are the most famous. Lisbon *fado* is sung by a single vocalist, who's usually accompanied by at least two instrumentalists, one playing the Portuguese guitar and the other playing the classical six-stringed guitar. Though the *fado corrido*, or fast *fado*, is captivating with its flair and liveliness, it is the standard slow *fado*, with its plaintive, sorrowful tale of tragedy and unrequited love, that holds the audience in thrall.

Coimbra, a centuries-old university town, is the birthplace of *Coimbra fado*. Usually sung by students, the Coimbra version of *fado* consists of slow, romantic ballads, with fewer anguished vocal trills than the Lisbon variety.

YOU MAY HEAR ...

bilhete	beelyet	ticket
bilheteira	beelytayruh	ticket office
entrada	engtrahduh	ticket
fadista	fuhdeeshtuh	fado singer
guitarra	geetahrruh	small 12-string guitar
grupo de rock	groopoo de rrohk	rock group
casa de fado	kahzuh de fahdoo	fado house
cantor/cantora	kangtor/kangtoruh	singer
concerto	kongsertoo	concert
lugar de pé	loogahr de peh	standing room
lugar reservado	loogahr rrzervahdoo	reserved seats
lugar sentado	loogahr sengtahdoo	seats
música	moozeekuh	music
noite de fados	noyt de fahdoosh	fado night
palco	pahlkoo	stage
rancho	rrangshoo	folk song/dance group
espectáculo	shpehtahkooloo	show
tuna	toonuh	university music group
viola	veeohluh	guitar

Fado is often played on the radio, and hundreds of recordings are available, but the *fado* experience is best enjoyed in a *casa de fado*, or *fado* house, where up to five or six different *fadistas*, or *fado* singers, can be heard each night.

Do you want to dance?
  kehrsh dangsahr?   *Queres dançar?*
Sorry, I'm a really bad dancer.
  dshkoolpuh muhzh dangsoo   *Desculpa, mas danço*
  mwingtoo muhl   *muito mal.*
What's your favourite kind of music?
  ke zhehnroo de moozeekuh   *Que género de música*
  eh ke gohshtuhzh maish?   *é que gostas mais?*

What radio station plays ...?	āy ke poshtoo de rrahdiw pohsoo oveer ..?	*Em que posto de rádio posso ouvir ...?*
classical music	moozeekuh klahseekuh	*música clássica*
easy-listening music	moozeekuh leezhayruh	*música ligeira*
jazz	dzhahz	*jazz*
rock music	rrohk	*rock*

Is it an FM or AM station?
  āy ke ongduh shtah es pohstoo?   *Em que onda está esse posto?*
  ehf ehm o ongduh mehdyuh?   *FM ou onda média?*

CINEMA & THEATRE   CINEMA E TEATRO

Most of Portugal's larger cities put out 'what's happening' guides free of charge or for a nominal fee. These include information on everything from film premieres, exhibitions and concerts to free, open-air entertainment.

Portugal is one of the few European countries where subtitles are preferred over dubbing. Many films in major cinemas are English-language productions, so you'll be able to see them in their original versions.

Most cinemas have reserved seating, and it's customary to tip the usher about 25 *escudos*. Some cinemas still have a 10-minute intermission, although this practice seems to be slowly dying out.

When you're purchasing concert or theatre tickets, you'll have to specify if you'd like seating in the *plateia*, 'orchestra seats', *camarotes*, 'box seats', the *primeira* or *segunda balcão*, 'first' or 'second balcony', or the *frisas*, 'wings'.

I feel like going to (see) a/the ...	tuhnyoo vongtahd deer ...	*Tenho vontade de ir ...*
comedy	ver oomuh koomehdyuh	*ver uma comédia*
cinema	ow seenemuh	*ao cinema*
romance	ver oong feelm rroomangteekoo	*ver um filme romântico*
theatre	ow tyahtroo	*ao teatro*

Are there any tickets for cinema (one)?
    ah beelyetshs puhruh   *Há bilhetes para*
    uh sahluh (oong)?   *a sala (um)?*

What time does the (next) film start?
    uh ke ohruhsh koomehsuh   *A que horas começa*
    uh (prohseemuh) sesõw?   *a (próxima) sessão?*

I'd like two tickets for ...
    kreeuh doyzh   *Queria dois*
    beelyetshs puhruh ...   *bilhetes para ...*

It got great reviews.
    tev mwingtoo bouhsh kreeteekuhsh   *Teve muito boas críticas.*

Opinions Opiniões

Did you (inf/pol) like the ...?	gooshtahsht/ gooshto ...?	*Gostaste/ Gostou ...?*
film	doo feelm	*do filme*
play	duh pehsuh (de tyahtroo)	*da peça (de teatro)*
show	doo shpehtahkooloo	*do espectáculo*

I really liked it.	gooshtay mwingtoo	*Gostei muito.*
I didn't like it at all.	nõw gooshtay nahduh	*Não gostei nada.*

It was OK. It wasn't my favourite.
  maiz o menoosh nõw foy
  o/uh ke gooshtay maish

*Mais ou menos. Não foi
  o/a que gostei mais.*

I couldn't follow the story
very well because of the language.
  nõw kongsegee uhkongpuhnyahr
  bãy uh eeshtohryuh poor
  kowzuh duh ling-gwuh

*Não consegui acompanhar
  bem a história por
  causa da língua.*

MUSEUMS   ## MUSEUS

Don't overlook the small museums in towns outside Lisbon
and Oporto, which boast interesting displays ranging from
local archaeological finds to historical displays of agriculture,
fishing and handicrafts. Museums close at 5 pm and are closed
all day on Mondays.

Where are the museums/galleries in this town/city?
  ongd feekõw oozh mooze-wsh/   *Onde ficam os museus/*
  uhsh guhlreeuhsh nehshtuh   *as galerias nesta*
  veeluh/seedahd?   *vila/cidade?*

battle	uh buhtahlyuh	*a batalha*
century	oo sehkooloo	*o século*
the Discoveries	oozh	*os*
(of the New World)	deshkoobreemengtoosh	*Descobrimentos*
empire	oo ingpehriw	*o império*
king	oo rray	*o rei*
queen	uh rruheenyuh	*a rainha*
reign	oo rraynahdoo	*o reinado*
sea	oo mahr	*o mar*

ART   **ARTE**

Which works are exhibited here?
  kwaish sōw uhz ohbruhsh   *Quais são as obras*
  shpohshtuhsh?   *expostas?*
Where can I see the works of ...?
  ongd eh ke pohsoo ver   *Onde é que posso ver*
  uhz ohbruhzh de ...?   *as obras de ...?*
What kind of art are you interested in?
  ãy ke teepoo dahrt shtah   *Em que tipo de arte está*
  ingtresahdoo/uh?   *interessado/a?*

I'm interested in ... ingtrehsoo-m poor ...   *Interesso-me por ...*
  architecture   uhrkeetehtooruh   *arquitectura*

  ... art   ahrt ...   *arte ...*
    Baroque   buhrrokuh   *barroca*
    Contemporary   kongtengpooruhneeuh *contemporânea*
    modern   moodehrnuh   *moderna*
    Renaissance   rrnuhs-sengteeshtuh *renascentista*
    Roman   rroomuhneekuh   *românica*

  art nouveau   uh ahrt nohvuh   *a arte nova*
  drawing   dzuhnyoo   *desenho*
  graphic arts   ahrtshs grahfeekuhsh *artes gráficas*
  painting   pingtooruh   *pintura*
  sculpture   shkooltooruh   *escultura*

  antiquity   uh angteegwidahd   *a antiguidade*
  canvas   uh tehluh   *a tela*
  to exhibit   shpor   *expor*
  exhibition   uh shpoozeesōw   *a exposição*
  exhibition opening   oomuh   *uma*
                        eenowgooruhsōw   *inauguração*
  fine arts   uhsh behluhz ahrtsh *as belas artes*
  gallery   uh guhlreeuh   *a galeria*
  impressionist   ingprsiwneeshtuh   *impressionista*
  master   oo/uh mehshtr   *o/a mestre*
  masterpiece   uh ohbruhpreemuh   *a obra-prima*
  oil (painting)   (pingtahdoo uh) ohliw *(pintado a) óleo*

painter	oo pingtor/	*o pintor/*
	uh pingtoruh	*a pintora*
picture	oo kwadroo	*o quadro*
work (of art)	uh ohbruh (dahrt)	*a obra (de arte)*
porcelain	uh poorsluhnuh	*a porcelana*
sculptor	oo shkooltor;	*o escultor;*
	uh shkooltoruh	*a escultora*
studio	oo shtoodiw	*o estúdio*
style	oo shteeloo	*o estilo*
technique	uh tehkneekuh	*a técnica*

Opinions Opiniões

Do you like the works of …?
  gohshtuh duhz ohbruhsh de …?   *Gosta das obras de …?*
What do you think of this (palace)?
  oo ke eh ke ahshuhzh/ahshuh   *O que é que acha*
  desht (puhlahsiw)?   *deste (palácio)?*
It reminds me of …
  fahzh-m lengbrahr …   *Faz-me lembrar …*

I think it's …	ahshoo ke eh …	*Acho que é …*
beautiful	lingdoo/uh/	*lindo/a/*
	booneetoo/uh	*bonito/a*
dramatic	druhmahteekoo/uh	*dramático/a*
extraordinary	shtruhordeenahriw/yuh	*extraordinário/a*
incomprehensible	ingkongpre-engseevehl	*incompreensível*
interesting	ingtresangt	*interessante*
strange	shtruhnyoo/uh	*estranho/a*
ugly	fayoo/uh	*feio/a*

ARCHITECTURE   ARQUITECTURA

Portugal has many fine examples of a variety of architectural styles, ranging from Roman ruins to contemporary buildings. However, one distinctively Portuguese style that captures the spirit of the country's wealth and power during the 16th century is *Manuelino*, or 'Manueline'.

INTERESTS

I'm interested in ... architecture.	ingtrehsoo-m poor uhrkeetehtooruh ...	*Interesso-me por arquitectura ...*
Gothic	gohteekoo/uh	*gótico/a*
classical	klahseekuh	*clássica*
Greek	gregoo/uh	*grego/a*
Iberian	eebehreekoo/uh	*ibérico/a*
Manueline	muhnweleenoo/uh	*Manuelino/a*
Moorish	moroo/uh	*Mouro/a*
rococo	oo rrohkohkoh	*o rococó*
Romanesque	rroomuhneekoo/uh	*românico/a*
Visigothic	vezeegohteekoo/uh	*visigótico/a*

arch	oo ahrkoo	*o arco*
armillary sphere (an astronomical model of the globe associated with Manueline architecture)	uh shfehruh uhrmeelahr	*a esfera armilar*
brick	oo teezholoo	*o tijolo*
castle	oo kuhshtehloo	*o castelo*
chapel	uh kuhpehluh	*a capela*
church	uh eegruhzhuh	*a igreja*
cloister	oo klowshtroo	*o claustro*
coat of arms	oo bruhzõw	*o brazão*
column	uh kooloonuh	*a coluna*
convent	oo kongvengtoo	*o convento*
courtyard	oo pahtiw	*o pátio*
dome	uh koopooluh	*a cúpula*
earthquake	oo trruhmohtoo	*o terramoto*
fountain	uh fongt	*a fonte*
granite	oo gruhneetoo	*o granito*
marble	oo mahrmoor	*o mármore*
monastery	oo mooshtayroo	*o mosteiro*
palace	oo puhlahsiw	*o palácio*

park	oo zhuhrding	*o jardim*
refectory	oo rrfaytohriw	*o refeitório*
stone	uh pehdruh	*a pedra*
tile	oo uhzooluhzhoo	*o azulejo*
tower	uh torr	*a torre*
vault	uh koopooluh	*a cúpula*
Visigoth	veezeegodoo/uh	*visigodo/a*
(city) wall	uh moorahlyuh	*a muralha*
wood	uh muhdayruh	*a madeira*

LITERATURE   LITERATURA

There are several good English translations of Portuguese authors that can be found in centrally located *livrarias*, 'bookshops'. Portuguese authors popular with foreign readers include Fernando Pessoa, the modernist poet; Eça de Queiroz, the multi-talented 19th century novelist; and José Saramago, the 1998 Nobel Prize laureate for literature and Portugal's most commercially successful contemporary writer.

Os Lusíadas, 'The Lusiads', was written by the 16th century poet Luís de Camões, who's often referred to as the 'Portuguese Shakespeare'. *The Lusiads* pays tribute to the country's maritime achievements, recounting Vasco da Gama's heroic discovery of the sea route to India.

What type of books do you read?
ke zhehnroo de leevrooz eh ke lezh?	*Que género de livros é que lês?*

Who's your favourite ...?
kwal eh ... fuhvooreetoo/uh?	*Qual é ... favorito/a?*
author (m) oo te-w owtor	*o teu autor*
author (f) uh twuh owtoruh	*a tua autora*

I like the works of ...
gohshtoo mwingtoo duh ohbruh de ...	*Gosto muito da obra de ...*

I (don't) like …	(nōw) gohshtoo de …	(Não) gosto de …
biographies	biwgruhfeeuhsh	biografias
comics	bangduh dzenyahduh	banda desenhada
essays	engsaioosh	ensaio
fiction	feeksōw	ficção
… literature	leeteruhtooruh …	literatura …
classical	klahseekuh	clássica
contemporary	kongtengpooruhnyuh	contemporânea
erotic	eerohteekuh	erótica
(historical) novels	rroomangsez	romances
	(eeshtohreekoosh)	(históricos)
mysteries	leevroosh pooleeseeaish	livros policiais
poetry	pooesyuh	poesia
short stories	kongtoosh	contos

Opinions Opiniões

I think it/ he/she is …	ahshoo ke eh …	Acho que é …
brilliant	zhneeahl	genial
fun/amusing	deeverteedoo	divertido
interesting	ingtresangt	interessante
monotonous	moonohtoonoo	monótono
really boring (coll)	oomuh sehkuh	uma seca

I thought it was well/badly written.
  puhrese-wm bāy/mahl shkreetoo

*Pareceu-me
bem/mal escrito.*

I thought it was better/worse than his/her last novel.
  puhrese-wm mlyohr/peeohr do
  ke oo rroomangs angteryor

*Pareceu-me melhor/
pior do que o
romance anterior.*

TALKING ABOUT TRAVELLING

Do you travel a lot?
kooshtoomuh veeuhzhahr mwingtoo?

How long have you been travelling?
ah kwangtoo tengpoo eh ke shtalı de veeahzhãy?

I've been travelling now for (three weeks).
zhah shto uh veeuhzhahr ah (tresh smuhnuhsh)

What places have you been to so far?
ke tehrruhz eh ke zhah veezeeto?

I've just come from ...
uhkahboo de veer/shgahr de ...

I spent ... days/weeks/months in ...
puhsay ... deeuhsh/ smuhnuhsh/mezesh ãy ...

I've been to ...   zhah shteev ãy ...
I'm going to ...   vo puhruh ...
I want to go to ... kehroo ir puhruh ...

FALAR SOBRE VIAGENS

Costuma viajar muito?

Há quanto tempo é que está de viagem?

Já estou a viajar há (três semanas).

Que terras é que já visitou?

Acabo de vir/chegar de ...

Passei ... dias/ semanas/meses em ...

Já estive em ...
Vou para ...
Quero ir para ...

(See page 52 in Meeting People for placenames.)

INTERESTS

WHAT ARE YA?

esquerdóide	shkerdoyd	leftist
intelectual	ingtlehktwal	intellectual
menino/a bem	mneenoo/uh bãy	rich kid
novo-rico	novoo rreekoo	noveau riche
piroso/a	peerozoo/uh	tacky
(menino/a) queque	(mneenoo/uh) kehk	hip rich kid
rasca	rrahshkuh	grungy
reaccionário/a	rryahsiwnahriw/uh	reactionary
retrogrado/a	rretrohgruhdoo/uh	retro
sinistro/a	seeneeshtroo/uh	evil
yuppie	iwpee	yuppy

INTERESTS

What did you think of (Athens)?
oo ke eh ke uhsho de   *O que é que achou de*
(uhtenuhsh)?   *(Atenas)?*

I thought it was … uhshay ke ehruh …		*Achei que era …*
very beautiful	mwingtoo booneetoo/uh	*muito bonito/a*
touristy	mwingtoo tooreeshteekoo/uh	*muito turístico/a*
really dead	mwingtoo puhrahdoo/uh	*muito parado/a*
really ugly	mwingtoo fayoo/uh	*muito feio/a*

It was an exciting place.
teenyuh mwingtuh veeduh   *Tinha muita vida.*
Everything was really expensive.
toodoo ehruh mwingtoo kahroo   *Tudo era muito caro.*
I was robbed in …
fwi uhsahtahldoo/uh ãy …   *Fui assaltado/a em …*

The people	lah uhsh psouhsh	*Lá as pessoas*
there are very …	sõw mwingtoo …	*são muito …*
friendly	uhmahvaysh	*amáveis*
open	uhbehrtuhsh	*abertas*
reserved	fshahdoosh	*fechados*

What's there to do in …?
oo ke eh ke se pohd   *O que é que se pode*
fuhzer ãy … de ingteresangt?   *fazer em … de*
     interessante?

What are the hotels and
restaurants like?
komoo eh ke sõw oz otaysh   *Como é que são os hotéis*
ee oosh rrshtowrangtsh?   *e os restaurantes?*
What's the best time
of year to go there?
kwal eh uh mlyohr ehpookuh   *Qual é a melhor época*
puhruh eer uhteh lah?   *para ir até lá?*

STARS
Astrology Astrologia

ESTRELAS

What's your zodiac sign?
    kwal eh oo te-w seegnoo?   *Qual é o teu signo?*

I don't believe in astrology.
    now uhkrdeetoo noosh seegnoosh   *Não acredito nos signos.*

I'm a/an …	so …	*Sou …*
Aries	kuhrnayroo	*Carneiro*
Taurus	toroo	*Touro*
Gemini	zhehmiwsh	*Gémeos*
Cancer	kuhrang-guhzhoo	*Caranguejo*
Leo	leeōw	*Leão*
Virgo	veerzhãy	*Virgem*
Libra	buhlangsuh	*Balança*
Scorpio	shkoorpeeōw	*Escorpião*
Sagittarius	suhzheetahriw	*Sagitário*
Capricorn	kuhpreekohrniw	*Capricórnio*
Aquarius	uhkwariw	*Aquário*
Pisces	payshesh	*Peixes*

INTERESTS

That explains everything!
    eesoo shpleekuh toodoo!   *Isso explica tudo!*

I get do/don't get along well with (Virgos).
    dom bãy/mahl kong   *Dou-me bem/mal com*
    oosh (veerzhãy)   *os (Virgem).*

ascendant (rising sign)	oo uhsh-sengdengt	*o ascendente*
astrological chart	uh kahrtuh uhshtrahl	*a carta astral*
descendant	oo desh-sengdengt	*o descendente*
financial profile	pluhnoo muhtereeahl	*plano material*
romance profile	pluhnoo uhfehteevoo	*plano afectivo*
horoscope	oo ohrohskoopoo	*o horóscopo*
personality	uh persoonuh-leedahd	*a personalidade*
zodiac	oo zoodeeuhkoo	*o zodíaco*

INTERESTS

Astronomy Astronomia

Are you interested in astronomy?
   ingterehsuhsht peluh
   uhshtroonoomeeuh?   *Interessas-te pela*
                              astronomia?

I'm interested in astronomy.
   uh uhshtroonoomeeuh   *A astronomia*
   ingterehsuhm   *interessa-me.*

Do you (inf) have a telescope?
   táyz oong tleshkohpiw?   *Tens um telescópio?*

Is there an observatory near here?
   ah ahlgoong observuhtohriw   *Há algum observatório*
   uhkee pehrtoo?   *aqui perto?*

Where's the best place to
view the night sky?
   kwal eh oo mlyohr seetiw   *Qual é o melhor sítio*
   puhruh observahr uhz   *para observar as*
   shtreluhzh de noyt?   *estrelas de noite?*

When can you see …?	kwangdoo eh ke se ve …?	*Quando é que se vê …?*
Mars	mahrt	*Marte*
Mercury	merkooriw	*Mercúrio*
Pluto	plootõw	*Plutão*
Venus	vehnoosh	*Vénus*

astronomer	oong/oomuh uhshtrohnoomoo/uh	*um/uma astrónomo/a*
comet	oo koometuh	*o cometa*
Earth	uh tehrruh	*a Terra*
full moon	uh loouh shayuh	*a lua cheia*
last quarter	kwartoo ming-gwangt	*quarto minguante*
the Milky Way	uh veeuh lahktyuh	*a Via Láctea*
the North Star	uh shtreluh poolahr	*a Estrela Polar*
planet	oo pluhnetuh	*um planeta*
Ursa Major	uh oorsuh mayohr	*a Ursa Maior*
Ursa Minor	uh oorsuh mnohr	*a Ursa Menor*
space	oo shpahsoo	*o espaço*

THE UNEXPLAINED	O INEXPLICÁVEL

Do you believe that there's
life on other planets?

uhkredeetuh ke ah veeduh
fohruh duh tehrruh?

*Acredita que há vida
fora da Terra?*

Do you believe in …?	uhkredeetuh …?	*Acredita …?*
Have you ever seen …?	ahlgoomuh vezh viw …?	*Alguma vez viu …?*
black magic	nuh muhzheeuh negruh	*na magia negra*
extraterrestrial life forms	nooz ayshtruhterrchshtresh	*nos extraterrestres*
ghosts	noosh fangtahzhmuhsh	*nos fantasmas*
life after death	nuh veeduh puhruh ahlãy duh mohrt	*na vida para além da morte*
miracles	noozh meelahgresh	*nos milagres*
spiritual mediums	noozh mehdeeoongsh	*nos mediums*
telepathy	nuh tehlehpuhteeuh	*na telepatia*
UFOs	nooz ohvneesh	*nos Ovnis*
witchcraft	nuh brooshuhreeuh	*na bruxaria*

Many people in my country are (not) …	uhsh psouhsh noo me-w puheesh nohrmahlmengt (nõw) sõw …	*As pessoas no meu país normalmente (não) são …*
believers	krengtsh	*crentes*
imaginative	eemuhzheenuh-teevuhs	*imaginativas*
realists	rryuhleeshtuhsh	*realistas*
religious	rrleezhyohzuhsh	*religiosas*
sceptics	sehteekoosh	*cépticas*
scientific	syengteefeekuhsh	*científicas*
superstitious	soopersteesyohzuhsh	*supersticiosas*

ACTIVITIES   ACTIVIDADES

SPORT   **DESPORTO**

Soccer is Portugal's most popular sport, followed by cycling. Track and field events are also very popular, and the country has had a number of champions, including Olympic marathon gold medallists Carlos Lopes (1984) and Rosa Mota (1988).

Traditional Portuguese games that are played mostly in country areas include *chinquilho*, which is similar to throwing horseshoes, and *jogo da malha*, where a metal disk is aimed at a wooden peg.

Do you play ...?	zhohguh ...?	*Joga ...?*
Would you like to play ...?	kehr zhoogahr ...?	*Quer jogar ...?*
I do ...	fahsoo ...	*Faço ...*
I play ...	pruhteekoo ...	*Pratico ...*
baseball	bayzbohl	*basebol (m)*
basketball	bahskehtbohl	*basquetebol (m)*
cricket	kreekeht	*críquete (m)*
cycling	seekleezhmoo	*ciclismo (m)*
diving	mergoolyoo	*mergulho (m)*
fencing	zhgreemuh	*esgrima (f)*
football (soccer)	footbohl	*futebol (m)*
martial arts	ahrtsh muhrsyaish	*artes marciais (f)*
rugby	rraygbee	*râguebi (m)*
sailing	vehluh	*vela (f)*
skiing	skee	*ski (m)*
surfing	suhrf	*surf (m)*
swimming	nuhtuhsõw	*natação (f)*
table tennis	ping-gpong-g	*ping-pong (f)*
tennis	tehneesh	*ténis (m)*

TALKING ABOUT SPORT

FALAR SOBRE DESPORTO

Do you like sport?	gohshtuh de deshportoo?	*Gosta de desporto?*
Very much.	gohshtoo mwingtoo	*Gosto muito.*
Not really.	nãy poor eesoo	*Nem por isso.*
I hate it!	dtehshtoo!	*Detesto!*

I like playing sport.
   gohshtoo de fuhzer deshportoo   *Gosto de fazer desporto.*
I prefer to watch rather than play sport.
   gohshtoo maizh de ver   *Gosto mais de ver*
   doo ke fuhzer deshportoo   *do que fazer desporto.*
Do you play any sports?
   pruhteekuh ahlgoong deshportoo?   *Pratica algum desporto?*
When's/Where's the game?
   kwangdoo/ongd eh oo zhogoo?   *Quando/Onde é o jogo?*
I (don't) like that team.
   (nõw) gohshtoo dehsuh eekeepuh   *(Não) gosto dessa equipa.*

Talking about a Game Falar Sobre um Jogo

Who's winning/losing?
   kãy eh ke vai uh   *Quem é que vai a*
   guhnyahr/perder?   *ganhar/perder?*
Who's playing?
   kãy eh ke zhohguh?   *Quem é que joga?*
Who do you think is going to win?
   kãy eh ke ahshuhsh   *Quem é que achas*
   ke vai guhnyahr?   *que vai ganhar?*
Where's my seat?
   ongd eh oo me-w loogahr?   *Onde é o meu lugar?*
What's the score?
   uh komoo eh ke vai?   *A como é que vai?*

What a …!	ke …!	*Que ...!*
move	zhoogahduh	*jogada*
pass	pahs	*passe*
shot	shootoo	*chuto*

How much longer to go?
    kwangtoo tengpoo eh ke fahltuh?   *Quanto tempo é que falta?*
What was the score?
    kwal foy oo rrzooltahdoo?   *Qual foi o resultado?*

A draw.   engpaht   *Empate.*
Who won?   kãy guhnyo?   *Quem ganhou?*

BAD PORTUGUESE

Que chatice!	ke shuhtees!	What a drag!
Isto é uma merda!	eeshtoo eh oomuh mehrduh!	This sucks! This is shit!
Estou lixado/a!	shtoo leeshahdoo/uh!	I'm screwed!
Foda-se!	foduhs!	Fuck it!
Fogo!	fogoo!	Damn!
Filho da puta!	feelyoo duh pootuh!	Son of a bitch! (lit: son of a whore!)
Não me sarnes!	nõw me sahrnsh!	Get off my back!
Não me chateies!	nõw me shuhtuhee-esh!	Don't bug me!
Vai à merda!	vai ah mehrduh!	Fuck off! (lit: go to shit!)
Vai para o raio que te purta!	vai puhruh oo rraioo ke te pahrtuh!	Go to hell! (lit: may a lightning bolt strike you!)
Vai pentear macacos!	vai pengtyahr muhkahkoosh!	Get lost! (lit: go comb monkeys!)
Cretino/a!	krteenoo/uh!	You jerk!
Anormal!	uhnohrmahl!	Retard!
Sua besta!	swuh beshtuh!	You animal!
Cabrão/Cabra!	kuhbrõw/kahbruh!	You bastard/bitch!
Puta!	pootuh!	Whore!
Emplastro!	engplahshtroo!	You freak!
Caraças!	kuhrahsuhsh!	Damn!
Caralho!	kuhrahlyoo!	Godammit! (lit: dick!)
Estou-me a cagar!	shtom uh kuhgahr!	I don't give a shit!

We/they lost (2)-(1).
    perdemoosh/perderõw
    (doyz) uh (oong)

Perdemos/Perderam
(dois) a (um).

We/they won (3)–(nil).
    guhnyahmoosh/guhnyahrõw
    (trez) uh (zehroo)

Ganhámos/Ganharam
(três) a (zero).

Great game!
    foy oong zhogoo shpehtuhkoolahr!

Foi um jogo espectacular!

What a boring game!
    ke zhogoo tõw shahtoo!

Que jogo tão chato!

The referee was on the take!
    oo ahrbeetroo shtahvuh
    kongprahdoo!

O árbitro estava
comprado!

Let's do the Mexican wave!
    vuhmoosh fuhzer uh ongduh!

Vamos fazer a onda!

Where's (Benfica) in the league table?
    ãy ke loogahr shtah
    (oo bãyfeekuh)
    noo kangpiwnahtoo?

Em que lugar está
(o Benfica)
no Campeonato?

They're in (second) place.
    shtah ãy (sgoongdoo) loogahr

Está em (segundo) lugar.

SOCCER   FUTEBOL

Would you like to go to a
football game?
    kehr eer ver oong
    zhogoo de footbohl?

Quer ir ver um
jogo de futebol?

Which is your team?
    eh de ke eekeepuh?

É de que equipa?

I'm a (Benfica) supporter.
    so doo bãyfeekuh

Sou do (Benfica).

What a lousy team!
    ke eekeepuh tõw mah!

Que equipa tão má!

Boavista is much better/worse!
    oo bouhveeshtuh eh mwingtoo
    mlyohr/peeohr!

O Boavista é muito
melhor/pior!

CHAMPIONSHIPS

the National League Championship	
kangpiwnahtoo nuhsiwnahl	Campeonato Nacional
the Portuguese Cup	
tahsuh de poortoogahl	Taça de Portugal
the UEFA Cup	
tahsuh duh ooehfuh	Taça da UEFA
the European Championship	
kangpiwnahtoo duh e-wrohpuh	Campeonato Campeonato da Europa
the World Cup	
oo kangpiwnahtoo doo mungdoo	O Campeonato do Mundo

The Players Will ... Os Jogadores Vão ...

attack	
zhoogahr ow uhtahk	jogar ao ataque
defend	
zhoogahr ah dfezuh	jogar à defesa
trip a player up	
pregahr oomuh rruhshtayruh	pregar uma rasteira
kick	
dahr oong pongtuhpeh	dar um pontapé
mark a player (m/f)	
muhrkahr oong/ oomuh zhooguhdor/uh	marcar um/ uma jogador/jogadora
score a goal	
muhrkahr oong goloo	marcar um golo

take a ...	muhrkahr ...	marcar ...
corner kick	oong kangtoo	um canto
free kick	oomuh fahltuh	uma falta
penalty kick	oong pehnahltee	um penalty

FOOTY LINGUS

failed save by a goalkeeper or defender	oo frang-goo	o frango
foul	uh fahltuh	a falta
goal	oo goloo	o golo
kick	oo shootoo	o xuto
off side	oo fohruh de zhogoo	o fora de jogo
red card	kuhrtõw vermuhlyoo	cartão vermelho
shot on goal	oo rrmaht	o remate
yellow card	kuhrtõw uhmuhrehloo	cartão amarelo

the coach	oo/uh traynuhdor/uh	o treinador/a treinadora
corner	oo kangtoo	o canto
defenders	oozh dfezuhsh	os defesas
extra time	oo proolong-guhmengtoo	o prolongamento
fan	oo/uh fang	o/a fã
field (pitch)	oo kangpoo	o campo
forwards (strikers)	oozh muhrkuhdorsh	os marcadores
the goal	uh buhleezuh	a baliza
goalkeeper	oo/uh gwarduhrredsh	o/a guarda-redes
inside/outside	dengtroo/fohruh	dentro/fora da
the penalty area	duh ahryuh	área
linesman	oo ahrbeetroo de leenyuh	o árbitro de linha
midfielders	oozh mehdiwsh	os médios
premier division	uh preemayruh deeveezõw	a Primeira Divisão
ranking	uh kluhseefeekuhsõw	a classificação
second division	uh sgoongduh deeveezõw dongrruh	a Segunda Divisão de Honra
the referee	oo ahrbeetroo	o árbitro
to send off (a player)	shpoolsahr (oong zhooguhdor)	expulsar (um jogador)
to substitute (a player)	soobshteetwir (oong zhooguhdor)	substituir (um jogador)

ACTIVITIES

FOOTBALL TEAMS

SL Benfica 'the Eagles'	ehs ehle bǎyfeekuh uhz ahgeeuhsh	SL Benfica as águias
Sporting CP 'the Lions'	spohrting-g se pe oosh leeōysh	Sporting CP os leoes
FC Porto 'the Dragons'	ehf se portoo oozh druhgōysh	FC Porto os drugoẽs
Boavista 'the Checkered Ones'	bouhveeshtuh ooz uhshuhdrezahdoosh	Boavista os axadrezados
CF Belenenses	se ehf blnengsesh	CF Belenenses

HIKING

(See In the Country, page 192, for hiking terms.)

TENNIS — TÉNIS

ACTIVITIES

Would you like to play tennis?
kelır zhoogahr ow tehneesh? — *Quer jogar ao ténis?*

How much is it to rent a court?
kwangtoo eh ke kooshtuh
uhloogahr oong kohrt de tehneesh? — *Quanto é que custa alugar um court de ténis?*

Can you play at night?
tangbǎy se pohd
zhoogahr de noyt? — *Também se pode jogar de noite?*

Can you rent racquets and balls?
pohds uhloogahr uhsh rrahkehtsh
ee uhsh bohluhsh? — *Pode-se alugar as raquetes e as bolas?*

What kind of surface does the court have?
ke teepoo de sooperfeesee-e
tǎy oo kohrt de tchneesh? — *Que tipo de superfície tem o court de ténis?*

advantage for	vangtahzhãy puhruh	*vantagem para*
deuce	engpuhtahdoosh kwuhrengtuh-kwuhrengtuh	*empatados* *quarenta-quarenta*
clay court	kohrt de tehrruh peezahduh	*court de terra* *pisada*
fault	fahltuh	*falta*
grass court	kohrt kong rrehlvahdoo	*court com* *relvado*
match	oo zhogoo	*o jogo*
net	uh rred	*a rede*
love	zehroo uh zehroo	*zero a zero*
out	fohruh	*fora*
playing doubles	zhoogahr owsh pahrsh	*jogar aos pares*
score point	oo pongtoo	*o ponto*
serve	oo serveesoo	*o serviço*
set	oo seht	*o set*
tennis tournament	toornayoo de tehneesh	*torneio de ténis*

CYCLING

CICLISMO

What's the circuit?
  kwal eh oo seerkooeetoo? *Qual é o circuito?*
Who's winning?
  kãy eh ke vai uh guhnyahr? *Quem é que vai a ganhar?*
How many kilometres is today's stage?
  kwangtoosh keelohmtroosh *Quantos quilómetros*
  tãy uh eetahpuh de ozh? *tem a etapa de hoje?*
Where does it finish?
  ongd eh ke uhkahbuh? *Onde é que acaba?*

stage	eetahpuh	*etapa*
time trial	kongtruh rrlohzhiw	*contra-relógio*
tour (road race)	vohltuh	*volta*
yellow jersey	kuhmeezohluh uhmuhrehluh	*camisola* *amarela*

(See pages 73 and 195 for more cycling terms.)

BULLFIGHTING   TOURADAS

Bullfighting has a long tradition in Portugal. The traditional Portuguese bullfight, *tourada à antiga portuguesa*, doesn't include a matador doing capework. Contrary to Spanish practice, since the 17th century, the killing of the bull in the arena has been forbidden. If the bullfight is done more according to the Spanish style, with a matador and capework, the kill at the end is simulated.

The authentic Portuguese event centres primarily around the *toureio a cavalo*, 'fighting on horseback', and the *forcados*, 'bull wrestlers'. The *toureio a cavalo* is the main event, and features a *cavaleiro*, 'horseman', lavishly clad in 18th century attire. In an amazing display of horsemanship, the *cavaleiro* artfully dodges and leads the bull, trying to thrust three different sized darts into its back. The horseman is followed by the *forcados* – nine men, completely unprotected and on foot, who stand in front of the bull and provoke it into a head-on assault by calling out *eh touro*. The lead *forcado* takes the full force of the charge, while the rest of the group jumps on and surrounds the animal in an attempt to immobilise it.

Fortunately (for the *forcados* that is), the bull's horns have been sawed off and wrapped in leather straps so no-one can be gored. At the end, another *forcado* brings in a herd of bullocks that help lead the wounded animal out of the ring.

ACTIVITIES

Are bullfights popular in this region?
    uhsh torahduhsh sōw   *As touradas são*
    poopoolahrsh nehshtuh rrezheeōw? *populares nesta região?*
Would you like to go to a bullfight?
    kehr eer uh oomuh torahduh?   *Quer ir a uma tourada?*
Do you think bullfighting is right?
    ahshuh bāy uhsh torahduhs?   *Acha bem as touradas?*
(No) I do(n't).
    (nōw) ahshoo bāy   *(Não) acho bem.*

Are there any bullfights ...	ah ahlgoomuh torahduh ...	*Há alguma tourada ...*
today	ozh	*hoje*
this week?	ehshtuh smuhnuh?	*esta semana?*

Where's the bullring?
   ongd feekuh uh
   prahsuh de toroosh?
          Onde fica a
          praça de touros?

Where can I get tickets for the bullfight?
   ongd eh ke se kongprŏw
   oosh beelyets puhruh
   uh torahduh?
          Onde é que se compram
          os bilhetes para
          a tourada?

In the Ring Na Arena

(untamed) bull	oo toroo (brahvoo)	*o touro (bravo)*
bullfighter	oo torayroo	*o toureiro*
bullfighting	uh leed	*a lide*
bullring	uh prahsuh de toroosh	*a praça de touros*
cape	uh kahpuh	*a capa*
a charge (by the bull)	uh ingveshteeduh	*a investida*
to close in on the bull	fshahr oo toroo	*fechar o touro*
darts (thrust into	oosh fehrroosh (uhsh	*os ferros*
the bull's back)	bangdayreelyuhsh)	*(bandarilhas)*
head *forcado* (takes	oo foorkahdoo	*o forcado*
the initial blow	duh kahruh	*da cara*
from the bull)		
horse	oo kuhvahloo	*o cavalo*
horseman	oo kuhvuhlayroo	*o cavaleiro*
immobilise the bull	pgahr oo toroo	*pegar o touro*
to spear the bull	peekahr oo toroo	*picar o touro*
(with darts)		

Ringside Nas Bancadas

What's this bullfighter's name?
   komoo eh ke se
   shuhmuh oo torayroo?
          Como é que se
          chama o toureiro?

What's happening now?
   oo ke se pahsuh uhgohruh?
          O que se passa agora?

TV & VIDEO

TV E VIDEO

Nearly all foreign films and TV series are shown in their original languages with Portuguese subtitles.

Can I turn the TV on?
  pohsoo leegahr uh
  tleveezõw/teve?

*Posso ligar a
televisão/TV?*

Turn off the TV.
  deshleeguh uh tleveezõw

Desliga a televisão.

Turn the volume up/down.
  põy maiz ahltoo/baishoo

Põe mais alto/baixo.

Do you mind changing the channel?
  ingpohrtuhsht de
  moodahr de kuhnahl?

*Importas-te de mudar de
canal?*

What channel would
you like to watch?
  ke kuhnahl kehrsh ver?

Que canal queres ver?

I feel like watching   uhpteseeuhm ver ...   *Apetecia-me ver ...*
a/the ...

cartoons	dzuhnyoosh	*desenhos*
	uhneemahdoosh	*animados*
documentary	oomuh	*uma*
	rrpoortahzhãy/oong	*reportagem/um*
	dookoomengtahriw	*documentário*
game show	oong kongkoorsoo	*um concurso*
movie	oong feelm	*um filme*
news	oong nooteesyahriw/	*um noticiário/*
	telılehzhoornahl	*telejornal*

Where's the remote control?
  ongd eh ke shtah oo
  koomangdoo ah deeshtangsyuh?

*Onde é que está o
comando à distância?*

The TV's not working.
  uh tleveezõw shtah
  uhvuhreeahduh

*A televisão está
avariada.*

ACTIVITIES

antenna	uh angtenuh	a antena
cable TV	uh teve kahboo	a TV cabo
channel	oo kuhnahl	o canal
dials	oosh bootōysh	os botões
picture	uh eemahzhãy	a imagem
remote control	oo koomangdoo	o comando
	(ah deeshtangseeuh)	(à distância)
satellite dish	uh angtenuh	a antena
	puhruhbohleekuh	parabólica
schedule of	uh proogruhmuhsōw	a programação
programming		
sound	oo song	o som
TV	uh teve	a TV
TV series	oomuh sehree-e	uma série
	(de tleveezōw)	(de televisão)
TV set	oo uhpuhruhlyoo	o aparelho
	de tleveezōw	de televisão
weather forecast	oo tengpoo	o tempo

Video Video

You usually have to become a member of a video library to rent videos in Portugal. To do this, you'll need to give your name and address and to show ID. If you're just passing through, it's easier to buy a video than to rent one.

Where do you rent videos?
ongd eh ke se
uhloogōw veediwsh?

*Onde é que se
alugam vídeos?*

Are you a member?
eh sohsiw?

É sócio?

How much is it to rent a movie for …?	kwangtoo kooshtuh uhloogahr oong feelm poor …?	*Quanto custa alugar um filme por …?*
a day	deeuh	*dia*
three days	kuhduh trezh deeuhsh	*cada três dias*
a week	smuhnuh	*semana*

HORSE RACING CORRIDAS DE CAVALOS

Horse racing isn't very popular in Portugal. But there are horse races in tourist areas like the Algarve in southern Portugal, Cascais and Estoril (near Lisbon).

Where's the race track?
ongd feekuh oo eepohdroomoo? *Onde fica o hipódromo?*
Which horse is the favourite?
kwal eh oo kuhvahloo fuhvoorcetoo? *Qual é o cavalo favorito?*
Which horse should I bet on?
ay ke kuhvahloo ayd uhpooshtahr? *Em que cavalo é que hei-de apostar?*

What are the odds on this horse?
kwaish sōw uhsh *Quais são as*
proobuhbeeleedahdsh desht *probabilidades deste*
kuhvahloo? *cavalo?*

bet	uh uhpohshtuh	*a aposta*
bookmaker	oo koorrtor duhz	*o corretor das*
	uhpohshtuhsh	*apostas*
horse	oo kuhvahloo	*o cavalo*
horse race	uh koorreeduh	*a corrida*
jockey	oo zhohkay	*o jóquei*

ACTIVITIES

HORSE RIDING EQUITAÇÃO

Are there any riding schools nearby?
ah ahlgoomuh shkohluh de *Há alguma escola de*
eekeetuhsōw uhkee pehrtoo? *equitação aqui perto?*
Can I take a horse out for a ride?
eh pooseevehl dahr *É possível dar*
oong puhsayoo uh kuhvahloo? *um passeio a cavalo?*
How long will the ride take?
kwangtoo tengpoo *Quanto tempo*
dooruh oo puhsayoo? *dura o passeio?*
How much is it?
kwangtoo kooshtuh? *Quanto custa?*

I'm an experienced rider.		
so oong/oomuh zheenet	*Sou um/uma ginete*	
kong shpree-engsyuh	*com experiência.*	
I'm a beginner.		
so pringseepyangt	*Sou principiante.*	

Is it possible to rent a riding
hat and some riding boots?

eh pooseevehl uhloogahr oong   *É possível alugar um*
kuhpuhset ee oomuhsh   *capacete e umas*
bohtuhzh de mongtahr   *botas de montar.*

to ride at a ...	angdahr uh ...	*andar a ...*
canter	mayoo guhlohp	*meio galope*
gallop	guhlohp	*galope*
trot	troht	*trote*

colt	oo potroo	*o potro*
reins	uhsh rehdyuhsh	*as rédeas*
saddle	uh sehluh	*a sela*
stables	oo shtahbooloo	*o estábulo*
stirrup	oo shtreeboo	*o estribo*
whip	oo sheekoht	*o chicote*

CAR RACING   CORRIDAS DE CARROS

Car racing is a sport that appeals to many people and has wide
coverage on national television.

to crash	shookahr	*chocar*
Formula One	uh fohrmooluh oong	*a Fórmula Um*
go off the road	deshpeeshtahrs	*despistar-se*
km per hour	keelohmtroosh	*quilómetros*
	ah ohruh	*à hora*

... place	áy ... loogahr	*em ... lugar*
first	preemayroo	*primeiro*
second	sgoongdoo	*segundo*
third	tersayroo	*terceiro*

a lap	oomuh vohltuh	*uma volta*
overtake	uhdeeangtahr	*adiantar*
racing car	oo kahrroo de	*o carro de*
	koorreeduhs	*corridas*
racing car driver	oo/uh peelotoo/uh	*o/a pilato/u*
racing track	uh peeshtuh	*a pista*

TV EYE

Nearly all foreign films and TV series are shown in their original
languages with Portuguese subtitles. Most TV series are imported
from the US, though there's also a good sampling of British,
French and Italian fare.

Channels 1 and 2 (called RTP1 and RTP2) are state-run.
Though it does have public service announcements, RTP2
broadcasts without commercial breaks, and offers a range of
programming catering to the serious-minded viewer.

GAMES   JOGOS

Do you like ...?	gohshtuh de ...?	*Gosta de ...?*
Do you know how to play ...?	sahb zhoogahr ...?	*Sabe jogar ...?*
Let's play ...	vuhmoosh zhoogahr ...?	*Vamos jogar ...?*
billiards	ow beelyahr	*ao bilhar*
checkers	ahzh duhmuhsh	*às damas*
chess	ow shuhdresh	*ao xadrês*
draughts	ahzh duhmuhsh	*às damas*
the lottery	uh lootuhreeuh	*a lotaria*

How do you play?
  komoo eh ke se zhohguh?   *Como é que se joga?*
What are the rules?
  kwaish sōw uhsh rrehgruhsh?   *Quais são as regras?*

I'll teach you (inf).		
e-w engseenoot		*Eu ensino-te.*
Whose turn is it now?		
de kãy eh uh vezh uhgohruh?		*De quem é a vez agora?*
I'm winning/losing.		
shto uh guhnyahr/perder		*Estou a ganhar/perder.*
That's cheating.		
uhsing nõw vahl.		*Assim não vale.*
I'm not playing anymore.		
nõwzhohgoo maish		*Não jogo mais.*
I have really bad luck.		
so mezhmoo oong/oomuh		*Sou mesmo um/uma*
uhzuhrahdoo/uh		*azarado/a.*

GETTING LUCKY

A popular saying for gamblers is:

Sorte no jogo, azar no amor.
sohrt noo zhogoo uhzahr noo uhmor
Good luck in gambling, bad luck in love.

Cards Cartas

When the Portuguese refer to card games, they'll often say, *vamos jogar à batota*, 'let's have a game of cheating'.

Do you want to play ...?	kehr zhoogahr ...?	*Quer jogar ...?*
bridge	ow breedzh	*ao bridge*
cards	ahsh kahrtuhsh	*à cartas*
poker	ow pohkehr	*ao póquer*
patience	puhsee-engsyuh	*uma paciência*
rummy	ruhmee	*rummy*

You have to throw a card.
tãyzh duhteerahr oomuh kahrtuh   *Tens de atirar uma carta.*

I'll pass.
pahsoo — *Passo.*

I'll bet ... escudos.
uhpohshtoo ... shkoodoosh — *Aposto ... escudos.*

I'll see you.
uhpohshtoo oo mezhmoo — *Aposto o mesmo.*

I'll raise you ... escudos.
ee maish ... shkoodoosh — *E mais ... escudos.*

I'll call you.
kehroo ver oo te-w zhogoo — *Quero ver o teu jogo.*

You're (inf) bluffing!
shtahsh uh fuhzer bluhf — *Estás a fazer bluff.*

ace	oo ahsh	o ás
king	oo rray	o rei
queen	uh duhmuh	a dama
jack	oo vuhleht	o valete
joker	oo deeahboo	o diabo
three	oo ternoo	o terno
a suite	oozh naipsh	os naipes
spades	uhsh shpahduhsh	as espadas
hearts	uhsh kohpuhsh	as copas
diamonds	oozh oroosh	os ouros
clubs	oosh powsh	os paus
the deck	oo buhrahlyoo	o baralho
shuffle	buhruhlyahr	baralhar
trump	oo troongfoo	o trunfo

ACTIVITIES

THEY MAY SAY ...

Don't cheat.	nōw fahsuh buhtohtuh;	Não faça batota;
	nōw vahl fuhzer buhtohtuh	Não vale fazer batota.
What luck!	ke sohrt!	Que sorte!
What bad luck!	ke uhzahr!	Que azar!

Chess Xadrês

How about a game of chess?
vai oong zhogoo de shuhdresh? *Vai um jogo de xadrês?*

The whites begin.
koomehsõw uhsh brangkuhsh *Começam as brancas.*

Now I play.
uhgohruh so e-w (uh zhoogahr) *Agora sou eu (a jogar).*

Hurry up! Don't think so much!
deshpahshuht! *Despacha-te!*
nõw pengsesh tangtoo! *Não penses tanto!*

check	shehk ow rray	*Xeque ao rei*
checkmate	shehk maht	*Xeque mate*
chessboard	tuhboolayroo	*tabuleiro*
	de shuhdresh	*de xadrês*
chess championship	kangpiwnahtoo	*campeonato*
	de shuhdresh	*de xadrês*
to open	uhbertooruh	*abertura*
to tie	engpuhtahr	*empatar*
rook	uh torr	*a torre*
knight	oo kuhvahloo	*o cavalo*
bishop	oo beeshpoo	*o bispo*
pawn	oo peeõw	*o peão*

ACTIVITIES

SOCIAL ISSUES

TEMAS SOCIAIS

POLITICS

POLÍTICA

Three topics tend to come up over and over again in both political speeches and general conversation – education, public health and the economy – especially Portugal's low salaries in comparison with the rest of the European Union.

The Portuguese Constitution is a modified version of the constitution drafted after the April 1974 revolution. It underwent successive changes that eliminated some ideological characteristics associated with the previous communist regime.

The *Diário da República* is the official government paper that publishes new laws, decrees and announcements about public service jobs and government contracts.

Did you hear about …?		
zhah sob ke …?		*Já soube que …?*
Have you heard about the new law on …?		
zhah oveeoo fuhlahr duh nohvuh lay sobr …?		*Já ouviu falar da nova lei sobre …?*
What do you think of the … government?	oo ke ahshuh …?	*O que acha …?*
current	doo goovernoo uhtwal?	*do governo actual*
new	doo novoo goovernoo	*do novo governo*
I (don't) agree with its policy on (the) …	(nōw) kongkohrdoo kong uh swuh pooleeteekuh sobr …	*(Não) concordo com a sua política sobre …*
drugs	uh drohguh	*a droga*
education	uh eedookuhsōw	*a educação*
economy	uh eekohnoomeeuh	*a economia*
environment	oo mayoo angbee-engt	*o meio ambiente*

military service	oo serveesoo meeleetahr	*o serviço militar*
privatisation	uhsh preevuhteezuhsōysh	*as privatizações*
public health care	uh suhood poobleekuh	*a saúde pública*

I support the	so peloo	*Sou pelo*
... party.	puhrteedoo ...	*partido ...*
communist	koomooneeshtuh	*comunista*
green	oosh verdsh	*'os verdes'*
popular	poopoolahr	*popular*
social-democratic	sooseeahl-dmookrahtuh	*social-democrata*
socialist	sooseeuhleeshtuh	*socialista*

DID YOU KNOW ... The 25 April 1974 revolution is also know as the 'carnation revolution' because on that day a woman handed out carnations to soldiers.

| I'm an anarchist. so uhnahrkeeshtuh | *Sou anarquista.* |
| I don't vote. uhbshtuhnyoom | *Abstenho-me.* |

In my country we have a	noo me-w paysh temooz oong	*No meu país temos um*
... government.	goovernoo ...	*governo ...*
conservative	kongservuhdor	*conservador*
leftist	de shkerduhsh	*de esquerdas*
liberal	leeberahl	*liberal*
right wing	de deeraytuhsh	*de direitas*

All politicians are alike.
todooz osh pooleeteekoosh sōw eegooaish

Todos os políticos são iguais.

SOCIAL ISSUES

Do you agree with Portugal's
decolonisation policies?

ahshuh ke foy uhdkwahduh
uh pooleeteekuh duh
deshkoolooneezuhsõw
poortoogezuh?

Acha que foi adequada
a política da
descolonização
portuguesa?

What do you think about the
Salazar regime?

oo ke eh ke ahshuh doo
goovernoo suhluhzuhreeshtuh?

O que é que acha do
governo salazarista?

What's your opinion of the
'Carnation Revolution'?

ke opeenecõw tãy sohre uh
rrvooloosõw doosh krahvoosh?

Que opiniao tem sobre a
'revolução dos cravos'?

Political Terms Expressões Políticas

bill	uh proopohshtuh de lay	*a proposta de lei*
campaign	uh kangpuhnyuh	*a campanha*
court decision	oo uhkohrdõw	*o acórdão*
demonstration	uh muhneefeshtuhsõw	*a manifestação*
... elections	uhz eelaysõysh ...	*as eleições ...*
local/municipal	mooneeseepaish	*municipais*
national	nuhsiwnaish	*nacionais*
presidential	przeedengseeaish	*presidenciais*
government	oo goovernoo	*o governo*
minister	oo/uh meeneeshtroo/uh	*o/a ministro/a*
polls	uhsh songdahzhãysh	*as sondagens*
President	oo/uh prezeedengt	*o/a Presidente*
of the Republic	duh rrehpoobleekuh	*da República*
prime minister	oo/uh preemayroo/uh	*o/a primeiro/a*
	meeneeshtroo/uh	*ministro/a*
political platform	oo proogruhmuh	*o programa*
	pooleeteekoo	*político*
rally	uh kongsengtruhsõw	*a concentração*

SOCIAL ISSUES

strike	uh grehv	*a greve*
term of office	oo mangdahtoo	*o mandato*
to vote	vootahr	*votar*

ABBREVIATIONS

CDU	se de oo	Unified Democratic Coalition (left)
PSD	pe es de	Social Democratic Party
PPD	pe pe de	Popular Democratic Party
PP	pe pe	Popular Party
CDS	se de es	Social Democratic Central Party (right)
PS	pe es	Socialist Party
UGT	oo zhe te	General Workers Union
UE	oo eh	European Union
PALOP	pahlohp	African Countries with Portuguese as the Official Language
OTAN/ NATO	otang/ nahtoo	NATO-North Atlantic Treaty Organisation
AMI	ahmee	International Medical Assistance
ONU	ohnoo	United Nations

ABREVIATURAS

THEY MAY SAY ...

(Não) concordo.	(nōw) kongkohrdoo	I (don't) agree.
Exactamente!	eezahtuhmengt!	Exactly!
Claro que sim!	klahroo ke sing	Of course!
Claro que não!	klahroo ke nōw!	Of course not!
Nem pensar!	nãy pengsahr!	No way!
Está fora de questão!	shtah fohruh de kshtōw!	It's out of the question!
Isso (não) é verdade!	eesoo (nōw) eh verdahd!	That's (not) true!
Pois não.	poyzh nōw	Well, no.
Deve estar a brincar!	dehv shtahr uh bringkahr!	You've got to be kidding!
Sim! Sim! Não haja dúvida!	sing! sing! nōw ahzhuh dooveeduh!	Yes! Yes! There's no doubt about it!
Só se for na tua cabeça!	soh se for nuh twuh kuhbesuh!	In your dreams!
Como queira!	komoo kayruh!	Whatever!

ENVIRONMENT   MEIO AMBIENTE

One of the more serious ecological problems troubling the Portuguese is forest fires. Nearly every summer, thousands of hectares of forest lands are destroyed by forest fires, many of which deliberately set. Neither public campaigns nor stiff legal penalties, such as prohibiting the use of the resulting wood, have been able to stop these fires.

Does Portugal have a pollution problem?
ah prooblemuhzh de poolwisow   *Há problemas de poluição*
ay poortoogahl?   *em Portugal?*
Does (Oporto) have a recycling programme?
ah proogruhmuhzh de   *Há programas de*
rrseeklahzhǎy (noo portoo)?   *reciclagem (no Porto)?*
Are there any protected ...?
ah ... prootzheedoosh/uhsh?   *Há ... protegidos/as?*
Where do you stand on ...?
oo ke eh ke ahshuh ...?   *O que é que acha ...?*
What do you think should be done?
oo ke eh ke pengsuh   *O que é que pensa*
ke se dvreeuh fuhzer?   *que se deveria fazer?*

Is this a   esht/chshtuh ...   *Este/Esta ...*
protected ...?   eh prootzheedoo/uh?   *é protegido/a?*
  forest   floorehshtuh   *floresta (f)*
  park   pahrk   *parque (m)*
  species   shpehsee-e   *espécie (f)*

antinuclear group   groopoo angteenooclyahr   *grupo anti-nuclear*
biodegradable   beeohdgruhdahvehl   *biodegradável*
conservation   uh kongservuhsǒw   *a conservação*
dam   uh rrprezuh   *a represa*
deforestation   duh dzuhrbooreezuhsǒw   *da desarborização*
    duhsh floorehshtuhsh   *das florestas*
drought   uh sehkuh   *a seca*
ecosystem   oo ekohseeshtemuh   *o ecossistema*
endangered   uhz shpehcee-es ǎy   *as espécies em*
  species   preegoo de shtingsǒw   *perigo de extinção*

SOCIAL ISSUES

forest fires	dooz ingsengdiwsh	*dos incêndios*
	floorshtaish	*florestais*
hunting	uh kahsuh	*a caça*
nuclear testing	doosh tehshtzth	*dos testes*
	nooklyahrsh	*nucleares*
ozone layer	uh kuhmahduh	*a camada*
	doo ozonoo	*do ozono*
(industrial)	uh poolwisōw	*a poluição*
pollution	(ingdooshtreeahl)	*(industrial)*
recyclable	rrseeklahvehl	*reciclável*
water supply	uh deeshtreebwisōw	*a distribuição*
	duh ahgwuh	*da água*

SOCIAL ISSUES   TEMAS SOCIAIS

Up until the 1980s, Portugal was a country of emigration. Large
numbers of Portuguese settled in countries like France, Germany
and the US. Now, though, the rate of emigration has dropped
sharply. In fact, the trend seems to be reversing, with both Portuguese emigrants and their children returning to the homeland, as
well as citizens from Portugal's former colonies.

What do you think about the
current (immigration) policy?
  oo ke eh ke pengsuh sobr uh   *O que é que pensa sobre a*
  pooleeteekuh uhtwahl de   *política actual de*
  (eemeegruhsōw)?   *(imigração)?*
Do you think the country can
absorb more immigrants?
  ahshuh ke oo paysh tāy   *Acha que o país tem*
  kongdeesōys puhruh uhkoolyer   *ondições para acolher*
  maiz uhbeetangtsh?   *c mais habitantes?*
Does the Social Security
system work well?
  uh sgoorangsuh soosyahl   *A Segurança Social*
  foongsyohnuh bāy?   *funciona bem?*

Do all citizens have access to
medical care in public hospitals?

todooz oosh seeduhdōwsh tãyãy
deeraytoo uh uhseeshtengsyuh
mehdeekuh ãy oshpeetaish
poobleekoosh?

*Todos os cidadãos têm
direito a assistência
médica em hospitais
públicos?*

abortion	oo uhbortoo	*o aborto*
aged	uh tersayruh eedahd	*a terceira idade*
animal rights	oozh deeraytoozh dooz uhneemaish	*os direitos dos animais*
equal opportunity	uh eegwaldahd de ohpoortooneedahdsh	*a igualdade de oportunidades*
euthanasia	uh e-wtuhnahzyuh	*a eutanásia*
homeless	oosh sãy uhbreegoo	*os sem-abrigo*
immigration	uh eemeegruhsōw	*a imigração*
party politics	uh pooleeteekuh puhrteedahryuh	*a política partidária*
racism	oo rahseezhmoo	*o racismo*
unemployed	oosh dzengpre-gahdoosh	*os desempregados*
unions	oosh singdeekahtoosh	*os sindicatos*

DRUGS   DROGA

Recreational drugs, except alcohol, are prohibited in Portugal. That
doesn't mean that there's no drug use, however, and you could
find yourself in situations where drugs are being discussed, used
or offered to you. It's wise to exercise the utmost discretion.

I'm not interested in drugs.
uh drohguh nōw me uhtrai — *A droga não me atrai.*

I use (cocaine) occasionally.
tohmoo (kokuheenuh)
de vez āy kwangdoo — *Tomo (cocaína)
de vez em quando.*

Let's have a smoke.
foomuhmoozh oong shahrroo? — *Fumamos um charro?*

Where can I get new syringes?
ongd pohsoo kongsgeer
sring-guhsh nohvuhsh? — *Onde posso conseguir
seringas novas?*

I'm out of it.
shto notruh — *Estou noutra.*

I'm trying to get off it.
shto uh tengtahr
dzingtohkseekahrm — *Estou a tentar
desintoxicar-me.*

drug dependence/ addiction	uh tohkseekoh-dpengdengsyuh	a toxico-dependência
drug dealer	oo/uh truhfeekangt de drohguhsh	o/a traficante de drogas
inject	ingzhehtahrs/ shootahrs	injectar-se/ chutar-se (coll)
LSD	oo ehl ehs de	o LSD
needle exchange	uh trohkuh de sring-guhz oozahduhsh	a troca de seringas usadas

SHOPPING   FAZER COMPRAS

There are still some good bargains to be had in Portugal. Leather shoes are stylish and cheaper than in other Western European countries, especially in Oporto.

Gold and silver filigree make popular gifts. Even though gold isn't cheap, as it's over 19 carats, it's generally considered good value. Ask for *ouro de lei* (lit: legal gold). Silver bracelets and charms are often delicate in design and inexpensive.

Portugal is also home to Port and Madeira wines. For a similar price, you can usually get a better quality Madeira than Port.

Shopping centres and supermarkets are often open until 11 pm, including Saturdays. Small shops open from 9 or 10 am until 7 pm, but most close for lunch between 1 and 3 pm. On Saturdays, many shops are open only until 1 pm.

LOOKING FOR ...   À PROCURA DE ...

Where's the	ongd eh ... maish	*Onde é ...*
nearest ...?	prohseemoo/uh?	*mais próximo/a?*
bookshop	uh leevruhreeuh	*a livraria*
camera shop	uh lohzhuh de footogruhfeeuhsh	*a loja de fotografias*
chemist (pharmacy)	uh fuhrmahsyuh	*a farmácia*
clothes store	uh lohzhuh de rropuh	*a loja de roupa*
crafts shop	uh lohzhuh de uhrtzuhnahtoo	*a loja de artesanato*
general store	oo meenee merkahdoo	*o mini-mercado*
grocery store	uh mersyuhreeuh	*a mercearia*
laundry	uh luhvangduhreeuh	*a lavandaria*
market	oo merkahdoo; uh prahsuh	*o mercado; a praça*
souvenir shop	uh lohzhuh de rrkoorduhsoysh	*a loja de recordações*
supermarket	oo soopehrmerkahdoo	*o supermercado*

155

SHOPPING

MAKING A PURCHASE

FAZER UMA COMPRA

You'll often hear the expression *conto*, which is the equivalent of 1000 escudos – three *contos* makes 3000 escudos. If you're paying with cash, the cashier will ask for the correct change in most stores, so be prepared! A bonus when buying presents is that giftwrapping is usually free of charge.

I'd like to buy ...	kreeuh kongprahr ...	*Queria comprar ...*
I don't like it.	nōw gohshtoo desht	*Não gosto deste.*
Can I look at it?	pohsoo veloo/luh?	*Posso vê-lo/la?*
Is it hand made?	eh faytoo/uh ah mōw?	*É feito/a à mão?*
I'm just looking.	shto soh uh olyahr	*Estou só a olhar.*

Do you have other sizes/colours?
tāy otroozh noomroosh/ otruhsh korsh? — *Tem outros números/outras cores?*

How much is this/that?
kwangtoo eh ke kooshtuh eeshtoo/uhkeeloo? — *Quanto é que custa isto/aquilo?*

Can you write down the price?
pohd shkrverm oo presoo? — *Pode escrever-me o preço?*

Do you accept credit cards?
uhsaytuh kuhrtōw de krehdeetoo? — *Aceita cartão de crédito?*

BARGAINING

REGATEAR

Bargaining isn't standard practice in Portugal. Nearly everything is fixed price, except for goods at some outdoor markets and fairs.

I think it's too expensive.
ahshoo ke eh mwingtoo kahroo — *Acho que é muito caro.*

Can you lower the price?
pohd baishahr oo presoo? — *Pode baixar o preço?*

I'll give you (two) thousand escudos.
doly (doyzh) meel shkoodoosh — *Dou-lhe (dois) mil escudos.*

This is my last offer.
eh uh meenyuh oolteemuh ofehrtuh — *É a minha última oferta.*

THEY MAY SAY ...

Faz favor, desejava alguma coisa?
fahsh fuhvor dzezhahvuh ahlgoomuh koyzuh?
  Are you looking for anything in particular?

Posso ajudá-lo/la?
pohsoo uhzhoodghlnn/uh
  Can I help you?

Já só temos este número/esta cor.
zhah soh temoozh esht noomroo/ehstuh kor
  This is the only size/colour we have left.

Vai pagar com cartão (de crédito)?
vai puhgahr kong kuhrtōw (de krchdeetoo)?
  Will you be paying with a (credit) card?

Quer que embrulhe para prenda?
kehr ke engbrooly puhruh prengduh?
  Would you like it giftwrapped?

É tudo?	eh toodoo?	Will that be all?
Quer factura?	kehr fahtooruh?	Would you like a receipt?

ESSENTIAL GROCERIES

COMPRAS ESSENCIAIS

Where can I find ...?

  ongd pohsoo engkongtrahr ...?   *Onde posso encontrar ...?*

I'd like (a) ...	kreeuh ...	Queria ...
batteries	peelyuhsh	*pilhas*
bread	pōw	*pão*
butter	mangtayguh	*manteiga*
cheese	kayzhoo	*queijo*
chocolate	shookoolaht	*chocolate*
eggs	ohvoosh	*ovos*
flour	fuhreenyuh	*farinha*
gas canister	oong kuhrtooshoo de gahsh	*um cartucho de gás*
ham	feeangbr	*fiambre*

SHOPPING

prosciutto	przoongtoo	presunto
honey	mehl	mel
margarine	muhrguhreenuh	margarina
matches	fohshfooroosh	fósforos
milk	layt	leite
mineral water	ahgwuh meenrahl	água mineral
pepper	peemengtuh	pimenta
salt	sahl	sal
shampoo	shangpo	champô
soap	suhboonet	sabonete
sugar	uhsookahr	açúcar
toilet paper	puhpehl eezhyehneekoo	papel higiénico
toothpaste	pahshtuh doozh dengtsh	pasta de dentes
washing powder	dtergengt puhruh	detergente para
	uh rropuh	a roupa
yogurt	yogoort	iogurte

I'd like …	kreeeuuh …	Queria …
a kilo	oong keeloo	um quilo
half a kilo	mayoo keeloo	meio quilo
… grams	… gruhmuhsh	… gramas
litre	oong leetroo	um litro
milligram	oomuhsh	umas
	meeleegruhmuh	miligrama

SOUVENIRS & SPECIALITIES

CORDAÇÕES E ESPECIALIDADES

Nearly every region has its own distinctive style of pottery at reasonable prices. The well-known 'cabbageware' is produced at the Bordalo Pinheiro factory in Caldas da Rainha.

Other towns famous for their pottery are Viana do Castelo, Coimbra, Mafra, Alcobaça, Redondo, Óbidos, and Lisbon, where Viúva Lamego and Sant'Ana pottery are produced.

For something at the higher end of the price range, you could try hand-made woollen rugs from Arraiolos, or embroidery from Madeira.

SHOPPING

ceramics
  sruhmeekuh
  cerâmica

ceramic tiles
  uhzooluhzhoosh
  azulejos

clay pottery
  oluhreeuh/uhrteegoosh
  áy bahrroo
  olaria/artigos em barro

copperware
  truhbahlyooz áy kohbr
  trabalhos em cobre

embroidery
  boordahdoosh
  bordados

gold/silver filigree
  feeleegruhnuh áy
  oroo/áy prahtuh
  *filigrana em
  ouro/em prata*

leather footwear
  kahlsahdoo áy pehl
  calçado em pele

pewter ware
  uhrteegoozh áy
  shtuhnyoo
  artigos em estanho

pottery
  sruhmeekuh
  cerâmica

rugs
  tuhpetsh
  tapetes

... wine   veenyoo ...   *vinho ...*
  Madeira   duh muhdayruh   *da Madeira*
  Port   doo porto   *do Porto*

SHOPPING

CLOTHING & ACCESSORIES

ROUPA E ACESSÓRIOS

bathrobe	oong rropõw	*um roupão*
belt	oong singtoo	*um cinto*
blouse	oomuh bloozuh	*uma blusa*
bra	oong sooteeang	*um soutien*
hat	oong shuhpehoo	*um chapéu*
jacket	oong kuhzahkoo	*um casaco*
raincoat	oomuh gahbahrdeenuh	*uma gabardina*
sandals	oomush sangdahlyuhsh	*umas sandálias*
shorts	oongsh kahlsõysh	*uns calções*
skirt	oomuh saiuh	*uma saia*
socks	oomush mayuhsh/ peeoogush	*umas meias/ peúgas*
trousers (pants)	oomush kahlsuhsh	*umas calças*
underwear	rropuh ingtryor	*roupa interior*

TRYING THINGS ON

PROVAR ROUPA/SAPATOS

Where's the fitting room?
  ongd eh,oo guhbeenet
  de prohvuhsh?

*Onde é o gabinete
de provas?*

It doesn't fit.
  nõw me sehrv

Não me serve.

I need a larger/smaller size.
  prseezoo doong noomroo
  mayohr/maish pkenoo

*Preciso dum número
maior/mais pequeno.*

It doesn't look good on me.
  nõw me feeekuh bãy

Não me fica bem.

Do you have it/them in another colour?
  tãy otruhsh korsh?

Tem outras cores?

It's too ...	eh mwingtoo ...	*É muito ...*
tight	zhooshtoo/uh	*justo/a*
loose	lahrgoo/uh	*largo/a*
short	koortoo/uh	*curto/a*
long	kongpreedoo/uh	*comprido/a*

MATERIALS

MATERIAIS

brass	luhtőw	*latão*
copper	kohbr	*cobre*
ceramic	sruhmeekuh	*cerâmica*
clay	bahrroo	*barro*
cork	koorteesuh	*cortiça*
cotton	ahlgoodőw	*algodão*
crystal	kreeshtahl	*cristal*
gold	oroo	*ouro*
iron	fehrroo	*ferro*
ivory	muhrfing	*marfim*
linen	leenyoo	*linho*
lycra	leekruh	*licra*
marble	mahrmoor	*mármore*
mother-of-pearl	mahdrpehrooluh	*madrepérola*
pewter	shtuhnyoo	*estanho*
polyester	feebruh	*fibra*
silk	seduh	*seda*
silver	prahtuh	*prata*
stainless steel	ahsoo	*aço*
	eenohkseedahvehl	*inoxidável*
tile	uhzooluhzhoo	*azulejo*

COLOURS

CORES

dark ...	... shkooroo	*... escuro*
light ...	... klahroo	*... claro*
black	pretoo	*preto*
blue	uhzool	*azul*
brown	kuhshtuhnyoo	*castanho*
green	verd	*verde*
grey	singzengtoo	*cinzento*
orange	kor de luhrangzhuh	*cor-de-laranja*
pink	kor de rrohzuh	*cor-de-rosa*
purple	viwletuh/rroshoo	*violeta/roxo*
red	vermelyoo	*vermelho*
white	brangkoo	*branco*
yellow	uhmuhrehloo	*amarelo*

SHOPPING

TOILETRIES		PRODUTOS HIGIÉNICOS
Band-Aid	pengsoosh rrahpeedoosh	*pensos rápidos*
condoms	przervuhteevoosh	*preservativos*
deodorant	dzohdooreezangt	*desodorizante*
hairbrush	shkovuh (puhruh oo kuhbeloo)	*escova (para o cabelo)*
moisturiser	krehm eedruhtangt	*creme hidratante*
razor	mahkeenuh de buhrbyahr	*máquina de barbear*
sanitary napkins	pengsooz eezhyehneekoosh	*pensos higiénicos*
shampoo	shangpo	*champô*
shaving cream	krehm de fuhzer uh bahrbuh	*creme de fazer a barba*
soap	suhboonet	*sabonete*
sunblock	prootehtor doo sohl	*protector do sol*
tampons	tangpõysh	*tampões*
toilet paper	puhpehl eezhyehneekoo	*papel higiénico*
toothpaste	pahshtuh de dengtsh	*pasta de dentes*
toothbrush	shkovuh de dengtsh	*escova de dentes*

FOR THE BABY		PARA O BEBÉ
tinned baby food	koomeeduh engluhtahduh de behbeh	*comida enlatada de bebé*
baby powder	poh de tahlkoo puhruh behbeh	*pó de talco para bebé*
bib	beeb	*bibe*
cotton swabs	kohtohnehtsh	*cotonetes*
feeding bottle	beebrõw	*biberão*
nappy rash cream	krehm kongtruh uh uhsuhdooruh	*creme contra a assadura*
powdered milk	layt ãy poh	*leite em pó*
teats	teteenyuhsh	*tetinhas*
towelettes	twuhlyeenyuhsh	*toalhinhas*

STATIONERY & PUBLICATIONS

MATERIAL DE PAPELARIA E PUBLICAÇÕES

You can find English-language books and magazines in most major bookstores in Lisbon and Oporto. Most city news stands also carry international newspapers and magazines.

Is there an English-language ... here?	ah ahlgoomuh ... de leevrooz ãy ing-glesh?	Há alguma ... de livros em ingles?
bookshop	leevruhreeuh	livraria
section	sehksõw	secção
Is there a local entertainment guide?	ah ahlgoong gecuh lookahl de uhtceveedahdsh?	Há algum guia local de actividades?
Do you sell ...?	vengd ...?	Vende ...?
city maps	plangtuhzh duh seedahd	plantas da cidade
dictionaries	deesiwnahrywsh	dicionários
envelopes	engvlohpsh	envelopes
magazines	rrveeshtuhsh	revistas
maps	mahpuhsh	mapas
(English-language) newspapers	zhoornaiz (ãy ing-glesh)	jornais (em inglês)
notebooks	blohkoozh de nohtush	blocos de notas
pens	shfehrohgrah-feekuhsh	esferográficas
postcards	pooshtaish	postais
regional maps	mahpuhsh rrzhiwnaish	mapas regionais
road maps	mahpuhzh duhzh shtrahduhsh	mapas das estradas
stamps	seloosh	selos
writing paper	puhpehl de kahrtuh	papel de carta

MUSIC   MÚSICA

I'm looking for a ... CD.
   prohkooroo oong sede de ...   *Procuro um CD de ...*
Do you have any ...?
   täy ...?   *Tem ...?*
I heard a band/singer called ...
   ovee fuhlahr doong groopoo/   *Ouvi falar dum grupo/*
   kangtor shuhmahdoo ...   *cantor chamado ...*

Can you recommend a CD of ...?	pohd rrkoomengdahr oong sede de ...?	*Pode recomendar um CD de ...?*
fado music	fahdoo	*fado*
Portuguese (folk) music	moozeekuh (folklohreekuh) poortoogezuh	*música (folclórica) portuguesa*
a good Portuguese pop group	oomuh bouh bangduh poortoogezuh de moozeekuh leezhayruh	*uma boa banda portuguesa de música ligeira*

I need a ...	prseezoo de ...	*Preciso de ...*
blank tape	oomuh kahseht veerzhäy	*uma cassette virgem*
headphones	oonzh owshkooltuhdorsh	*uns auscultadores*

PHOTOGRAPHY   FOTOGRAFIA

How much is it to process this film?
   kwangtoo kooshtuh   *Quanto custa*
   rrvlahr esht rroloo?   *revelar este rolo?*
When will it be ready?
   kwangdoo eh ke shtah prongtoo?   *Quando é que está pronto?*
I'd like a roll of film for this camera.
   kreeuh oong rroloo puhruh   *Queria um rolo para*
   ehshtuh mahkeenuh   *esta máquina.*

SHOPPING

Do you do one-hour developing?
    fahzãy uh rrvluhsõw   *Fazem a revelação*
    noomuh ohruh?   *numa hora?*
I'd like to have some
passport photos taken.
    kreeuh ke me feezeلis oomuhsh   *Queria que me fizesse umas*
    footoogruhfeeuhsh teepoo pahs   *fotografias tipo passe*

flash bulb	oo flahsh	o flash
light metre	oo footohmtroo	o fotómetro
slides	oosh slaidsh/	os slides/
	deeuhpoozeeteevoosh	diapositivos
videotape	uh kahseht de veediw	a cassette de vídeo

SMOKING   FUMAR

Most restaurants and cafés don't have separate sections for non-
smokers. Restaurants, bars and coffee-shops can get fairly smoky,
but the person sitting next to you won't usually mind if you
politely ask them to blow their smoke the other way.

A packet of cigarettes, please.
    oong mahsoo de tuhbahkoo/   *Um maço de tabaco/*
    oong mahsoo de seegahrroosh   *um maço de cigarros,*
    se fahsh fuhvor   *se faz favor.*
Do you have a light?
    tãy loom?   *Tem lume?*
Do you mind blowing the
smoke the other way?
    ingpohrtuhs de   *Importa-se de*
    dshveeahr oo foomoo?   *desviar o fumo?*
Please don't smoke.
    poor fuhvor nõw foom   *Por favor, não fume.*
May I smoke?
    pohsoo foomahr?   *Posso fumar?*
I'm trying to quit.
    shto uh tengtahr   *Estou a tentar*
    dayshahr de foomahr   *deixar de fumar.*

SHOPPING

PROIBIDO FUMAR; NÃO FUMADORES	NO SMOKING

ashes	uh singzuh	*a cinza*
filtered	kong feeltroo	*com filtro*
pipe	oo kuhshingboo	*o cachimbo*
(non)smoking section	zonuh de (nõw) foomuhdorsh	*zona de (não) fumadores*
tobacco	oo tuhbahkoo	*o tabaco*

SIZES & COMPARISONS

TAMANHOS E COMPARAÇÕES

small	pkenoo/uh	*pequeno/a*
big	grangd	*grande*
heavy	pzahdoo/uh	*pesado/a*
light	lehv	*leve*
more	maish	*mais*
less	menoosh	*menos*
little (amount)	pokoo/uh	*pouco/a*
few	pokoosh/uhsh	*poucos/as*
too much/many	dmuhzeeahdoo/ oosh/uhsh	*demasiado/ os/as*
many	mwingtoosh/uhsh	*muitos/as*
enough	soofeesyengt	*suficiente*
a lot	mwingtoo/uh	*muito/a*

FOOD   COMIDA

The typical Portuguese breakfast is bread with ham or cheese and
a cup of coffee. Lunch often consists of soup, a main dish, dessert
and coffee, and there's a similar menu for dinner. It's also very
common to have a mid-morning and mid-afternoon snack of a
salgadinho, 'savoury' or 'cake'.

breakfast (between 8 and 10 am)
  oo pkenoo ahlmosoo   *o pequeno-almoço*
lunch (between noon and 2 pm)
  oo ahlmosoo   *o almoço*
afternoon snack (between 4 and 5 pm)
  oo langsh   *o lanche*
dinner (between 7 and 8 pm)
  oo zhangtahr   *o jantar*

VEGETARIAN   REFEIÇÕES
& SPECIAL MEALS VEGETARIANAS
E ESPECIAIS

Traditional Portuguese cuisine is rarely vegetarian, with main
meals almost invariably centring around meat or fish. You'll find,
though, that these are served with a fairly wide variety of side
dishes such as green beans, broccoli and cabbage, depending on
the season, and rice, potatoes, pulses or chickpeas.

I'm vegetarian.
  so vzhetuhreeuhnoo/uh   *Sou vegetariano/a.*
Do you have any vegetarian dishes?
  tãy ahlgoong prahtoo   *Tem algum prato*
  vzhetuhreeuhnoo?   *vegetariano?*
Does this dish have any meat in it?
  esht prahtoo tãy kahrn?   *Este prato tem carne?*
Can I get this without meat?
  pohdm serveer eeshtoo   *Pode-me servir isto*
  sãy kahrn?   *sem carne?*

Is this organic?		
esht eh oong proodootoo		*Este é um produto*
biwlohzheekoo?		*biológico?*
Does it contain eggs?		
lehvuh ohvoos?		*Leva ovos?*

I don't eat ...	nõw komoo ...	*Não como ...*
chicken	frang-goo	*frango*
dairy products	luhkteeseeniwsh	*lacticínios*
fish	paysh	*peixe*
meat	kahrn	*carne*

I'm allergic to ...	so uhlehrzheekoo/uh	*Sou alérgico/a*
	uh ...	*a ...*
peanuts	uhmengdooingsh	*amendoins*

EATING OUT   COMER FORA

Cervejarias specialise in *cerveja*, 'beer', *bifes*, 'steaks' and *petiscos*, 'snacks'. *Cervejarias* are open until late and are a popular place to socialise. A *marisqueira* specialises in *marisco*, 'shellfish' and often serves fresh fish as well. These are also usually open late.

Cafés are everywhere in Portugal. They serve sandwiches, snacks and other drinks as well as coffee. Some also serve complete meals.

At the Restaurant No Restaurante

Normally, bread and olives are served as an hors d'oeuvre, and are usually included in the *couvert*, 'cover charge'. Main dishes are usually served on a platter from which the customers take what they want.

Service and tax are included in the bill, but many people leave a small tip anyway. Tips normally run to no more than 10 per cent of the bill and, if the bill is large, can be even less.

Table for (five), please.	
oomuh mezuh puhruh (singkoo),	*Uma mesa para (cinco),*
se fahsh fuhvor	*se faz favor.*
Excuse me!	
fahsh fuhvor!	*Faz favor!*

May we see the menu?
   truhzeeuh uh kahrtuh/eemengtuh?   *Trazia a carta/ementa?*
The wine list, please.
   uh kahrtuh de veenyoosh,   *A carta de vinhos,*
   poor fuhvor   *por favor.*
The house wine, please.
   oo veenyoo duh kahzuh,   *O vinho da casa,*
   poor fuhvor   *por favor.*
What's the daily special?
   kwal eh oo menoo/   *Qual é o menu/*
   prahtoo doo deeuh?   *prato do dia?*
What's the house speciality?
   kwal eh uh shpesuhleedahd   *Qual é a especialidade*
   duh kahzuh?   *da casa?*
What's in this dish?
   oo ke eh ke lehvuh   *O que é que leva*
   es prahtoo?   *esse prato?*

FOOD

I'd like a(n) ...   kreeuh ...   *Queria ...*
  apéritif   oong uhpreeteevoo   *um aperitivo*
  main dish   oo prahtoo pringseepahl   *o prato principal*

Please bring   poor fuhvor,   *Por favor,*
(a/the) ...   trahguh ...   *traga ...*
  ashtray   oong singzayroo   *um cinzeiro*
  bill   uh kongtuh   *a conta*
  fork   oong galirfoo   *um garfo*
  glass of wine/   oong kohpoo de   *um copo de*
  water   veenyoo/ahgwuh   *vinho/água*
  knife   oomuh fahkuh   *uma faca*
  napkin   ong gwuhrduhnahpoo   *um guardanapo*
  spoon   oomuh koolyehr   *uma colher*
  toothpick   oong puhleetoo   *um palito*

Is it ...?   shtah ...?   *Está ...?*
  spicy   peekangt   *picante*
  very salty   mwingtoo   *muito*
    sahlgahdoo/uh   *salgado/a*

FOOD

MENU DECODER

à *alentejana*	ah uhlengtzhunuh	garlic, olive oil, paprika (and usually small clams)
à *cabidela*	ah kuhbeedehluh	any dish (especially chicken) made with the blood of the animal
à *cebolada*	ah sboolahduh	with onions sautéed in olive oil with garlic and often tomatoes
à *espanhola*	ah shpuhnyohluh	in a tomato and onion sauce
à *madeirense*	ah muhdayrengs	cooked with tomatoes, onions and garlic, and possibly bananas or Madeira wine
à *minhota*	ah meenyotuh	bits of ham, blood sausage, fried pig's blood or liver
à *padeira*	ah pahdayruh	baked in an earthenware casserole, served with oven roasted potatoes
à *transmontana*	ah trangzh-mongtuhnuh	hearty dish usually made with dried beans and bits of sausage
açorda	uhsorduh	bread-based dish the consistency of porridge and flavoured with garlic and cilantro
aletria	uhltreeuh	angel-hair pasta
amêijoas à Bulhão Pato	uhmayzhwuhsh ah boolyõw pahtoo	small clams in white wine and garlic sauce with cilantro
arroz ...	uhrrozh ...	rice ...
de tomate	de toomaht	cooked in a tomato broth seasoned with garlic and onions
de feijão	de fayzhõw	with red beans
de ervilhas	derveelyuhsh	with peas
cozido	koozeedoo	boiled
de marisco	de muhreeshkoo	in a casserole of seafood in tomato sauce
de pato	de pahtoo	cooked in an oven-baked casserole with duck and sausages
batatas fritas	buhtahtuhsh freetuhsh	chips
batatas à murro	buhtahtuhsh ah moorroo	new, baked potatoes with the skin on, slightly smashed
beringelas	bringzhehluhsh	eggplant/aubergine

bifana ...	beefuhnuh ...	pork ...
no pão	noo pōw	thin pork steak sandwich
bife (de vaca) ...	beef (de vahkuh) ...	... steak (beef)
da alcatra	duh uhlkahtruh	rump
da vazia	duh vuhzeeuh	sirloin
do lombo	doo longboo	fillet
bem passado	bay puhsahdoo	well done
mal passado	mahl puhsahdoo	rare
bolo inglês	boloo ing-glesh	cake with dried fruits and nuts
bolo de mel	boloo de mehl	honey and spice cake, studded with candied fruits
bolo de noz	de nohzh	walnut cake
bolo-rei	booloorray	richly decorated cake with glazed fruits
costeletas	kooshtletuhzh	lamb chops
de borrego	de boorregoo	
caldeirada	kahldayrahduh	stew of assorted fish and sea-
de peixe	de paysh	food in a tomato and wine sauce
caldo	kahldoo	chicken broth
de galinha	de guhleenyuh	
caldo verde	kahldoo verd	potato-based soup with shredded Galician cabbage and garlicky sausage
caramelo	kuhruhmehloo	caramel
chanfana	shangfuhnuh	hearty stew with goat or mutton in a heavy wine sauce
chocos (com/	shohkoosh (kong/	cuttlefish (without/with ink)
sem tinta)	sãy tingtuh)	
chouriço	shoreesoo	garlicky sausage
codornizes	koodoorneezesh	quail
com molho	kong molyoo	with sauce, gravy or salad dressing
com todos	kong todoosh	with boiled potatoes and vegetables and a boiled egg (served with boiled fish)
couve	kov	cabbage
cozido à	koozeedoo ah	Portuguese boiled dinner. A
portuguesa	poortoogezuh	hearty one-dish meal made with chunks of different meats, sausages, vegetables, rice and beans
cozido/a	koozeedoo/uh	cooked/boiled
creme de	krehm de	spicy shrimp/prawn soup
marisco/	muhreeshkoo/	
camarão	kuhmuhrōw	

FOOD

croquete	krohkeht	meat croquette
digestivo	deezhesteevoo	after-dinner drink, usually a liqueur or brandy
dobrada	doobrahduh	tripe with white beans and rice
doce da casa	dos duh kahzuh	(lit: house sweet) can be any specialty dessert but is often made of cream or condensed milk, crumbled cookies and chopped nuts
dose	dohz	single portion
empada	engpahduh	miniature pot pie with chicken or meat filling
enchidos	engsheedoosh	sausages
ensopado	engsoopahdoo	lamb or other meat stew served on top of toasted or deep-fried bread
esparguete	shpahrgeht	spaghetti
esparregado (de espinafres)	shpuhrrgahdoo (de shpeenahfresh)	puréed spinach or other greens, flavoured with garlic, onion and olive oil
especialidade da casa	shpseeuhleedahd duh kahzuh	house specialty
espetada ...	shptahduh ...	... kebab
mista	meeshtuh	mixed grill
de lulas	de looluhsh	squid
estufado/a	shtoofahdoo/uh	stewed
farinheira	fuhreenyayruh	sausage made largely of a spiced flour-based filling that may include bits of pork fat
favada	fuhvahduh	stew made of fava (like lima) beans and sausage, and sometimes poached eggs
feijoada	fayzhwahduh	hearty bean stew with sausages or other meat; each region has its own variations
filetes de pescada	feelehtsh de pshkahduh	breaded and fried hake fillets
frango (assado)	(frang-goo) uhsahdoo	(roasted) chicken
frito/a	freetoo/uh	deep-fried
fruta da época	frootuh duh ehpookuh	seasonal fruit
frutos secos	frootoosh sekoosh	dried fruit and nuts
fumado	foomahdoo	smoked

garrafa ...	guhrrahfuh ...	... bottle
pequena	pkenuh	small
de meio litro	de mayoo leetroo	half-litre
de um litro	doong leetroo	litre
gila/chila	zheeluh/sheeluh	spaghetti squash
guisado/a	goozahdoo/uh	braised
hortaliça	ortuhleesuh	boiled green leafy vegetables
cozida	koozeeduh	
iscas	eeshkuhsh	pork liver
joaquinzinhos	zhwahking zeenyoosh	small fried mackerel
lebre	lehbr	hare
leitão	laytow	suckling pig
linguiça	ling-gwisuh	thin, long garlicky sausage
lombo de	longboo de	roast pork loin
porco assado	porkoo uhsahdoo	
mini-prato	meenee prahtoo	very small serving
miolos	myohloosh	brains
molho branco	molyoo brangkoo	white sauce
molho de	molyoo de	melted butter sauce
manteiga	mangtayguh	
na(s) brasa(s)	nuh(sh) brahzuh(sh)	charcoal grilled
na pedra	nuh pehdruh	grilled and served on a stone
na sertã	nuh sertang	skillet-fried
natas	nahtuhsh	cream
no forno	noo fornoo	baked
ovo ...	ovoo ...	... egg
cozido	koozeedoo	boiled
escalfado	shkahlfahdoo	poached
mexido	msheedoo	scrambled
ovos moles	ohvoozh mohlsh	beaten egg yolks cooked in sugary broth and used primarily as a filling
ovos verdes	ohvoosh verdsh	boiled, halved eggs, stuffed with egg yolks, parsley and onion then breaded and fried
paio	paioo	smoked pork tenderloin
panado/a	puhnahdoo/uh	breaded
para duas	puhruh dwuhsh	for two people
pessoas	psouhsh	
pataniscas	puhtuhneeshkuhsh	salt cod fritters
peito de	paytoo de	chicken breast
frango	frang-goo	
peixe frito	paysh freetoo	fried fish

FOOD

FOOD

peixinhos da horta	paysheenyoosh duh ohrtuh	green beans fried in batter
perdiz	perdeezh	partridge
perna de ...	pehrnuh de ...	leg of ...
pescadinhas de rabo na boca	peshkuhdeenyuhzh de rrahboo nuh bokuh	small whole fried hakes with their tails put into their mouths
pezinhos de porco	pehzeenyoosh de porkoo	pig's feet made with cilantro
prato do dia	prahtoo doo deeuh	daily special
prego no pão	prehgoo noo pōw	small steak sandwich
presunto	prezungtoo	prosciutto
queijo fresco	kayzhoo freshkoo	very fine curd fresh cheese
recheado/a	rreshyahdoo/uh	stuffed
rissol	rreesohl	fried pasty with shrimp, meat or fish filling
robalo	rroobahloo	sea bass
rojões	rroozhōysh	chunks of pork, marinated and browned, then stewed in wine; often garnished with bits of fried pork liver
salada ... mista russa	suhlahduh ... meeshtuh rroosuh	... salad tomato, lettuce and onion potato salad with peas and carrots and lots of mayonaise
salada de frutas	suhlahduh de frootuhsh	fruit salad
salsicha fresca	sahlseeshuh freshkuh	fresh sausage
salteado/a	sahltyahdoo/uh	sautée
sardinha (assada)	suhrdeenyuh (uhsahd)	(grilled) sardine
sarrabulho	suhrruhboolyoo	a variety of meats cooked in pig's blood
arroz de sarrabulho	uhrrozh de suhrruhboolyoo	casserole of meats cooked in pig's blood with rice sometimes
semifrio	smeefreeoo	a soft or homemade ice cream, layered with a biscuit-type crust or cake
tornedó	toorndoh	thick tender steak fillet
trouxa de ovos	troshuh dohvoosh	poached thin layers of beaten egg yolk rolled into little bundles and soaked in sugar syrup
vinha de alhos	veenyuh dahlyoosh	meat marinated in wine, olive oil and garlic

DRINKS
BEDIDAS

Non-Alcoholic Drinks Bebidas Não Alcoólicas

(orange) juice	oong soomoo (de luhrangzhuh)	*um sumo (de laranja)*
lemonade	leemoonahduh	*limonada*
milk	layt	*leite*

... tea	oong shah ...	*um chá ...*
herbal	dehrvush	*de ervas*
black	pretoo	*preto*

with/without ...	kong/sāy ...	*com/sem ...*
milk	layt	*leite*
sugar	uhooookahr	*açúcar*
artificial sweetener	uhdoosangt/ eedoolkorangt	*com adoçante/ edulcorante*

... water	ahgwa ...	*água ...*
carbonated	kong gahsh	*com gás*
non-carbonated	sāy gahsh	*sem gás*
mineral	meenrahl	*mineral*

FOOD

Coffee Café

Portuguese coffee is among the best in the world. It's strong and full-bodied, without being bitter. It's typically drunk as espresso, either black during the day or with milk in the morning

Many cafés have coffee and hot milk prepared in advance for the popular morning drinks *meia de leite* and *galão*. If you want your coffee with milk freshly made, ask for it *de máquina*.

espresso coffee

| kuhfeh; oomuh beekuh; | café; uma bica; um cimbalino |
| oong singbuhleenoo | (this last one's used in the north) |

espresso coffee with a dash of milk

| kuhfeh ping-gahdoo | café pingado |

short shot of espresso coffee

| eetuhleeuhnuh | italiana |

full shot of espresso coffee

| kuhfeh shayoo | café cheio |

coffee with milk, espresso size

| guhrotoo | garoto |

café au lait

| mayuh de layt | meia de leite |
| (de mahkeenuh) | (de máquina) |

coffee with milk in a glass

| oong guhlōw | um galão |

Alcoholic Drinks Bebidas Alcoólicas

I'd like a …,	kreeuh … ,	Queria … ,
please.	se fahsh fuhvor	se faz favor.
brandy	oomuh ahgwardengt	uma aguardente
gin & tonic	oong dzheen tohneek	um gin tonic
shot	oomuh oonyuh	uma unha
slammer	oong boong boong	um bum-bum
vodka and orange	oong vohdkuh	um vodka
	luhrangzhuh	laranja
whisky	oong wiskee	um whisky

Wine Vinho

Portugal produces many excellent wines that are well worth trying and relatively inexpensive. Although the Portuguese drink more red wine than white, there are also some good Portuguese whites.

Vinho verde (lit: green wine) is produced in the north. It's a light, refreshing effervescent white wine with a low alcohol content that should be served very well chilled, and is ideal to drink with fish, shellfish or spicy foods. Portugal also produces *vinho verde tinto* (lit: red green wine).

The most well-known of all Portuguese wines are Port and Madeira wines. These are fortified wines which can be served as an after-dinner drink or as an apéritif, chilled or on ice. Moscatel and Carcavelos wines are other popular dessert wines.

What kind of wine would you recommend?	ke teepoo de veenyoo eh ke rrekoomengduh?	*Que tipo de vinho é que recomenda?*
dry	sekoo	*seco*
medium dry	mayoo sekoo	*meio seco*
sweet	dos	*doce*
I'd like a (half) bottle of ... , wine, please.	kreeuh oomuh (mayuh) guhrrahfuh de ... , poor fuhvor	*Queria uma (meia) garrafa de ... , por favor.*
champagne	shangpuhny	*champanhe*
green	veenyoo verd	*vinho verde*
house	veenyo duh kahzuh	*vinho da casa*
red	veenyoo tingtoo	*vinho tinto*
white	veenyoo brangkoo	*vinho branco*

A glass of Port/Madeira wine, please.

oong kahlees de veenyoo doo portoo/duh muhdayruh poor fuhvor

Um cálice de vinho do Porto/da Madeira, por favor

FOOD

BEER

beer	
oomuh servuhzhuh	uma cerveja
draft beer, very small glass	
oong feenoo	um fino
draft beer, large glass	
oomuh kuhnehkuh	uma caneca
dark beer	
oomuh servuhzhuh pretuh	uma cerveja preta
half dark and half light	
oomuh servuhzhuh meeshtuh	uma cerveja mista

INTERPRETING WINE LABELS

adega	uhdehguh	wine produce
casta	kahshtuh	grape variety
colheita	koolyaytuh	vintage (year)
engarrafado por ...	enguhrruhfahdoo poor ...	bottled by ...
garrafão	guhrruhfōw	5-litre jug
produzido por	proodoozeedoo poor	produced by

FOOD

engarrafado na origem/quinta
  enguhrruhfahdoo nuh oreezhāy/kingtuh
  estate-bottled

reserva
  rrzehrvuh
  a reserve or higher-quality wine

quinta
  kingtuh
  vineyard and wine-producing estate

DOC (Denominação de Origem Controlada)
  de oh se (dnoomeenuhsōw de
  oreezhāy kongtroolahduh)
  Demarcated Wine Region
  (Portugal's top 19 regions)

IPR (Indicação de Proveniência Regulamentada)
  ee pe err (ingdeekuhsōw de
  proovnyengsyuh rrgooluhmengtahduh)
  Indication of Regulated Provenance (28 regions)

TYPICAL DISHES   PRATOS TÍPICOS

Portuguese menus don't usually list what's served with meat or
fish because there are standard combinations. Fried meat, fish and
grilled meat are normally served with rice and/or chips and a bit
of lettuce and tomato. Grilled or boiled fish is normally served
with boiled potatoes and vegetables. Oven-roasted meat and fish
are normally served with roasted potatoes.

Appetisers Entradas

amêijoas à Bulhão Pato   ulmuayzhwuhzh ah boolyow pahtoo
  small clams in wine and garlic sauce with cilantro (coriander)

camarões com piripiri   kuhmuhrōysh kong peereepeeree
  shrimp sautéed in garlic, seasoned with hot pepper

chouriço assado   shoreesoo uhsahdoo
  grilled sausage

cogumelos recheados   koogoomehloozh rresheeahdoosh
  stuffed mushrooms

gambas fritas com alho   gangbuhsh freetuhsh kong ahlyoo
  prawns sautéed with garlic

pasta de atum   pahshtuh duhtoong
  tuna pâté

melão com presunto   melōw kong przoongtoo
  prosciutto and melon

queijo fresco   kayzhoo freshkoo
  very fine curd fresh cheese

requeijão   rrekayzhōw
  similar to Italian ricotta

salgados   sahlgahdoosh
  savoury pastries

Soups Sopas

In Portugal, a soup that's called *creme de ...*, 'cream of ...', doesn't
contain either cream or milk. It simply means it has a creamy
texture because it's been puréed.

caldo verde   kahldoo verd
  potato-based soup with shredded Galician cabbage
  and garlicky sausage
creme de camarão   krehm de kuhmuhrōw
  spicy shrimp soup
sopa de espinafres   sopuh de shpeenahfresh
  spinach soup
sopa de feijão verdes   sopuh de fayzhōw verd
  green bean soup
sopa de pedra   sopuh de pehdruh
  hearty vegetable soup with red beans and sausages
sopa de tomate com ovo   sopuh de toomaht kong ovoo
  tomato soup with poached egg

Rice & Bean Dishes Pratos de Arroz e Feijão

arroz de cabidela   uhrrozh de kuhbeedehluh
  chicken and rice casserole prepared with fresh chicken blood
arroz de marisco   uhrrozh de muhreeshkoo
  casserole of seafood and rice in tomato sauce
arroz de pato   uhrrozh de pahtoo
  oven-baked casserole of rice with duck and sausages
ervilhas com ovos   eerveelyuhsh kong ohvoosh
  a dish made of peas, sausages and herbs, served with poached eggs
favada   fuhvahduh
  like the pea dish above, but made with fava beans
feijoada   fayzhwaduh
  hearty bean stew with sausages or other meat; each region has its
  own variation

FOOD

Fish & Seafood Dishes Pratos de Peixe e Marisco

açorda de marisco   uhsorduh de muhreeshkoo
bread-based dish the consistency of porridge, studded with sea
food, flavoured with garlic and cilantro

amêijoas na cataplana   uhmayzhwazh nuh kuhtuhpluhnuh
small clams prepared with tomato, green pepper and onions
in a special copper cooking vessel

caldeirada   kahldayrahduh
stew of assorted fish and seafood in a tomato and wine sauce

espetada de lulas   shpetahduh de looluhsh
squid kebab

peixe assado no forno   paysh uhsahdoo noo fornoo
oven baked fish

Dried Salt Cod Bacalhau

Bacalhau is a special favourite of the Portuguese, and it's said that
the Portuguese know hundreds of different ways to prepare it.
Here are a few you're likely to find on the menu.

bacalhau à Brás   buhkuhlyow ah brahsh
casserole of shredded salt cod, fried potatoes
and scrambled eggs

bacalhau à Gomes de Sá   buhkuhlyow ah gomezh de sah
oven-baked casserole of flaked salt cod
with potatoes and onion

bacalhau com natas   buhkuhlyow kong nahtuhsh
casserole of creamed salt cod and potatoes

bacalhau á lagareiro/   buhkuhlyow ah luhguhrayroo/
com batatas á murro   kong buhtahtuz ah moorroo
grilled salt cod served with baked potatoes (skin on)
and garlic scented olive oil

pataniscas de bacalhau   puhtuhneeshkuhsh de buhkuhlyow
salt cod fritters, served with seasoned rice and red beans

FOOD

Meat Dishes Pratos de Carne

bife à casa (or *bife à* plus   beef ah kahzuh
the name of the restaurant)
   thin, pan-fried steak served with chips, rice and a bit of salad

cabrito assado   kuhbreetoo uhsahdoo
   kid, roasted with wine, garlic and bay laurel. Lamb (*borrego*) is
   also prepared this way.

coelho à caçador   kwuhlyoo ah kuhsuhdor
   (lit: hunter's style rabbit) rabbit stewed with red wine and tomato

cozido à portuguesa   koozeedoo ah poortoogezuh
   (lit: Portuguese boiled dinner) a hearty one-dish meal made with
   chunks of different meats, sausages and vegetables

frango no churrasco   frang-goo noo shoorrahshkoo
   grilled chicken seasoned with garlic, bay leaves, paprika and
   olive oil, and sometimes hot pepper

leitão   laytōw
   suckling pig, roasted in an oven; may be served hot or cold

carne de porco à   kahrn de porkoo ah
alentejana   uhlengtzhuhnuh
   cubes of marinated pork and clams simmered with onions,
   garlic and tomatoes

rojões   rroozhōysh
   a typical northern dish made with chunks of pork, marinated
   and browned, then stewed in wine; often garnished with fried
   pork liver

Side Dishes Acompanhamentos

arroz de tomate   uhrrozh de toomaht
   rice cooked in a tomato broth seasoned with garlic and onions.

esparregado   shpuhrrgahdoo
   puréed spinach or other greens, flavoured with garlic, onion and
   olive oil

pimentos assados   peemengtooz uhsahdoosh
   strips of roasted sweet pepper, marinated in vinegar and oil

salada   suhlahduh
   lettuce with oil and vinegar. A *salada mista* also includes
   sliced tomato and onions

FOOD

Desserts & Sweets Sobremesas e Doces

In general, desserts tend to be very sweet and rich. Lemon and cinnamon are preferred flavourings.

Regional specialities include almond and fig desserts from the Algarve, such as excellent *maçapão*, 'marzipan', shaped into fruits and other objects with tiny centres of *fios de ovos*, 'sweetened egg yolk'; *ovos moles*, sweet soft eggs, from Aveiro, and *pastéis de Tentugal*, a flaky filled pastry. Larger cakes and tarts are served by the slice.

bolo de amêndoa   boloo de uhmengdoouh
   cake made of ground almonds, usually of two layers with a
   filling of *doce de ovos* (see *ovos moles*, page 184)
bolo de bolacha   boloo de boolahshuh
   cake made with biscuit layered with sweetened buttercream
   frosting to form a cake
pão de ló (de Alfeizarão)   pōw de loh (de ahlfayzuhrōw)
   a rich yellow sponge cake, eaten plain or used as a base for other
   desserts
tarte de amêndoa   tahrt de uhmengdoouh
   sweet almond filling in a pastry shell
toucinho do céu   toseenyoo doo sehoo
   (lit: bacon from heaven) rich cinnamon-flavoured dessert made
   with eggs and pumpkin or *chila*, a kind of squash

Many Portuguese desserts are *doces de colher*, soft and creamy concoctions, eaten with a spoon rather than a fork.

doce da avó/doce da casa   dos duh uhvoh/dos duh kahzuh
   many restaurants serve these chilled desserts, typically made of
   cream or condensed milk, d*oce de ovos*, 'sweet egg', crumbled
   biscuit and chopped nuts
gelado   zhelahdoo
   ice cream
leite creme   layt krehm
   custard cream with caramelised sugar (similar to crème brûlée)

FOOD

FOOD

ovos moles   ohvoozh mohlesh
  sweetened egg yolks thickened to a soft creamy texture. These
  can be eaten plain, but a similar concoction, *doce de ovos*, is also
  used as an ingredient in other breads and cakes.
pudim molotov   pooding molohtohv
  poached meringue with caramel sauce

AT THE PASTRY SHOP   NUMA PASTELERIA
Cakes & Sweets Bolos e Doces
arrepiadas   uhrrpeeahduhsh
  clusters of sliced almonds, held together with meringue
bolo de arroz   boloo de uhrrozh
  cake made with rice and wheat flour topped with sugar
bolo de mel   boloo de mehl
  honey and spice cake, studded with candied fruits
palmier   pahlmee-ehr
  flat, palm-shaped puff pastry. Variations include *simples* (plain),
  recheado (two *palmiers* sandwiched with sweet egg-based
  filling), *coberto* (with icing)
pastel de nata   puhshtehl de nahtuh
  small rich custard cream tart in flaky pastry shell. You can ask to
  have it sprinkled with cinnamon. Many *pastelarias* boast their
  own
  special recipes for this delicious pastry.
sonhos   sohnyoosh
  fried sweet dough, sprinkled with sugar and cinnamon
torta   tohrtuh
  cake roll with filling

Savouries Salgados
um croquete   oong krohkeht
  meat croquette
um rissol de   oong rreesohl de
camarão/carne/peixe   kuhmuhrõw/kahrn/paysh
  fried pasty with shrimp/meat/fish filling

um folhado de vitela/   oong foolyahdoo de veetehluh/
salsicha/galinha/carne/legumes sahlseeshuh/kahrn/lgoomesh
  puff pastry filled with veal/sausage/chicken/ground
  meat/vegetables
um pastel de bacalhau   oong puhshtehl de buhkuhlyow
  deep fried, oval-shaped patties of seasoned potato,
  onion and salt cod
um crepe de   oong krehp de
galinha/legumes   guhleenyuh/lgoomesh
  chicken/vegetable filled crepe, fried to a crisp

SELF-CATERING   COMPRAR PROVISÕES

For an authentic Portuguese shopping experience, you can go to a
mercearia, a small grocery store which sells most of the basics.

Fresh meat is sold at a *talho*. In city shopping districts, you can
find small shops, called *charcutarias*, that specialise in traditional
regional foods like sausages, cheeses, dried fruits and nuts and wines.
Some shops that specialise in dried salt cod, a favourite fish of the
Portuguese.

... bread	pōw ...	*pão ...*
corn	de meelyoo	*de milho*
whole grain	ingtegrahl	*integral*
biscuits (cookies)	beeshkoytoosh	*biscoitos*
butter	mangtayguh	*manteiga*
cheese	kayzhoo	*queijo*
chocolate	shookoolaht	*chocolate*
crackers	boolahshuhsh	*bolachas*
eggs	ohvoosh	*ovos*
flour	fuhreenyuh	*farinha*
ham	feeangbr	*fiambre*
honey	mehl	*mel*
margarine	muhrguhreenuh	*margarina*
milk	layt	*leite*
... olives	uhzaytonuhsh ...	*azeitonas ...*
black	pretuhsh	*pretas*
green	verdesh	*verdes*
olive oil	uhzayt	*azeite*

FOOD

pasta	mahsuh	*massa*
pepper	peemengtuh	*pimenta*
reduced fat	mayoo gordoo	*meio gordo*
(brown) rice	uhrroz (ingtegrahl)	*arroz (integral)*
salt	sahl	*sal*
sugar	uhsookahr	*açúcar*
vegetable oil	ohliw uhleemengtahr	*óleo alimentar*
yogurt	eeohgoort	*yogurte/iogurte*

FOOD

AT THE MARKET   NO MERCARDO
Meat Carne

When the type of meat isn't specified, as in *sandes de carne assada*, 'roast meat sandwich', it will usually be pork.

The Portuguese word for steak is *bife*, 'steaks', which shouldn't be confused with 'beef'. You can have *bifes* of any kind of meat.

bacon	baykong	*bacon*
beef	kahrn de vahkuh	*carne de vaca*
blood sausage	morcela	*moorsehluh*
(with rice)	(de arroz)	*(de uhrrosh)*
chourizo	shoreesoo	*chouriço*
(garlicky sausage)		
hot dogs	sahlseeshuhsh	*salsichas*
kid (goat)	kuhbreetoo	*cabrito*
lamb	boorregoo	*borrego*
liver	feeguhdoo	*fígado*
meat	kahrn	*carne*
pork	kahrn de porkoo	*carne de porco*
smoked bacon	toseenyoo foomahdoo	*toucinho fumado*
veal	veetehluh	*vitela*
venison	vyahdoo	*veado*
wild boar	zhuhvuhlee	*javali*

Poultry & Game Aves

chicken	frang-goo	*frango*
duck	pahtoo	*pato*
partridge	perdeesh	*perdiz*
pheasant	faizõw	*faisão*
rabbit	kwuhlyoo	*coelho*
turkey	proo	*perú*

Fish Peixe

Bacalhau is usually translated into English as 'codfish'. This can lead the unsuspecting tourist looking at an English version of a menu to believe that they're ordering fresh fish. But in Portugal *bacalhau* is always dried salt cod unless stated otherwise.

Peixe-espada will often be translated on an English menu as 'swordfish'. A better translation is 'scabbard fish', as this fish is shaped like a long blade. It has delicately-flavoured, flaky white flesh completely unlike the dense and meaty swordfish. The Portuguese word for swordfish is *espadarte*.

FOOD

FOOD

dory	dorahduh	*dourada*
eel	eng-geeuh	*enguia*
red mullet	sahlmoonet	*salmonete*
roe	ohvuhzh de peshkahduh	*ovas de pescada*
salmon	sahlmōw	*salmão*
sardines	suhrdeenyuh	*sardinha*
scabbard fish	paysh shpahduh	*peixe-espada*
sea bass	roobahloo	*robalo*
sea bream	bzoogoo	*besugo*
sole	ling-gwahdoo	*linguado*
trout	trootuh	*truta*
tuna	uhtoong	*atum*
whiting	peshkuhdeenyuh	*pescadinha*

Shellfish Mariscos

crab (spider or spiny)	sangtohluh	*santola*
crayfish	luhgooshtingsh	*lagostins*
clams	uhmayzhwuhsh	*amêijoas*
cuttlefish (without/with ink)	shohkoosh (kong/sãy tingtuh)	*chocos (com/sem tinta)*
lobster	luhgoshtuh	*lagosta*
mussels	msheelyōysh	*mexilhões*
prawns	gangbuhsh	*gambas*
octopus	polvoo	*polvo*
oysters	oshtruhsh	*ostras*
shrimp	kuhmuhrōw	*camarão*
baby squid (without/with ink)	looluhsh (kong/sãy tingtuh)	*lulas (com/sem tinta)*

Vegetables Hortaliças/Vegetais

Normally, fresh produce is sold by the kilogram. When speaking of quantities, use the singular form (such as *dois quilos de cenoura*, literally, 'two kilos of carrot'). Avoid ever saying the word *tomates*, 'tomato' in the plural, as the plural form is also slang for 'testicles'.

artichoke	ahlkuhshohfruh	*alcachofra*
asparagus	shpahrgoosh	*espargos*
beans (green)	fayzhōw (verd)	*feijão (verde)*
cabbage	kov	*couve*
capsicum	peemengtoo	*pimento*
(red/green)	(vermelhoo/verd)	*(vermelho/verde)*
carrots	snoruh	*cenoura*
cauliflower	kov flor	*couve-flor*
corn	meelyoo dos	*milho doce*
cucumber	pepeenoo	*pepino*
eggplant	bringzhehluh	*beringela*
garlic	ahlyoo	*alho*
lettuce	ahlfahs	*alface*
mushrooms	koogoomehloosh	*cogumelos*
onion	sboluh	*cebola*
peas	eerveelyuhsh	*ervilhas*
potato	buhtahtuh	*batata*
pumpkin	uhbohbooruh	*abóbora*
spinach	shpeenahfresh	*espinafres*
tomato	toomaht	*tomate*

Fruit Fruta

apple	muhsang	*maçã*
avocado	uhbuhkaht	*abacate*
banana	buhnuhnuh	*banana*
cantaloupe	mlouh	*meloa*
fig	feegoo	*figo*
lemon	leemōw	*limão*
mango	mang-guh	*manga*
orange	luhrangzhuh	*laranja*

FOOD

peach	pesgoo	*pêssego*
pear	peruh	*pêra*
pineapple	uhnuhnahsh	*ananás*
strawberry	moorang-goo	*morango*
watermelon	mlangseeuh	*melancia*

Herbs, Spices & Condiments / Ervas, Especiarias e Temperos

Portuguese cooks use relatively few herbs and spices in their cooking, but nevertheless manage to prepare a wide variety of delicious foods.

bay laurel	loroo	*louro*
coriander (cilantro)	kooengtroosh	*coentros*
curry powder	kuhreel	*caril*
garlic	ahlyoo	*alho*
ginger	zhengzheebr	*gengibre*
hot pepper	peeree peeree/ muhluhgetuh	*piri piri/ malagueta*
mayonnaise	maiohnez	*maionese*
mint	ortlang	*hortelã*
mustard	mooshtahrduh	*mostarda*
oregano	orehgõwsh	*orégãos*
paprika	kooloorow	*colorau*
parsley	sahlsuh	*salsa*
pepper	peemengtuh	*pimenta*
salt	sahl	*sal*
vinegar	veenahgr	*vinagre*

IN THE COUNTRY NO CAMPO

CAMPING   ## CAMPISMO

Most camping sites in Portugal are in coastal areas. In summer, they tend to fill up fast, so it's best to make a reservation ahead of time. The range of services – water, showers, gas supply, telephone, type of access, hours – should be posted at the entrance to the camping site.

Where's the nearest campsite?

ongd feekuh oo uhkangpuhmengtoo maish prohseemoo? — *Onde fica o acampamento mais próximo?*

Do you have any sites available?

tãy alilgoomuh puhtsehluh vahguh? — *Tem alguma parcela vaga?*

I'd like to speak to the manager.

kreeuh fuhlahr kong oo zherengt — *Queria falar com o gerente.*

How much is it per …?	kwangtoo kooshtuh poor …?	Quanto custa por …?
person	psouh	*pessoa*
tent	tengduh	*tenda*
vehicle	vuheekooloo	*veículo*

Are there shower facilities?

tãy doosh? — *Tem duche?*

What are the operating hours?

kwahl eh oo orahriw de foongsiwnuhmengtoo? — *Qual é o horário de funcionamento?*

Do you supply gas?

foornehsãy gahzh? — *Fornecem gás?*

Where can I hire a tent?

ongd pohsoo uhloogahr oomuh tengduh? — *Onde posso alugar uma tenda?*

Can we camp here?

poodemooz uhkangpahr uhkee? — *Podemos acampar aqui?*

backpack	uh moosheeluh	a mochila
camping	(fuhzer) kangpeezhmoo	(fazer) campismo
campsite	oo uhkangpuhmengtoo	o acampamento
can/tin opener	oo ahbrlahtuhsh	o abre-latas
compass	uh boosooluh	a bússola
gas stove	oo foogõw uh gahzh	o fogão a gás
hammer	oo muhrtehloo	o martelo
mattress	oo kolshõw	o colchão
pad	uh shtayruh	a esteira
pocket knife	uh nuhvahlyuh	a navalha
rope	uh kohrduh	a corda
sleeping bag	oo sahkoo kuhmuh	o saco-cama
tent	uh tengduh	a tenda
tent peg	uh shtahkuh	a estaca
thermos	oo termoo	o termo
torch (flashlight)	uh langtehrnuh	a lanterna
wood	uh luhnyuh	a lenha

HIKING   CAMINHADAS E MONTANHISMO

Every year, hiking trips are organised in places such as Sintra, near Lisbon, or the *Serra de Sicó*, the Sicó mountain range, in the interior of the country. Hiking gear and equipment can be hired. Consult the local Tourist Information Centre for details.

Where's the nearest village?
   ongd feekuh uh veeluh   *Onde fica a vila*
   maish prohseemuh?   *mais próxima?*
Is it safe to climb this mountain?
   eh sgooroo shkuhlahr   *É seguro escalar*
   ehshtuh mongtuhnyuh?   *esta montanha?*
Is there a shelter up there?
   lah ah ahlgoong uhbreegoo?   *Lá há algum abrigo?*
Where can I find out about
hiking trails in the region?
   ongd eh ke me pohsoo   *Onde é que me posso*
   ingfoormahr sobr kuhmeenyoozh *nformar sobre caminhos*
   nuh rrzheeõw?   *ina região?*

Are there guided treks?
  ah shkoorsõysh geeahduhsh?   *Há excursões guiadas?*

I'd like to talk to someone
who knows this area.
  gooshtahvuh de fuhlahr   *Gostava de falar*
  kong ahlgäy ke koonyesuh   *com alguém que conheça*
  bay uh zonuh   *bem a zona.*

How long is the trail?
  kwahl eh oo tuhmuhnyoo   *Qual é o tamanho*
  doo perkoorsoo?   *do percurso?*

Is the track well marked?
  oo perkoorsoo shtah bäy   *O percurso está bem*
  uhseenuhlahdoo?   *assinalado?*

How high is the climb?
  uhteh ke ahltooruh eh uh   *Até que altura é a*
  shkuhlahduh?   *escalada?*

Which is the shortest/easiest route?
  kwahl eh oo perkoorsoo maish   *Qual é o percurso mais*
  koortoo/fahseel?   *curto/fácil?*

When does it get dark?
  kwangdoo eh ke shkoorehs?   *Quando é que escurece?*

Where can I hire mountain gear?
  ongd eh ke pohsoo uhloogahr   *Onde é que posso alugar*
  muhtryahl de mongtuhnyeezhmoo?   *material de montanhismo?*

Where can we buy food supplies?
  ongd eh ke poodemoosh   *Onde é que podemos*
  kongprahr koomeeduh?   *comprar comida?*

On the Path   No Caminho

Where have you come from?
  dongd väy?   *De onde vem?*

How long did it take you?
  kwangtoo tengpoo eh   *Quanto tempo é*
  ke dmooroo?   *que demorou?*

Does this path go to ...?
  esht kuhmeenyoo vai puhruh ...?   *Este caminho vai para ...?*

IN THE COUNTRY

Where can we spend the night?
   ongd eh ke poodemoosh   *Onde é que podemos*
   puhsahr uh noyt?   *passar a noite?*
Is the water safe to drink?
   uh ahgwuh eh pootahvehl?   *A água é potável?*
I'm lost.
   shto perdeedoo/uh   *Estou perdido/a.*

binoculars	oozh beenohkooloosh	*os binóculos*
to climb	shkuhlahr	*escalar*
crampons	oosh grangpoozh de fehrroo	*os grampos de ferro*
downhill	engkohshtuh uh baishoo	*encosta a baixo*
first-aid kit	oo shtozhoo de	*o estojo de*
	preemayroosh sookohrroosh	*primeiros socorros*
guide	oo geeuh	*o guia*
guided trek	uh shkoorsõw geeahduh	*a excursão guiada*
harness	oo singtoo de shkuhlahduh	*o cinto de escalada*
hiking	puhsyahr uh peh	*passear a pé*
hiking boots	uhzh bohtuhzh de	*as botas de*
	mongtuhnyuh	*montanha*
knots	oozh nohsh	*os nós*
ledge	uh suhlyengsyuh	*a saliência*
lookout	oo meeruhdoroo	*o miradouro*
map	oo mahpuh	*o mapa*
mountain climbing	oo ahlpeeneezhmoo	*o alpinismo*
peak	oo topoo/oo ahltoo	*o topo/o alto*
pick	uh peekuhretuh	*a picareta*
provisions	uhsh prooveezõysh/	*as provisões/os*
	oozh mangteemengtoosh	*mantimentos*
rock climbing	shkuhlahr	*escalar*
signpost	uh plahkuh	*a placa*
steep	ing-grem	*íngreme*
trek	uh shkoorsõw	*a excursão*
uphill	engkohshtuh uhseemuh	*encosta acima*
to walk	angdahr	*andar*

CYCLING   CICLISMO

In Portugal, cycling races are fairly traditional. Both national and
international teams participate in the *Volta a Portugal*, 'Tour of
Portugal'. On the amateur level, cycling races are organised by
different cycling associations and local organisations. (See pages
73 and 136 for more cycling terms.)

bell	uh kangpuheenyuh	*a campainha*
(front/rear) brakes	oosh truhvõyzh	*os travões*
	(duh frengt/de trahsh)	*(da frente/de trás)*
cycling	oo seekleezhmoo	*o ciclismo*
cycling course	uh vohltuh	*a volta*
cyclist	oo/uh seekleeshtuh	*o/a ciclista*
handlebars	oo geeuhdor	*o guiador*
helmet	oo kuhpuhset	*o capacete*
level of difficulty	oo grow de deefeekooldahd	*o grau de dificuldade*
meeting point	oo lookahl de kongsengtruhsõw	*o local de concentração*
pedal	oo pdahl	*o pedal*
route/trail	oo perkoorsoo/ oo treelyoo	*o percurso/ o trilho*
starting time	uh ohruh duh purteeduh	*a hora da partida*
steepest point	oo dezhneevehl mahseemoo	*o desnível máximo*
tyre	oo pne-w	*o pneu*
water bottle	uh guhrrahfuh dahgwuh	*a garrafa de água*
wheel	uh rrohduh	*a roda*

AT THE BEACH   NA PRAIA

At almost every beach in Portugal, there are stands where you can buy all the essentials for a day at the beach, including sunscreen, beach towels and sun hats. Food is sold at kiosks and by vendors who walk along the beach selling chips, ice cream and sweets.

Before heading into the water, check the colour of the flag on the beach. Red means it isn't safe to swim; yellow means to be careful, it may be dangerous; and green means it's safe to swim. A blue flag means that the beach has passed tests of quality and hygiene, but doesn't necessarily mean it's safe to swim at the time.

Is it safe to swim here?
    eh sgooroo nuhdahr uhkee?   *É seguro nadar aqui?*
What time is high/low tide?
    uh ke ohruhz eh ke uh muhreh   *A que horas é que a maré*
    shtah baishuh/ahltuh?   *está baixa/alta?*

coast	uh kohshtuh	*a costa*
fishing	peshkahr	*pescar*
reef	oo rrooshedoo	*o rochedo*
rock	uh rrohshuh	*a rocha*
sand	uh uhrayuh	*a areia*
sea	oo mahr	*o mar*
snorkelling	uh nuhtuhsõw soobuhkwateekuh	*a natação subaquática*
sunblock	oo krehm de prootehsõw soolahr	*o creme de protecção solar*
sunglasses	ooz ohkooloozh de sohl	*os óculos de sol*
surf	oo suhrf	*o surf*
surfing	fuhzer suhrf	*fazer surf*
surfboard	uh prangshuh de suhrf	*a prancha de surf*
swimming	nuhdahr	*nadar*
towel	uh twalyuh	*a toalha*
waterskiing	skee uhkwateekoo	*esqui aquático*
waves	uhz ongduhsh	*as ondas*
windsurfing	fuhzer wingdsuhrf	*fazer windsurf*

Diving   Fazer Mergulho

Are there good diving sites here?
ah seetiwsh bongsh puhruh
mergoolyahr uhkee?

*Há sítios bons para
mergulhar aqui?*

Can we hire a diving boat?
poodemoosh uhloogahr oong
bahrkoo de mergoolyoo?

*Podemos alugar um
barco de mergulho?*

Can we hire a guide?
poodemoosh kongtruhtahr oong
geeuh de mergoolyoo?

*Podemos contratar um
guia de mergulho?*

We'd like to hire diving equipment.
kreeuhmooz uhloogahr
eekeepuhmengtoo de mergoolyoo

*Queríamos alugar
equipamento de mergulho.*

I'm interested in exploring wrecks.
shto ingtresahdoo/uh ãy
shploorahr nowfrahzhiwsh

*Estou interessado/a em
explorar naufrágios.*

WEATHER   O CLIMA

The climate in Portugal is mild – neither too cold in winter, nor too hot in summer. There's a rainy season, though, from October until spring, and particularly in the north this can mean a lot of rain. Summers are hotter in the southern regions of the Alentejo and the Algarve, with temperatures reaching 35° C and higher.

What's the weather like?
komoo shtah oo tengpoo?   *Como está o tempo?*
It's raining heavily/lightly.

  shtah uh shoover mwingtoo/   *Está a chover*
  pokoo   *muito/pouco.*

Today it's ...	ozh shtah ...	*Hoje está ...*
cloudy	kong noováysh	*com nuvens*
cold	freeoo	*frio*
foggy	nvooayroo	*nevoeiro*
hot	kuhlor	*calor*
warm	kengt	*quente*
windy	vengtoo	*vento*

downpour	uh trongbuh dahgwuh	*a tromba d'água*
dry season	ehpookuh sekuh	*época seca*
rainy season	ehpookuh duhsh	*época das*
	shoovuhsh	*chuvas*
snow	uh nehv	*a neve*
sun	oo sohl	*o sol*
typhoon	oo toofów	*o tufão*

GEOGRAPHICAL   TERMOS
TERMS   GEOGRÁFICOS

bridge	uh pongt	*a ponte*
cave	uh grootuh	*a gruta*
cliff	uh fuhlehzyuh	*a falésia*
countryside	oo kangpoo	*o campo*
desert	oo dzehrtoo	*o deserto*

IN THE COUNTRY

footpath	oo kuhmeenyoo/ oo treelyoo	o caminho/ o trilho
forest	uh floorehshtuh	a floresta
gap (narrow pass)	uh puhsahzhãy shtraytuh/ oo sengdayroo	a passagem estreita/ o sendeiro
harbour	oo portoo	o porto
hill	uh kooleenuh	a colina
hot spring	uh nuhshsengt	a nascente
island	uh eelyuh	a ilha
lake	oo lahgoo	o lago
mountain	uh mongtuhnyuh	a montanha
mountain range	uh sehrruh	a serra
pass	uh puhsahzhãy	a passagem
pasture	oo pahshtoo	o pasto
peak	oo ahltoo/oo koom	o alto/o cume
plain	uh pluhneeruh	a planície
river	oo reeoo	o rio
stream	oo rreeahshoo	o riacho
tide	uh muhreh	a maré
valley	oo vahl	o vale
waterfall	uh kuhshkahduh	a cascada

IN THE COUNTRY

SEASONS
ESTAÇÕES DO ANO

summer	oo vrõw	o Verão
autumn (fall)	oo otonoo	o Outono
winter	oo ingvehrnoo	o Inverno
spring	uh preemuhvehruh	a Primavera

FAUNA
FAUNA

What do you call this animal?
    komoo eh ke se shuhmuh
    esht uhneemahl/beeshoo?

*Como é que se chama
este animal/bicho?*

Help! A mouse!
    sookorroo! oong rrahtoo!

Socorro! Um rato!

What a beautiful bird!
    ke pahsuhroo tõw booneetoo!

Que pássaro tão bonito!

IN THE COUNTRY

Wildlife Vida Selvagem

bear	oo oorsoo	o urso
bee	uh uhbuhlyuh	a abelha
butterfly	uh boorbooletuh	a borboleta
deer	oo veeahdoo	o veado
fish	oo paysh	o peixe
fly	uh moshkuh	a mosca
fox	uh rruhpozuh	a raposa
monkey	oo muhkahkoo	o macaco
mosquito	oo mooshkeetoo	o mosquito
mouse	oo rrahtoo	o rato
snake	uh kohbruh	a cobra
wild boar	oo zhuhvuhlee	o javali
wolf	oo/uh loboo/uh	o/a lobo/a
shark	oo toobuhrõw	o tubarão
rat	uh rruhtuhzuhnuh	a ratazana
spider	uh uhruhnyuh	a aranha
wasp	oo zang-gõw	o zangão

Birds Pássaros

bird	oo pahsuhroo	o pássaro
canary	oo kuhnahriw	o canário
crow	uh grahlyuh	a gralha
eagle	uh ahgyuh	a águia
hawk	oo guhveeõw	o gavião
owl	oo moshoo	o mocho
parakeet	oo pereekeetoo	o periquito
parrot	oo puhpuhgaioo	o papagaio
pigeon	oo/uh pongboo/uh	o/a pombo/a
raven	oo korvoo	o corvo
seagull	uh gaivohtuh	a gaivota
songbird	oo tengteelyõw	o tentilhão
sparrow	oo puhrdahl	o pardal
stork	uh sgonyuh	a cegonha
woodpecker	oo peekuhpow	o pica-pau

Farm Animals Animais Domésticos

bull	o boy	o boi
cat	oo/uh gahtoo/uh	o/a gato/a
chicken	uh guhleenyuh;	a galinha;
	oo frang-goo	o frango
cow	uh vahkuh	a vaca
dog (m/f)	oo kōw/	o cão/
	uh kuhdehluh	a cadela
donkey	oo boorroo	o burro
duck	oo/uh pahtoo/uh	o/a pato/a
goat	uh kahbruh	a cabra
horse	oo kuhvahloo	o cavalo
pig	oo porkoo	o porco
rabbit	oo kwuhlyoo	o coelho
sheep	uh oovuhlyuh	a ovelha
rooster	oo gahloo	o galo

Pets Animais de Estimação

I (don't) like animals.
(nōw) gohshtoo duhneemaish   *(Não) Gosto de animais.*
I'm afraid of animals.
tuhnyoo medoo dooz uhneemaish   *Tenho medo dos animais.*
What a cute puppy!
ke kuhshorroo tōw kreedoo!   *Que cachorro tão querido!*
What's his/her name?
komoo eh ke se shuhmuh?   *Como é que se chama?*
How old is s/he?
ke eedahd eh ke tãy?   *Que idade é que tem?*
What breed is it?
de ke rahsuh eh?   *De que raça é?*
Does it bite?
mohrd?   *Morde?*
It's very tame and affectionate.
eh mwingtoo mangsoo   *É muito manso*
ee kuhreenyozoo   *e carinhoso.*

FLORA & AGRICULTURE

FLORA E AGRICULTURA

agriculture	uh uhgreekooltooruh	*a agricultura*
cane sugar	oo uhsookahr de kuhnuh	*o açúcar de cana*
crops	uhsh kooltooruhsh	*as culturas*
grapevine	uh veedayruh	*a videira*
planting	plangtahr	*plantar*
rice field	oo kangpoo duhrrozh	*o campo de arroz*
sowing	koolteevahr	*cultivar*
terraced land	tehrruh āy sookahlkoo	*terra em socalco*
tree	uh ahrvoor	*a árvore*

Flowers Flores

camelia	uh kuhmehlyuh	*a camélia*
carnation	oo krahvoo	*o cravo*
daisy	uh muhrguhreeduh	*a margarida*
geranium	uh suhrdeenyayruh	*a sardinheira*
hydrangea	uh ohrtengs	*a hortense*
iris	oo leeriw	*o lírio*
rose	uh rrohzuh	*a rosa*
sunflower	oo zheeruhsohl	*o girassol*
tulip	uh tooleepuh	*a túlipa*

FESTIVALS & HOLIDAYS

Most Portuguese people holiday in the summer between July and September. Lisbon slows down in August, so expect to find many small businesses, shops and restaurants closed. It's a good idea to avoid travelling on Friday and Sunday afternoons, when people from Lisbon make a mass exodus to nearby Costa da Caparica beach or the Algarve for the weekend.

Happy Holidays! (Christmas and Easter)		
bouhsh fehshtuhsh/ fehshtuhsh fleezsh!		*Boas festas/ Festas Felizes!*
Congratulations! (for a birthday)		
puhruhbáysh!		*Parabéns!*
to celebrate	selbrahr/feshtezhahr	*celebrar/festejar*
gift	prengduh	*prenda*
official holiday	freeahdoo	*feriado*

CROSSING THAT BRIDGE

A day that falls between an official holiday and the weekend is declared a holiday for public service workers. These days are called *ponte*, which literally means 'bridge'.

NATIONAL HOLIDAYS

The most important national holiday in Portugal is celebrated on 25 April. On this day in 1974, the 'Carnation Revolution' established a democratic regime.

On 10 June, the Portuguese commemorate *Camões* Day. *Camões*, who lived in the 16th century, is considered Portugal's greatest poet and one of the greatest epic writers of all time.

This day also celebrates Portuguese communities around the world. (Portugal was, until recently, an emigrant country and there are large Portuguese communities in many countries worldwide. People sometimes refer to Paris, where more than a million Portuguese live, as being the second largest Portuguese city.)

For most Portuguese, 1 December is just a day off work, but actually commemorates the Restoration of Independence from Spain in 1640.

RELIGIOUS HOLIDAYS
Christmas Natal

FERIADOS RELIGIOSOS

At Christmas, presents are exchanged on the *noite da consoada*, 'night of Christmas Eve', after the *missa do galo*, 'midnight mass', or during or after Christmas Eve dinner.

The Portuguese are passionate about their salt cod, and a traditional Christmas Eve dinner usually consists of boiled salt cod with chick peas and cabbage. After midnight, fried savouries and sweets are served, such as *filhozes*, *sonhos*, sweet fritters, and *fatias douradas*, egg-dipped bread, fried and sprinkled with cinnamon sugar.

Although the Epiphany on 6 January isn't a holiday in Portugal, eating *bolo rei* (lit: king cake) on this day has become a tradition. This cake is richly decorated with candied fruits and has a fava bean (similar to a lima bean) and a token gift baked inside. The person who ends up with the fava bean has to provide the *bolo rei* the next year.

Merry Christmas!	fleezh nuhtahl!	*Feliz Natal!*
Blessed Christmas!	sangtoo nuhtahl!	*Santo Natal!*
Christmas Eve	noyt de kongswahduh	*Noite de Consoada*

Easter Páscoa

Easter is another important holiday in Portugal. Easter fare usually consists of roast lamb or kid and a special sweet bread that's flavoured with cinnamon and anise and decorated with boiled whole eggs (in the shell!) on the top. A more recent tradition is to eat candied almonds and chocolate eggs.

Happy Easter!	pahshkwuh fleesh!	*Páscoa feliz!*
Good Friday	suhshtuh fayruh sangtuh	*Sexta-Feira Santa*
Holy Week	smuhnuh sangtuh	*Semana Santa*
Palm Sunday	dooming-goo de rruhmoosh	*Domingo de Ramos*
Easter bread	foolahr	*folar*
chocolate eggs	ohvoosh de shookoolaht	*ovos de chocolate*
Easter eggs	ohvoosh duh pahshkwuh	*ovos da Páscoa*

Saint's Days   Dias de
& Patron Saints   Santos e Padroeiros

Each Portuguese city and village has a patron saint, and each celebrates this saint's day with a municipal holiday. Streets are decorated, and there's usually a religious procession. At night an *arraial*, or 'block party', is set up, and grilled sardines, bread and wine are provided free or for a nominal charge. You can eat while listening to music and dance to the sounds of *modinhas*, 'traditional songs'. St Anthony is the patron saint of Lisbon, and the Portuguese capital celebrates its municipal holiday on 13 June.

One of the highlights of this festival is the *marchas populares*. In this parade down the Avenida da Liberdade, brightly-costumed groups march, dance and sing to tunes composed especially for the occasion.

OTHER HOLIDAYS   OUTRAS FESTAS
New Year   Ano Novo

The new year is celebrated on New Year's Eve. One custom is to stand on a chair at midnight. Each person has 12 raisins, one for each month of the year. When the clock strikes midnight, one raisin is eaten with each chime to bring good luck for each month of the year. Afterwards, people bang pots and pans outside their windows.

New Year's Eve is celebrated in grand style on the Portuguese island of Madeira. People come from all around to enjoy the lavish parties and extravagant fireworks that have made Funchal, Madeira, a New Year's hot spot.

Happy New Year!
     fleesh/prohshproo uhnoo novoo!   *Feliz/Próspero Ano Novo!*
New Year's Eve
     noyt doo uhnoo novoo   *Noite do Ano Novo*

Mardi Gras Carnaval

Carnaval is celebrated in February. Although Portugal and Brazil have very strong language and cultural ties, Portugal's Carnaval is unlike that of Brazil, with its flamboyant world-famous parades.

While the island of Madeira boasts large, showy parades, on the continent, Carnaval is mainly celebrated by children, who set off firecrackers and play pranks.

Happy Mardi Gras!	bong kuhrnuhvahl!	*Bom Carnaval!*
parade	deshfeel/koortuhzhoo	*desfile/cortejo*
to play a prank	prgahr oomuh puhrteeduh	*pregar uma partida*
to wear a costume	muhshkuhrahrs	*mascarar-se*

TOASTS & CONDOLENCES

Here's to you!	ah twuh/vohsuh!	*À tua (sg)/vossa (pl)!*
Chin-Chin!	tshinh-tshing!	*Chim-Chim!*
Bottoms up!	bohtuh uhbaishoo!	*Bota-abaixo!*
Good luck!	bouh sohrt/mehrduh!	*Boa sorte/Merda (inf)!*
Hope it goes well!	ke toodoo korruh bāy!	*Que tudo corra bem!*
Get well soon!	uzh mlyohruhsh!	*As melhoras!*
My deepest sympathy.	oozh me-wsh pezuhmsh	*Os meus pêsames*

BIRTHDAYS

Happy Birthday!
  (mwingtoosh) puhruhbāysh!

Blow out the candles!
  uhpuhgahr uhsh vehluhsh!
When's your birthday?
  kwangdoo eh oo deeuh
  doosh te-wz uhnoosh?
Many happy returns
(and in good health)!
  ke fahsuhzh mwingtooszh
  maish (ee kong suhood)!
birthday party/cake
  fehshtuh/bolo duhnoosh

ANIVERSÁRIOS

(Muitos) parabéns!
(lit: (many) congratulations)

Apagar as velas!

Quando é o dia
dos teus anos?

Que faças muitos
mais (e com saúde)!

festa/bolo de anos

HEALTH   SAÚDE

Even if you don't have medical insurance, you won't be turned
away from a public hospital in an emergency. Many doctors in
Portugal speak English, and chances are there'll be at least one in
any hospital.

I'm sick.
   shto dooengt   *Estou doente.*
My friend (m/f) is sick.
   oo/uh me-w/meenyuh   *O/A meu/minha amigo/a*
   uhmeegoo/uh shtah dooengt   *está doente.*
Can you call a doctor for me?
   poodeeuhm shuhmahr   *Podia me chamar*
   oong mehdeekoo?   *um médico?*
I need a doctor who speaks English
   piseezoo doong mehdeekoo   *Preciso de um médico*
   ke fahl ing-glesh   *que fale inglês.*

Where's the	ongd feekuh ...	*Onde fica ...*
nearest ...?	maish prohseemoo/uh?	*mais próximo/a?*
dentist	oo dengteeshtuh	*o dentista*
doctor	oo mehdeckoo	*o médico*
hospital	oo oshpeetahl	*o hospital*
(after hours)	uh fuhrmahsyuh	*a farmácia*
pharmacy	(de serveesoo)	*(de serviço)*

AT THE DOCTOR   NO MÉDICO

I usually take this medication.
   kooshtoomoo toomahr   *Costumo tomar*
   esht rrmehdiw   *este remédio.*
All my vaccinations are up to date.
   tuhnyoo toduhz uhsh   *Tenho todas as*
   vuhseenuhz ãy deeuh   *vacinas em dia.*
Don't give me any blood transfusions.
   nõw me fahsõw oomuh   *Não me façam uma*
   trangshfoozõw de sang-g   *transfusão de sangue.*

HEALTH

HEALTH

I feel better now.
    zhah me singtoo mlyohr   *Já me sinto melhor.*
I have medical insurance.
    tuhnyoo sgooroo mehdeekoo   *Tenho um seguro médico.*
Could you give me a receipt for
    my medical insurance?
    pohd dahrm oomuh fahtooruh   *Pode dar-me uma factura*
    puhruh oo me-w sgooroo   *para o meu seguro*
    mehdeekoo?   *médico?*

THEY MAY SAY ...

O que é que tem?	oo ke eh ke tãy?	What's the matter?
Tem dores?	tãy dorsh?	Do you feel any pain?
Onde é que doi?	ongd eh ke doy?	Where does it hurt?
Bebe álcool?	behb ahlkohl?	Do you drink?
Fuma?	foomuh?	Do you smoke?
Toma drogas?	tohmuh drohguhsh?	Do you use drugs?
Está grávida?	shtah grahveeduh?	Are you pregnant?

Está assim há quanto tempo?
    shtah uhsing ah kwangtoo tengpoo?
    How long have you been like this?
Isto já lhe aconteceu antes?
    eeshtoo zhah ly uhkongtse-w angtesh?
    Have you had this before?
Tem alergias?
    tãy uhlerzheeuhsh?
    Are you allergic to anything?
Está a tomar algum medicamento?
    shtah uh toomahr ahlgoong mdeekuhmengtoo?
    Are you taking any medication?
Sofre de alguma doença (crónica)?
    sohfr dahlgoomuh dooengsuh (krohneekuh)?
    Do you have a medical condition?
Quando foi a última menstruação/o último período?
    kwangdoo foy uh oolteemuh mengshtrwuhsõw/oo
    oolteemoo preeoodoo?
    When was your last menstrual period?

AILMENTS

PROBLEMAS DE SAÚDE

HEALTH

I can't sleep.
nōw kongseegoo doormeer *Não consigo dormir.*

I've been vomiting.
tuhnyoo shtahdoo uh voomeetahr *Tenho estado a vomitar.*

I feel ...	shto ...	*Estou ...*
awful	mwingtoo mahl	*muito mal*
dizzy	kong tongtooruhsh	*com tonturas*
feverish	kong fehbr	*com febre*
nauseous	kong nowzyuhsh	*com naúseas*
weak	frahkoo/uh	*fraco/a*

I have (a/an) ...	tuhnyoo ...	*Tenho ...*
I'm on medication	shto uh tomahr	*Estou a tomar*
for (a/an) ...	mdeekuhmengtoosh	*medicamentos*
	puhruh ...	*para ...*
AIDS	seeduh	*SIDA*
asthma	ahzhmuh	*asma*
bite (insect)	oomuh peekahduh	*uma picada*
	(dingsehtoo)	*(de insecto)*
blister	oomuh bolyuh	*uma bolha*
bronchitis	brongkeet	*bronquite*
burn	oomuh kaymuhdooruh	*uma queimadura*
chills	kuhluhfreeoosh	*calafrios*
cold	oomuh	*uma*
	kongshteepuhsōw	*constipação*
constipation	obshteepuhsōw/	*obstipação/*
	preezōw de vengtr	*prisão de ventre*
cough	oomuh tohs	*uma tosse*
cramp	kãybrah	*câimbra*
diarrhoea	deeuhrrayuh	*diarreia*
fever	fehbr	*febre*
food poisoning	oomuh	*uma*
	ingtohkseekuhsow	*intoxicação*
	uhleemengtahr	*alimentar*
hay fever	fehbr doo fenoo	*febre do feno*

(bad) headache	oomuh dor de kuhbesuh (mwingtoo fohrt)	*uma dor de cabeça (muito forte)*
heartburn	uhzeeuh	*azia*
heart disease	oomuh dooengsuh kuhrdeeuhkuh	*uma doença cardíaca*
hepatitis	eepuhteet	*hepatite*
high/low blood pressure	tengsōw artreeahl ahltuh/baishuh	*tensão arterial alta/baixa*
indigestion	ingdeezheshtōw	*indigestão*
infection	oomuh infehsōw	*uma infecção*
inflammation	oomuh ingfluhmuhsōw	*uma inflamação*
influenza/the flu	oomuh greep	*uma gripe*
itch	koomeeshōw	*comichão*
lice	pyolyoosh	*piolhos*
lump	oong kuhrosoo	*um caroço*
migraine	oomuh engshuhkehkuh	*uma enxaqueca*
motion/sea sickness	engzho-oo de kahrroo/doo mahr	*enjoo de carro/do mar*
pacemaker	oong pays mayker	*um pacemaker*
pain	dorsh	*dores*
rash	oomuh eeroopsōw duh pehl	*uma erupção da pele*
rheumatism	rre-wmuhteezhmoo	*reumatismo*
sexually transmitted disease	oomuh dooengsuh vnehryuh	*uma doença venérea*
sore throat	dorzh de guhrgangtuh	*dores de garganta*
stomachache	dorzh de buhrreeguh	*dores de barriga*
sunburn	kaymuhdooruh doo sohl	*queimadura do sol*
sunstroke	oomuh ingsooluhsōw	*uma insolação*
swollen lymph nodes	gang-gliwz ingshahdoosh	*gânglios inchados*
urinary tract infection	oomuh ingfehsōw nuhsh veeuhz ooreenahryuhsh	*uma infecção nas vias urinárias*
worms	longbreeguhsh	*lombrigas*

HEALTH

SPECIAL HEALTH NEEDS

NECESSIDADES ESPECIAIS DE SAÚDE

I'm (a/an) ...	so ...	Sou ...
alcoholic	ahlkoo-ohleekoo/uh	alcoólico/a
anaemic	uhnehmeekoo/uh	anémico/a
diabetic	dyuhbehteekoo/uh	diabético/a
drug user	tohkseekohdpengdengt	toxico-dependente
haemophiliac	emohfeeleekoo/uh	hemofílico/a
HIV negative	sehrohnguhreevoo/uh	seronegativo/a
HIV positive	sehrohpoozeeteevoo/uh	seropositivo/a

I'm allergic to ...	so uhlerzheekoo/uh ...	Sou alérgico/a ...
(some types of) anaesthesia	uh (sehrtoosh teepoozh de) uhneshtzeeuh	a (certos tipos de) anestesia
antibiotics	owz angteebyohteekoosh	aos antibióticos
bee stings	ahsh peekahduhzh duhbuhlyuh	às picadas de abelha
codeine	ah koduheenuh	à codeína
gluten	owsh glootehnsh	aos glútens
lactose	ah luhktohz	à lactose
penicillin	ah pneeseeleenuh	à penicilina
pollen	ow pohlehn	ao pólen
sugars	ow uhsookahr	ao açúcar
Ventolin	uh vengtooleen	a Ventolin
wasp stings	ahsh peekahduhzh de veshpuhsh	às picadas de vespas
yeasts	ow fermengtoo/ah lvuhdooruh	ao fermento/à levedura

ALTERNATIVE TREATMENTS

TRATAMENTOS ALTERNATIVOS

aromatherapy	uh truhpeeuh duhromuhsh	a terapia de aromas
health spa	uhsh termuhsh	as termas
herbalist	oo ervulnahriw	o ervanário
homeopathy	uh omiwpuhteeuh	a homeopatia
massage	uh muhsahzháy	a massagem

masseur/masseuse	oo/uh muhsuhzheeshtuh	o/a massagista
meditation	uh mdeetuhsõw	a meditação
naturopathy	uh nuhtoorohpuhteeuh	a naturopatia
reflexology	uhh rrflehksooloozheeuh	a reflexologia
yoga	oo eeohguh	o ioga

WOMEN'S HEALTH   A SAÚDE DA MULHER

Note that diaphragms aren't currently available in Portugal, and access to medically-induced abortions is restricted.

I'd like a female doctor.
    kreeuh ke me uhtengdes
    oomuh mehdeekuh

Queria que me atendesse
uma médica.

I'm on the Pill.
    tohmoo uh peelooluh

Tomo a pílula.

I think I'm pregnant.
    ahshoo ke shto grahveeduh

Acho que estou grávida.

I'd like a pregnancy test.
    kreeuh fuhzer oo tehsht
    duh gruhveedesh

Queria fazer o teste
da gravidez.

I haven't had a period in … weeks.
    ah … smuhnuhsh ke nõw
    me vãy oo preeoodoo

Há … semanas que não
me vem o período.

I'd like to use a contraceptive.
    kreeuh oozahr oong
    mehtoodoo angteekongsehteevoo

Queria usar um
método anti-conceptivo.

I'd like to take the morning-after pill.
    kreeuh toomahr uh
    peelooluh doo deeuh sgingt

Queria tomar a
pílula do dia seguinte.

I'd like to terminate my pregnancy.
    kreeuh ingterrongper
    uh meenyuh gruhveedesh

Queria interromper
a minha gravidez.

HEALTH

abortion	oo uhbortoo proovookahdoo	*o aborto provocado*
condoms	przervuhteevoosh	*preservativos*
diaphragm	oo dyuhfrahgmuh	*o diafragma*
IUD	oo deeoo	*o DIU*
labour	oo pahrtoo	*o parto*
mammogram	uh muhmoogruhfeeuh	*a mamografia*
menstrual pain/cramps	uh dor mengshtrwal	*a dor menstrual*
miscarriage	oo uhbortoo shpongtuhniw	*o aborto espontâneo*
the Pill	uh peelooluh	*a pílula*
pregnancy	uh gruhveedesh	*a gravidez*
premenstrual tension	uh tengsõw prehmengshtrwal	*a tensão pré-menstrual*
spermicide	oomuh shpehrmeeseeduh	*uma espermicida*
ultrasound	uh ekogruhfeeuh	*a ecografia*

AT THE DENTIST

NO DENTISTA

My ... hurts.	doym ...	*Dói-me ...*
gum	zhengzheevuhsh	*a gengiva*
molar	oong dengt moolahr	*um dente molar*
tooth	oong dengt	*um dente*

I need to have my teeth cleaned.
prseezahvuh de fuhzer oomuh lingpezuh owzh dengtsh

Precisava de fazer uma limpeza aos dentes.

I don't want the tooth pulled.
nõw kehroo ke muhrrangk oo dengt

Não quero que me arranque o dente.

Can you give me an anaesthetic?
pohd uhneshtzyahrm?

Pode anestesiar-me?

Stop! You're hurting me!
pahr/shtah uh fuhzer dooer!

Pare! Está a fazer doer!

How much is it for the consultation?
kwangtoo eh uh kongsooltuh?

Quanto é a consulta?

O CORPO
THE BODY

A MÃO
HAND

O DEDO
FINGER

A CABEÇA
HEAD

O BRAÇ
ARM

O OMBR
SHOULDE

O PEITO
CHEST

O ESTÔMAG
STOMACH

A PERN
LEG

O JOELHO
KNEE

O PÉ
FOOT

BODY PARTS

PARTES DO CORPO

My ... hurts.	doym oo/uh ...	*Doi-me o/a ...*
abdomen	oo uhbdohmehn/ uh buhrreeguh	*o abdómen/ a barriga* (coll)
ankle	oo toornoozeloo	*o tornozelo*
arm	oo brahsoo	*o braço*
back	uhsh kohshtuhsh	*as costas*
bladder	uh bsheeguh	*a bexiga*
bone	oo osoo	*o osso*
breast	uh muhmuh/ oo paytoo	*a mama/ o peito* (pol)
buttocks	uhzh nahdguhsh	*as nádegas*
chest	oo paytoo/tohrahks	*o peito/tórax*
ear (exterior)	uh ooruhlynh	*a orelha*
ear (interior)	oo oveedoo	*o ouvido*
elbow	oo kootoovcloo	*o cotovelo*
eye(s)	oo olyoo/ooz ohlyoosh	*o(s) olho(s)*
finger	oo dedoo (duh mōw)	*o dedo (da mão)*
foot	oo pch	*o pé*
gall bladder	uh vzeekooluh	*a vesícula*
hand	uh mōw	*a mão*
head	uh kuhbesuh	*a cabeça*
heart	oo kooruhsōw	*o coração*
hip	uh angkuh	*a anca*
joints	uhz uhrteekooluhsōysh	*as articulações*
kidneys	oosh rringsh	*os rins*
knee	oo zhwuhlyoo	*o joelho*
leg	uh pehrnuh	*a perna*
lungs	oosh poolmōysh	*os pulmões*
mouth	uh bokuh	*a boca*
neck	oo pshkosoo	*o pescoço*
nose	oo nuhreezh	*o nariz*
rectum	oo rrehtoo	*o recto*
shoulder	oo ongbroo	*o ombro*
stomach	oo shtomuhgoo	*o estômago*
thigh	uh koshuh	*a coxa*
throat	uh guhrgangtuh	*a garganta*
toes	oozh dedoozh doo peh	*os dedos do pé*

HEALTH

HEALTH

AT THE CHEMIST

NA FARMÁCIA

Where's the nearest after-hours chemist?
ongd feekuh uh fuhrmahsyuh
de serveesoo maish prohseemuh?

*Onde fica a farmácia
de serviço mais próxima?*

I need something for …
prseezoo dahlgoomuh
koyzuh puhruh …

*Preciso de alguma
coisa para …*

I have a doctor's prescription.
tuhnyoo oomuh rrsaytuh
mehdeekuh

*Tenho uma receita
médica.*

How many times a day should
I take this medicine?
kwangtuhsh vezesh poor deeuh
devoo toomahr esht rrmehdiw?

*Quantas vezes por dia
devo tomar este remédio?*

Could you give me (a/an/some) …, please?	dahvuhm … se fash fuhvor?	*Dava-me … se faz favor?*
analgesic	oong uhnahlzhehzeekoo	*um analgésico*
antibiotic	oong angteebeeohteekoo	*um antibiótico*
aspirin	oomuh kaishuh duhshpeereenuhsh	*uma caixa de aspirinas*
contraceptive	oong angteekongsehteevoo	*um anticonceptivo*
something for cold symptoms	oong rrmehdiw puhruh uh kongshteepuhsōw	*um remédio para a constipação*
tranquillisers	oongsh kahlmangtsh	*uns calmantes*

SPECIFIC NEEDS   NECESSIDADES ESPECIAIS

DISABLED TRAVELLERS
VIAJANTES DEFICIENTES

New facilities, equipped with wheelchair ramps and bathrooms for people with physical disabilities, are only now starting to be built. Though many railway stations in larger cities have bathrooms designed for people with wheelchairs, there's no special access for people with disabilities at subway stations and on buses, and most buildings don't have ramps. Few street corners have ramped sidewalks.

Some of the newer subway stations in Lisbon have information plaques in Braille for the visually impaired, and some pedestrian crosswalks have audio beeps to signal light changes. Occasionally, television stations broadcast programs with signing.

Are there any services for
disabled people?
   ah ahlgoong serveesoo   *Há algum serviço*
   puhruh dfeesyengtesh?   *para deficientes?*
What types of services are available?
   ke teepoo de serveesooz eh ke ah?   *Que tipo de serviços é*
                       que há?

I need assistance because I'm ...	preseezoo duhseeshtengsyuh poork so ...	*Preciso de assistência porque sou ...*
blind	sehgoo/uh	*cego/a*
disabled	dfeesyengt feezeekoo	*deficiente físico*
hearing impaired	soordoo/uh	*surdo/a*
mute	moodoo/uh	*mudo/a*
visually impaired	ingveezwahl	*invisual*

Is there wheelchair access?
   ah asehsoo puhruh oomuh   *Há acesso para uma*
   kuhdayruh de rrohduhsh?   *cadeira de rodas?*

I may be in a wheelchair, but I'm
able to live independently!

    pohsoo angdahr de kuhdayruh   *Posso andar de cadeira*
    de rrohduhzh muhsh kongseegoo   *de rodas mas consigo*
    ter oomuh veeduh ingdpengdengt!   *ter uma vida independente!*

Are guide dogs allowed?

    eh permeeteeduh uh engtrahduh   *É permitida a entrada*
    uh kãysh geeuh?   *a cães-guia?*

Is there a guide service for the
visually impaired?

    ah ahlgoong serveesoo de   *Há algum serviço de*
    geeuhsh puhruh ooz   *guias para os invisuais?*
    ingveezwaysh?

Do you have any information
in Braille?

    tãy ahlgoong zhehnroo   *Tem algum género*
    dingfoormuhsōw ãy brail?   *de informação em braille?*

Are there any libraries with books
in Braille?

    ah ahlgoomuh beebliwtehkuh *Há alguma biblioteca*
    kong leevrooz ãy brail?   *com livros em braille?*

Please speak more slowly so
I can understand.

    poor fuhvor fahl maizh   *Por favor fale mais*
    dvuhgahr puhruh e-w engtengder *devagar para eu entender.*

Please speak into my left/right ear.

    poor fuhvor fahlm doo lahdoo   *Por favor, fale-me do lado*
    shkerdoo/deeraytoo   *esquerdo/direito.*

I use (a/an) ...	oozoo oong ...	Uso um ...
audiphone	owdeefoonoo dowdeesõw	audifono de audição
Braille	oo brail	o braille
cane	uh beng gahluh	a bengala
guide dog	oo kõwgeeuh	o cão-guia
hearing aid	uhpuhruhlyoo	aparelho
sign language	ling-gwahzhãy zhehshtwahl	a linguagem gestual
wheelchair	uh kuhdayruh de rrohduhsh	a cadeira de rodas

SPECIFIC NEEDS

GAY TRAVELLERS VIAJANTES HOMOSEXUAIS

While Lisbon has a substantial range of gay and lesbian restaurants, bars, discos, saunas, beaches and cruising areas, there are fewer places in Oporto and the Algarve, and fewer still elsewhere.

Are there any gay bars in this city?
eeseesht ahlgoong bahr gay
nehshtuh seedahd?

Existe algum bar gay nesta cidade?

Is there a gay information line?
ah ahlgoomuh leenyuh de tlefohn
puhruh ingfoormuhsõw gay?

Há alguma linha de telefone para informação gay?

Do you (pol) know of any gay magazines?
koonyehs ahlgoomuh
rrveeshtuh puhruh
ohmohsehkswaish?

Conhece alguma revista para homossexuais?

How do people here feel about homosexuals?
ke uhteetood tãyãy uhsh
psouhsh ãy rrluhsõw owz
ohmohsehkswaish?

Que atitude têm as pessoas em relação aos homossexuais?

Do homosexuals get harassed here?
ooz ohmohsehkswaish sõw
mahltruhtahdoosh/
ingkoomoodahdoosh
peloo fahktoo doo serãy?

Os homossexuais são maltratados/ incomodados pelo facto de o serem?

They are very open/conservative.
sōw mwingtoo uhbehrtuhsh/
kongservuhdoruhsh

*São muito abertas/
conservadoras.*

People respect each other's privacy.
uhsh psouhsh rreshpaytōw
uh ingteemeedahd uhlyayuh

*As pessoas respeitam
a intimidade alheia.*

Some people don't understand.
ah psouhsh ke nōw engtengdãy

Há pessoas que não entendem.

SEXUALIDADE

I'm (a) …	so …	Sou …
bisexual	beesehkswahl	bisexual
gay	gay	gay
heterosexual	ehtrohsehkswahl	heterossexual
homosexual	ohmohsehkswahl	homossexual
lesbian	lehzhbeekuh	lésbica
transsexual	trangshsehkswahl	transexual
transvestite	trahveshtee	travesti

TRAVELLING WITH A FAMILY

VIAJAR COM A FAMÍLIA

Except for some fast food chains, most restaurants in Portugal
don't have children's menus. You can try asking for a *meia dose*, a
'half serve'.

I'm travelling with my family.
shto uh veeuhzhahr kong uh
meenyuh fuhmeelyuh

*Estou a viajar com a
minha família.*

Are there special services for babies?
ah serveesoosh shpeseeaish
puhruh oozh behbehsh?

*Há serviços especiais
para os bébés?*

Is there a child-minding
service in the hotel?
oo ohtehl deeshpōy doong
shpahsoo puhruh kwidahr
dush kreeangsuhsh?

*O hotel dispõe de um
espaço para cuidar
das crianças?*

SPECIFIC NEEDS

Can you add another bed to the room?
 pohdāy uhkreshsengtahr
 oomuh kuhmuh noo kwartoo?
Podem acrescentar
uma cama no quarto?

Does this restaurant
have a children's menu?
 nesht rreshtowraangt tāyāy
 eemengtuh puhruh kreeangsuhsh?
Neste restaurante têm
ementa para crianças?

Could we have a child-sized portion?
 poodeeuh serveer oomuh dohz
 pkenuh puhruh uh kreeangsuh
 se fahsh fuhvor?
Podia servir uma dose
pequena para a criança,
se faz favor?

Do you have a highchair?
 deeshpōy de kuhdayruh de behbeh?
Dispõe de cadeira de bébé?

Is there a children's discount?
 fahzāy ahlgoong deshkongtoo
 ahsh kreeangsuhsh?
Fazem algum desconto
às crianças?

Do you have a special family price?
 fahzāy oong presoo shpesyahl
 puhruh oomuh fuhmeelyuh?
Fazem um preço especial
para uma família?

Is there a playground for children?
 ah ahlgoong zhuhrding
 puhruh kreeangsuhsh?
Há algum jardim
para crianças?

LOOKING FOR A JOB   À PROCURA DE EMPREGO

European Union nationals can compete for any job in Portugal
without a work permit. It's a good idea for non-EU citizens to
arrange a work permit before arrival. People who aren't regular em-
ployees of a company need to register themselves as self-employed.
They must use *recibos verdes*, 'green receipts', to bill for their services. These receipts aren't actually green, but at one time they were,
and the name has stuck.

I'm looking for a job.
 shto ah prokooruh dengpregoo
Estou à procura de emprego.

Where's the best place to find work?
 kwal eh oo mlyohr seetiw
 puhruh engkongtrahr truhbahlyoo?
Qual é o melhor sítio
para encontrar trabalho?

Do you have any positions
open for a/an …?
  ah ahlgoong poshtoo de   *Há algum posto de*
  truhbahlyoo puhruh   *trabalho para*
  oong/oomuh …?   *um/uma …?*

I have experience as a/an …
  tuhnyoo shpryengsyuh komoo …   *Tenho experiência como …*

(See page 55 the chapter on Meeting People for occupations.)

I have experience	tuhnyoo	*Tenho*
in/using …	shpryengsyuh …	*experiência …*
childminding	āy kwidahr de	*em cuidar de*
	kreeangsuhsh	*crianças*
computers	āy ingfoormahteekuh	*em informática*
construction work	nuh kongshtroosōw	*na construção*
	seeveel	*civil*

Academic Degrees Graus Académicos

compulsory education	engseenoo bahzeekoo	*ensino básico*
secondary education	engseenoo skoongdahriw	*ensino secundári*
bachelor's degree	buhshuhrlahtoo	*bacharelato*
(3-year university degree)		
doctoral degree	dotoruhmengtoo	*doutoramento*
licentiate's degree	leesengsyuhtooruh	*licenciatura*
(5-year university degree)		
master's degree	mehshtrahdoo	*mestrado*
postgraduate degree	pohshgruhdwuhsōw	*pós-graduação*
technical course	koorsoo tehkneekoo	*curso técnico*

I can …	say …	*Sei …*
cook	koozeenyahr	*cozinhar*
drive	kongdoozeer	*conduzir*
paint	pingtahr	*pintar*
type	shkrever ah	*escrever à*
	mahkeenuh	*máquina*

I'm looking for	Estou á procura	*Estou à procura*
… work.	de truhbahlyoo …	*de trabalho …*
casual	shpoorahdeekoo	*esporádico*
part-time	áy pahrt-taim	*em part-time*
full-time	uh tengpoo ingtayroo	*a tempo inteiro*

How much does it pay?
kwal eh oo suhlahriw? — *Qual é o salário?*

Do I have to pay tax?
tuhnyoo de puhgahr ingpohshtoosh? — *Tenho de pagar impostos?*

What are the working hours?
kwal eh oo orahriw? — *Qual é o horário?*

I'd like to apply.
kreeuh kangdeeduhtahrm — *Queria candidatar-me.*

When's the interview?
kwangdoo eh uh engtrveeshtuh? — *Quando é a entrevista?*

Here's my CV.
uhkee táy oo me-w koorreckooloo — *Aqui tem o meu currículo.*

I have a work permit.
tuhnyoo leesengsuh de truhbahlyoo — *Tenho licença de trabalho.*

I'm available to work here for (three months)/(until May).
tuhnyoo deeshpuuneeheeleedahd puhruh truhbuhlyahr ukee (trezh mezesh)/(uhteh maioo) — *Tenho disponibilidade para trabalhar aqui (três meses)/(até Maio).*

boss	oo/uh shehf	*o/a chefe*
certificate	oo serteefeekahdoo	*o certificado*
company	uh kongpuhnyeeuh	*a companhia*
contract	oo kongtrahtoo	*o contrato*
diploma	oo deeplomuh/	*o diploma/*
	oo kuhnoodoo	*canudo (inf)*
exploitation	uh shplooruhsőw	*a exploração*
harassment	oo uhsehdiw	*o assédio*
high school	oo leese-w	*o liceu*
income tax	oo ingposhtoo sobr	*o imposto sobre*
	oo rrengdeemengtoo	*o rendimento*
interview	uh engtrveeshtuh	*a entrevista*

job advertisement	oo uhnoongsiw de truhbahlyoo	*o anúncio de trabalho*
job position	oo poshtoo de truhbahlyoo	*o posto de trabalho*
Personal Income Tax	oo ee ehrr es	*o IRS*
qualification	uhz uhbeeleetuhsōysh	*as habilitações*
salary	oo suhlahriw	*o salário*
school	uh shkohluh	*a escola*
wage	oo suhlahriw	*o salàrio*
work permit	uh leesengsuh de truhbahlyoo	*a licença de trabalho*

ON BUSINESS

EM NEGÓCIOS

I'm here on business.
  shto uh fuhzer oomuh
  veeahzhāy de ngohsiwsh

Estou a fazer uma viagem de negócios.

We're attending a conference.
  shtuhmooz uh uhseeshteer
  uh oomuh kongfrengsyuh

Estamos a assistir a uma conferência.

I have an appointment with …
  tuhnyoo oong engkongtroo kong…

Tenho um encontro com …

Thank you for seeing me.
  obreegahdoo poor me rrseber

Obrigado por me receber.

I'm pleased to meet you.
  mwingtoo goshtoo
  āy oo/uh koonyser

Muito gosto em o/a conhecer.

Here's my (business) card.
  uhkee tāy oo me-w kuhrtōw
  (de veezeetuh)

Aqui tem o meu cartão (de visita).

I need to …	tuhnyo de …	*Tenho de …*
make	teerahr	*tirar*
photocopies	fohtohkohpyuhsh	*fotocópias*
use a computer	oozahr oong kongpootuhdor	*usar um computador*
send a(n) email/fax	engveeahr oong eemayl/fahks	*enviar um email/fax*

I need a(n) ...	prseezoo de ...	*Preciso de ...*
guide	oong/oomuh geeuh	*um/uma guia*
interpreter	oong/oomuh ingtehrpret	*um/uma intérprete*
translator	oong truhdootor/ oomuh truhdootoruh	*um tradutor/ uma tradutora*

agreement	oo uhkordoo	*o acordo*
billing	uh fahtooruhsõw	*a facturação*
branch office	uh sookoorsahl	*a sucursal*
business (deal)	oo ngohsiw	*o negócio*
client	oo/uh klyengt	*o/a cliente*
colleague	oo/uh koolehguh	*o/a colega*
contract	oo kongtrahtoo	*o contrato*
director	oo deerehtor/uh deerehtoruh	*o director/a directora*
distributor	oo deeshtreebuidor/uh deeshtreebuidoruh	*o distribuidor/a distribuidora*
financial transactions	uhz opruhsõysh feenangsayruhsh	*as operações financeiras*
(the company's) head office	uh sehd (duh engprezuh)	*a sede (da empresa)*
loss	oo prezhooeezoo	*o prejuízo*
modem	oo mohdehm	*o modem*
profit	oo lookroo	*o lucro*
profitable	rrengtahvehl	*rentável*
proposal	uh proopohshtuh	*a proposta*
sales department	oo dpuhrtuhmengtoo de vengduhsh	*o departamento de vendas*
stock exchange	uh bolsuh	*a Bolsa*

ON TOUR

I'm with a band/group.
  pertengsemooz uh oomuh bangduh/oong groopoo
I'm with a (football) team.
  vuhnyoo kong oomuh eekeepuh de (footbohl)

EM TOURNÉE

Pertencemos a uma banda/um grupo.

Venho com uma equipa de (futebol).

We're here for (three) nights.
feekuhmoosh (trezh) noytsh

Ficamos (três) noites.

We've lost our baggage.
perdemooz uhzh
nohsuhsh buhgahzhãysh

*Perdemos as
nossas bagagens.*

Would you like tickets to our concert?
kehr beelyetsh puhruh
oo nohsoo kongsertoo?

*Quer bilhetes para
o nosso concerto?*

We're doing	shtuhmooz uh fuhzer	*Estamos a fazer*
a tour of ...	oomuh toorneh poor ...	*uma tournée por ...*
Europe	toduh uh e-wrohpuh	*toda a Europa*
Portugal	poor poortoogahl	*Portugal*

We'll be staying	feekuhmooz uhteh	*Ficamos até*
until the ... is over.	uhkuhbahr oo ...	*acabar o ...*
championship	kangpiwnahtoo	*campeonato*
festival	feshteevahl	*festival*
tournament	toornayoo	*torneio*

Please talk	se fash fuhvor,	*Se faz favor,*
to the ...	fahl kong oo/uh ...	*fale com o/a ...*
group leader	rreshpongsahvehl	*responsável*
	peloo groopoo	*pelo grupo*
guide	geeuh	*guia*
manager	zhrengt	*gerente*

We're ... on	vuhmoosh ... noo	*Vamos ... no*
(Saturday).	(sahbuhdoo)	*(sábado).*
doing a show	rreprezengtahr	*representar*
playing (music)	tookahr	*tocar*
playing (sport)	zhoogahr	*jogar*
rehearsing	engsuhyahr	*ensaiar*

coach	oo traynuhdor/	*o treinador/*
	uh traynuhdoruh	*a treinadora*
equipment	oo eekeepuhmengtoo	*o equipamento*

group	oo groopoo	o grupo
guide	geeuh	guia
manager	zhrengt	gerente
member	oo/uh eelmengtoo	o/a elemento
team	uh eckeepuh	a equipa
van	uh kuhrreenyuh	a carrinha

FILM & TV

We're filming on location.
  shtuhmooz uh feelmahr
  oosh shtryorsh

We're filming here for (three days).
  vuhmoosh feelmahr
  uhkee (trezh deeuhsh)

Who should we ask for
permission to film here?
  uh kãy eh ke eh nsesahriw
  pdeer owtooreezuhsõw
  puhruh feelmahr uhkee?

We'd like to hire some extras.
  kreeuhmoosh kongtruhtahr
  feegoorangtesh

We're making a ...   shtuhmooz uh fuhzer ...
  feature   oomuh
  documentary   rrpoortahzhãy
  film   oong feelm
  soap opera   oomuh
                    tehlehnoovehluh
  television series oomuh sehree-e
                    puhruh uh tleveezõw

FILME E TV

Estamos a filmar
os exteriores.

Vamos filmar
aqui (três dias).

A quem é que é necessário
pedir autorização
para filmar aqui?

Queríamos contratar
figurantes.

Estamos a fazer ...
uma
reportagem
um filme
uma
telenovela
uma série
para a televisão

SPECIFIC NEEDS

actor	oo ahtor/uh ahtreesh	o actor/a actriz
camera	uh kuhmuhruh	a câmara
cameraman	oo kuhmuhruh muhn	o câmara man
director	oo rryuhleezuhdor/uh rryuhleezuhdoruh	o realizador/a realizadora
editor	oo eedeetor/uh eedeetoruh	o editor/a editora
first cuts	uhsh preemayruhsh prohvuhsh	as primeiras provas
host	oo uhprezengtuhdor/uh uhprezengtuhdoruh	o apresentador/a apresentadora
lights	uhsh loozesh	as luzes
make-up	uh muhkeelyahzhãy	a maquilhagem
producer	oo proodootor/uh proodootoruh	o produtor/a produtora
rehearsal	oo engsaioo	o ensaio
script	oo skreept/oo geeõw	o script/o guião
scriptwriter	oo/uh geeooneeshtuh	o/a guionista
set	oo snahriw	o cenário
sound	oo song	o som
wardrobe	oo gwarduhrropuh	o guarda-roupa

THEY MAY SAY ...

Estamos a filmar!
shtuhmooz uh feelmahr!   We're filming!

Vamos repetir!
vuhmoosh rrpeteer!   Let's do it again!

Take Um!	tayk oong!	Take one!
Acção!	ahsõw!	Action!
Cortem!	kohrtãy!	Cut!

PILGRIMAGE & RELIGION

PEREGRINAÇÃO E RELIGIÃO

Each town celebrates its own religious holiday – in honour of a saint or of the Virgin Mary – with a special Mass, procession and often a street festival. (See also Festivals and Holidays, page 203.)

One of the most well-known pilgrimages is to Our Lady of Fatima. Several days before the official day of celebration on 13 May, worshippers make their way on foot from their hometowns to the site where a miracle is said to have occurred.

Is there a church near here?
ah ahlgoomuh eegruhzhuh uhkee pehrtoo?
Há alguma igreja aqui perto?

Where can I go to pray?
ongd eh ke pohsoo rrzahr?
Onde é que posso rezar?

Can I take communion here?
pohsoo koomoong-gahr uhkee?
Posso comungar aqui?

What time does Mass start?
uh ke ohruz eh ke se rrehzuh uh meesuh?
A que horas é que se reza a missa?

When's the cathedral/church open?
uh ke ohruhz ch ke ahbr uh seh/eegruhzhuh?
A que horas é que abre a Sé/igreja?

I'm making a pilgrimage to Fatima.
shto uh fuhzer oomuh pregreenuhsõw uh fahteemuh
Estou a fazer uma peregrinação a Fátima.

altar	oo ahltahr	o altar
the Bible	uh beeblyuh	a Bíblia
chapel	uh kuhpehluh	a capela
church	uh eegruhzhuh	a igreja
communion	uh koomoonyõw	a comunhão
confession	uh kongfeesõw	a confissão
the confessional	oo kongfsiwnahriw	o confessionário
the cross	uh kroosh	a cruz
convent	oo kongvengtoo	o convento

SPECIFIC NEEDS

funeral	oo foonrahl	*o funeral*
God	de-wsh	*Deus*
the Koran	oo koorőw	*o Corão*
mass	uh meesuh	*a missa*
monastery	oo mooshtayroo	*o mosteiro*
monk	oo mongzh	*o monge*
mosque	uh meshkeetuh	*a mesquita*
nun	uh frayruh	*a freira*
pastor	oo puhshtor	*o pastor*
place of worship	oo tengploo	*o templo*
the Pope	oo pahpuh	*o Papa*
prayer	uh oruhsőw	*a oração*
prayer book	oo leevroo doruhsőysh	*o livro de orações*
priest	oo pahdr/oo snyor preeor	*o padre/o senhor prior*
Protestant	prooteshtangt	*Protestante*
rabbi	oo rrahbee/oo rruhbeenoo	*o rabi/o rabino*
saint	sangtoo/uh	*santo/a*
synagogue	uh seenuhgohguh	*a sinagoga*
tomb	oo toomooloo	*o túmulo*
the Torah	uh tohrah	*a Torá*
worship	uh dvoosőw	*a devoção*

TIME & DATES

TEMPO E DATAS

Portugal is on Greenwich Mean Time, which is one hour earlier than the most of the rest of the European Union. Business hours in Portugal vary depending on the type of business.

TELLING THE TIME

DIZER AS HORAS

When telling the time in Portuguese, the hours are given in the plural, except for *uma hora*, '1.00 o'clock', *meio-dia*, 'noon', and *meia-noite*, 'midnight'.

To make it clear whether a time like 6 o'clock, *às seis horas*, is in the morning or in the afternoon, add the expression *da manhã*, 'in the morning' or *da tarde*, 'in the afternoon'. For very early hours you can say *da madrugada*, 'in the early morning'.

Another way to avoid confusion is to use a 24-hour clock, which is common in Portugal.

Could you tell me the time,
please? (pol)
   poodeeuh deezerm uhz ohruhs?   *Podia dizer-me as horas?*

What time is it?
   ke ohruhsh sōw   *Que horas são?*

It's one o'clock.
   eh oomuh ohruh.   *É uma hora.*

It's noon.
   eh mayoo dccuh   *É meio-dia.*

It's midnight.
   eh mayuh noyt   *É meia-noite.*

It's ten o'clock.
   sōw dehz ohruhsh   *São dez horas.*

It's half past one (in the morning/
afternoon).
   eh oomuh ee mayuh   *É uma e meia*
   (duh muhnyang/tahrd)   *(da manhã/tarde).*

It's a quarter past one.
    eh oomuh ee oong kwartoo   *É uma e um quarto.*
It's two twenty-five.
    sōw doouhz ee vingt ee singkoo   *São duas e vinte e cinco.*
It's twenty to five.
    sōw singkoo menoosh vingt   *São cinco menos vinte.*

DAYS   OS DIAS

According to legend, at some point the Portuguese refused to adopt the names of pagan gods for the days of the week, preferring instead to refer to them as numbered market or fair days, except for *sábado* and *domingo*. *Segunda-feira*, 'Monday', literally means 'second fair'. *Terça-feira*, 'Tuesday', is 'third fair' and so on. No one has properly explained, though, why there's no first fair day.

You'll often see the ending *-feira* dropped, with 'Monday' becoming simply *segunda* (or *2ª*). It's also quite common for people to do this in conversation. The days of the week aren't capitalised in Portuguese.

What day is it?	ke deeuh eh ozh?	*Que dia é hoje?*
Monday	uh sgoongduh fayruh	*a segunda-feira*
Tuesday	uh tersuh fayruh	*a terça-feira*
Wednesday	uh kwartuh fayruh	*a quarta-feira*
Thursday	uh kingtuh fayruh	*a quinta-feira*
Friday	uh sayshtuh fayruh	*a sexta-feira*
Saturday	oo sahbuhdoo	*o sábado*
Sunday	oo dooming-goo	*o domingo*
weekend	oo fing de smuhnuh	*o fim de semana*

MONTHS

While in Brazil the names of the months aren't capitalised, in Portugal they are.

OS MESES

January	zhuhnayroo	*Janeiro*
February	fevrayroo	*Fevereiro*
March	mahisoo	*Março*
April	uhbril	*Abril*
May	maioo	*Maio*
June	zhoonyoo	*Junho*
July	zhoolyoo	*Julho*
August	uhgoshtoo	*Agosto*
September	stengbroo	*Setembro*
October	otoobroo	*Outubro*
November	noovengbroo	*Novembro*
December	dzengbroo	*Dezembro*

DATES

What's today's date?
  uh kwangtoosh
  shtuhmoosh ozh?
It's 18 October 1999.
  eh deeuh dzoytoo de otoobroo
  de meel nohvsengtoosh
  ee noovengtuh ee nohv

AS DATAS

*A quantos
estamos hoje?*

*É dia 18 de Outubro
de 1999.*

Present Presente

now	uhgohruh	*agora*
this morning	ehshtuh muhnyang	*esta manhã*
today	ozh	*hoje*
tonight	ehshtuh noyt	*esta noite*
this week	ehshtuh smuhnuh	*esta semana*
this month	esht mesh	*este mês*
this year	esht uhnoo	*este ano*

Past Passado

yesterday	ongtãy	*ontem*
day before yesterday	angteeongtãy	*anteontem*
yesterday morning/	ongtãy de	*ontem de*
afternoon	muhnyang/	*manhã/*
	ah tahrd	*à tarde*
last night	ongtãy ah noyt	*ontem à noite*
last week	uh smuhnuh	*a semana*
	puhsahduh	*passada*
last month	oo mesh puhsahdoo	*o mês passado*
last year	oo uhnoo puhsahdoo	*o ano passado*
I was there for …	shteev lah …	*Estive lá …*
I've been here	shto uhkee	*Estou aqui*
since/for …	dezhd …	*desde …*
a short time	ah bookahdoo	*há um bocado*
an hour	ah oomuh ohruh	*há uma hora*
5 June	oo deeuh singkoo	*o dia 5*
	de zhoonyoo	*de Junho*
July	zhoolyoo	*Julho*
five months	singkoo mezesh	*cinco meses*
two years	doyz uhnoosh	*dois anos*
1995	meel nohvsengtoosz	*1995*
	ee noovengtuh	
	ee sinkoo	

DID YOU KNOW …

Centuries in Portuguese are expressed using cardinal numbers, unlike English, which uses ordinal numbers. The 15th century is o *século quinze* (lit: the century 15).

Future Futuro

in a little while	duhkee uh bookahdoo	*daqui a bocado*
tomorrow	ahmuhnyang	*amanhã*
tomorrow morning	ahmuhnyang de muhnyang	*amanhã de manhã*
tomorrow afternoon	ahmuhnyang ah tahrd	*à tarde*
tomorrow evening	ahmuhgyang ow fing duh tahrd	*amanhã ao fim da tarde*
day after tomorrow	dpoysh de ahmuhnyang	*depois de amanhã*
a week from today	duhkee uh oomuh smuhnuh	*daqui a uma semana*
a week from Monday	de sgoongduh uh oytoo deeuhsh	*de segunda a oito dias*
next week	(puhruh) uh smuhnuh ke vãy	*(para) a semana que vem*
next month	(puhruh) o mesh ke vãy	*(para) o mês que vem*
next year	(puhruh) o uhnoo ke vãy	*(para) o ano que vem*

within (six) …	dengtroo de (saysh) …	*dentro de (seis) …*
hours	ohruhsh	*horas*
days	deeuhsh	*dias*
months	mezesh	*meses*
years	uhnoosh	*anos*

by/until …	uhteh …	*até …*
15 October	ow deeuh kingz de otoobroo	*ao dia 15 de Outubro*
November	noovengbroo	*Novembro*
2010	doyzh meel ee dehsh	*2010*

TIMES & DATES

DURING THE DAY — DURANTE O DIA

early	sedoo	*cedo*
late	tahrd	*tarde*
afternoon	uh tahrd	*a tarde*
dawn	uh muhdroogahduh	*a madrugada*
day	oo deeuh	*o dia*
early evening	ow fing duh tard	*ao fim da tarde*
at lunch time	ah ohruh doo ahlmosoo	*à hora do almoço*
midnight	mayuh noyt	*meia-noite*
morning	muhnyang	*manhã*
night	noyt	*noite*
noon	mayoo deeuh	*meio-dia*
sunrise	uhmuhnyser	*amanhecer*
sunset	por doo sohl	*pôr do sol*
(Monday) ...	(sgoongduh fayruh) ...	*(Segunda-feira)* ...
morning	de muhnyang	*de manhã*
afternoon	ah tahrd	*à tarde*
evening	ah noyt	*à noite*

NUMBERS & AMOUNTS

NÚMEROS E QUANTIAS

CARDINAL NUMBERS

OS NÚMEROS CARDINAIS

Keep in mind that the numbers 'one' and 'two' have both masculine and feminine forms.

0	zehroo	*zero*
1	oong/oomuh	*um/uma*
2	doysh/dwuhsh	*dois/duas*
3	tresh	*três*
4	kwatroo	*quatro*
5	singkoo	*cinco*
6	saysh	*seis*
7	seht	*sete*
8	oytoo	*oito*
9	nohv	*nove*
10	dehsh	*dez*
11	ongz	*onze*
12	doz	*doze*
13	trez	*treze*
14	kuhtorz	*catorze*
15	kingz	*quinze*
16	dzuhsaysh	*dezasseis*
17	dzuhseht	*dezassete*
18	dzoitoo	*dezoito*
19	dzuhnohv	*dezanove*
20	vingt	*vinte*
21	vingt ee oong/oomuh	*vinte e um/uma*
22	vingt ee doysh/dwuhsh	*vinte e dois/duas*

NUMBERS

239

30	tringtuh	*trinta*
40	kwuhrengtuh	*quarenta*
50	singkwengtuh	*cinquenta*
60	sesengtuh	*sessenta*
70	stengtuh	*setenta*
80	oytengtuh	*oitenta*
90	noovengtuh	*noventa*
100	sãy	*cem*
101	sengtoo ee ong	*cento e um*
110	sengtoo ee ongz	*cento e dez*
111	sengtoo ee doz	*cento e onze*
120	sengtoo ee vingt	*cento e vinte*
200	doozengtoosh/uhsh	*duzentos/as*
300	trezengtoosh/uhsh	*trezentos/as*
400	kwatroosengtoosh/uhsh	*quatrocentos/as*
500	keenyengtoosh/uhsh	*quinhentos/as*
600	sayshsengtoosh/uhsh	*seiscentos/as*
700	sehtsengtoosh/uhsh	*setecentos/as*
800	oytoosengtoosh/uhsh	*oitocentos/as*
900	nohvsengtoosh/uhsh	*novecentos/as*
1000	meel	*mil*
2000	doysh meel	*dois mil*
one million	oong meelyõw	*um milhão*
two million	doysh meelyõysh	*dois milhões*

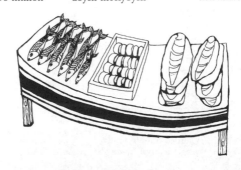

HOW MUCH IS TOO MUCH?

How many/much ...?	kwangto/uh(sh) ...?	Quanto/a(s) ...?
Enough!	sheguh!	Chega!
all	todoo	todo
half	mtahd	metade
double	oo dobroo	o dobro
a little	oong pokoo	um pouco
a half dozen	mayuh doozyuh	meia dúzia
a dozen	oomuh doozyuh	uma dúzia
a pair	oong pahr	um par
per cent	poor sengtoo	por conto
once	oomuh vesh	uma vez
twice	doouhsh vezsh	duas vezes

ORDINAL NUMBERS

OS NÚMEROS ORDINAIS

Ordinal numbers, like adjectives, vary depending on gender (-o for masculine and -a for feminine), and also for number (-s for plural). Ordinal numbers can be abbreviated to 1º, 1ª, 2º, 2ª and so on.

1st	preemayroo/uh	primeiro/a
2nd	sgungdoo/uh	segundo/a
3rd	tersayroo/uh	terceiro/a
4th	kwartoo/uh	quarto/a
5th	kingtoo/uh	quinto/a
6th	suhshtoo/uh	sexto/a
7th	sehteemoo/uh	sétimo/a
8th	oytahvoo/uh	oitavo/a
9th	nonoo/uh	nono/a
10th	dehseemoo/uh	décimo/a

NUMBERS

In English, only the last part of a number is given in the ordinal form, as in 'twenty-fifth'. In Portuguese, all parts of a number are in the ordinal form, as is *vigésimo quinto* (lit: twentieth fifth).

20th	veezhehzeemoo/uh	*vigésimo/a*
30th	treezhehzeemoo/uh	*trigésimo/a*
40th	kwuhdruhzhehzeemoo/uh	*quadragésimo/a*
50th	kingkwuhzhehzeemoo/uh	*quinquagésimo/a*
60th	sehkswuhzhehzeemoo/uh	*sexagésimo/a*
70th	sehptwuhzhehzeemoo/uh	*septuagésimo/a*
80th	oktozhehzeemoo/uh	*octogésimo/a*
90th	nonuhzhehzeemoo/uh	*nonagésimo/a*
100th	sengtehzeemoo/uh	*centésimo/a*

FRACTIONS FRACÇÕES

a quarter	oong kwartoo	*um quarto*
a third	oong tersoo	*um terço*
a half	mayoo/uh	*meio/a*
three quarters	tresh kwartoosh	*três quartos*

EMERGENCIES EMERGÊNCIAS

The telephone number in Portugal for emergencies is 112.

Help!	sookorroo!; nhkoodõwm!	*Socorro!; Acudam-me!*
Stop!	pahr!	*Pare!*
Go away!	vahs engbohruh!	*Vá-se embora!*
Thief!	luhdrõw!	*Ladrão!*
Fire!	fogool	*Fogo!*
Watch out!	kwidahdoo!	*Cuidado!*

It's an emergency.
  eh oomuh emerzhengsyuh! · *É uma emergência!*
Call a doctor!
  shuhmãy oong mehdeekoo! · *Chamem um médico!*
Call an ambulance!
  shuhmãy oomuh angboolangsyuh! · *Chamem uma ambulância!*
Call the police!
  shuhm uh pooleesyuh! · *Chame a polícia!*
Could you help me please?
  pohd uhzhoodahrme, fahsh fuhvor? · *Pode ajudar-me, faz favor?*
Could I use the telephone?
  pohsoo oozahr oo telfohn? · *Posso usar o telefone?*
Where's the police station?
  ongd eh uh shkwadruh duh pooleesyuh? · *Onde é a esquadra da polícia?*
I've been raped.
  fwi viwlahduh · *Fui violada.*
I've/We've been robbed.
  fwi/fomooz uhsahltahdoosh/uhsh · *Fui/Fomos assaltados/as.*

My ... was/ were stolen.	rrobahrõwm ...	*Roubaram-me ...*
backpack	uh (meenyuh) moosheeluh	*a (minha) mochila*
bags	uhzh (meenyuhsh) mahluhsh	*as (minhas) malas*
camera	uh (meenyuh) mahkeenuh footoograhfeekuh	*a (minha) máquina fotográfica*
car	oo kahrroo	*o carro*
car radio	oo rrahdiw doo kahrroo	*o rádio do carro*
handbag	a (meenyuh) kuhrtayruh (de snyoruh)	*a (minha) carteira (de senhora)*
money	oo deenyayroo	*o dinheiro*
travellers cheques	oosh (me-wsh) trahvelersh shehkesh	*os (meus) travellers cheques*
passport	oo (me-w) pahsuhpohrt	*o (meu) passaporte*
video camera	uh meenyuh kuhmuhruh de veedeeoo	*a (minha) camera de vídeo*
wallet	uh (meenyuh) kuhrtayruh (de nohtuhsh)	*a (minha) carteira (de notas)*

DEALING WITH THE POLICE
LIDAR COM A POLÍCIA

Larger cities have their own police departments, known as the *PSP (Polícia de Segurança Pública)*. Everywhere else, policing is carried out by the *GNR (Guarda Nacional Republicana)*.

We want to report an offence.
    kreeuhmuhs dnoongseeahr   *Queríamos denunciar*
    oong kreem   *um crime.*
I didn't realise I was doing anything wrong.
    nõw me uhpersbee ke   *Não me apercebi que*
    shtahvuh uh fuhzer mahl   *estava a fazer mal.*
I didn't do it.
    nõw feez eesoo   *Não fiz isso.*
My possessions are insured.
    oosh me-wsh bãysh shtõw   *Os meus bens estão*
    sgoorahdoosh   *segurados.*

I want to contact my embassy/consulate.

> kreeuh kongtuhktahr kong
> uh meenyuh engbaishahduh/
> oo me-w kongsoolahdoo

*Queria contactar com
a minha embaixada/o
meu consulado.*

Can I call someone?

> pohsoo shuhmahr ahlgãy?

Posso chamar alguém?

Can I have a lawyer who speaks English?

> pohsoo tei oong uhdvoogahdoo
> ke fahl ing glesh?

*Posso ter um advogado
que fale inglês?*

Is there a fine we can pay to clear this?

> ah ahlgoomuh mooltuh ke
> poosuhmoosh puhgahr puhruh
> rrsolver uh seetwuhsõw?

*Há alguma multa que
possamos pagar para
resolver a situação?*

I don't understand.

> nõw kongpryengdoo

Não Compreendo.

I know my rights.

> (e-w) koonyesoo oosh
> me-wsh deeraytoosh

*(Eu) conheço os
meus direitos.*

arrested	oo/ uh prezoo/uh	o/a preso/a
cell	uh sehluh	a cela
consulate	oo kongsoolahdoo	o consulado
embassy	uh engbaishahduh	a embaixada
fine (payment)	uh mooltuh	a multa
	(puhguhmengtoo)	(pagamento)
guilty	oo/uh koolpahdoo/uh	o/a culpado/a
lawyer	oo/uh uhdvoogahdoo/uh	o/a advogado/a
not guilty	eenoosengt	inocente
police officer	oo/uh pooleesyuh/	o/a polícia/
	gwarduh	guarda
police station	uh shkwadruh	a esquadra
	duh pooleeseeuh	de polícia
GNR (National	oo poshtoo duh	o posto da
Guard) post	gwarduh	guarda
prison	uh preezõw	a prisão
trial	oo zhoolguhmengtoo	o julgamento

EMERGENCIES

What am I accused of?
de ke eh ke so uhkoozahdoo?   *De que é que sou acusado?*

You/he/she will be charged with ...	vohse/el/ehluh vai ser uhkoozahdoo/uh de ...	*Você/ele/ela) vai ser acusado/a de ...*
anti-government activity	uhteeveedahdsh angteegoovernoo	*actividades anti-governo*
assault	uhsahltoo	*assalto*
disturbing the peace	pertoorbuhsõw duh pahzh	*perturbação da paz*
illegal entry .	uhrrongbuhmengtoo	*arrombamento*
not having a visa	nõw ter veeshtoo	*não ter visto*
overstaying your visa	eshsder oo leemeet de vuhleedahd doo veeshtoo	*exceder o limite de validade do visto*
possession (of illegal substances)	pohs (de soobshtangs yuhsh eelgaish)	*posse (de substâncias ilegais)*
rape	viwluhsõw	*violação*
shoplifting	foortoo de lohzhuhsh	*furto de lojas*
theft	rroboo	*roubo*
traffic violation	ingfrahsõw duhzh nohrmuhsh de trangzeetoo	*infracção das normas de trânsito*
working without a permit	truhbuhlyahr sãy leesengsuh	*trabalhar sem licença*

Generally, nouns ending in -o are masculine, while those ending in -a are feminine. In the dictionary that follows, the gender of nouns that don't follow this rule is indicated in parentheses after the noun.

For nouns that may be either masculine or feminine (as with nouns referring to people), the masculine then the feminine endings are given, as in:

adeptos/as   uhdehptoosh/ulish   fans (of a team)

When a word changes according to whether it's masculine or feminine, both forms are given.

actor/actriz   uhtor/ahtreezh   actor

For adjectives, both masculine and feminine endings are given.

barulhento/a   buhroolyengtoo/uh   noisy

If the same ending is used for both masculine and feminine adjectives, this is indicated in parentheses.

alegre (m/f)   uhlehgr   happy

(See Grammar pages 25 and 26 for an explanation on gender.)

A

able (to be); can pooder; ser
  kuhpahzh de
  poder; ser capaz de

  Can you show me on the map?
  poodeeuh mooshtrahrm
  noo mahpuh?
  Podia mostrar-me no mapa?

aboard uh bordoo *a bordo*

abortion uhbortoo *aborto*

above ãy seemuh; poor seemuh
  de; sobr *em cima; por cima
  de; sobre*

abroad noo shtrang-zhayroo;
  fohruh *no estrangeiro; fora*

to accept uhsaytahr *aceitar*

accident uhseedengt
  acidente (m)

accommodation uhloozhuh
  mengtoo *o alojamento*

across uhtruhvehsh; poor; ãy
  frengt *através; por; em frente*

activist meeleetangt
  militante (m/f)

actor ahtor/ahtreezh *actor* (m)
  actriz (f)

addict droogahdoo/uh
  drogado/a

addiction dpengdengsyuh
  dependência

address moorahduh *morada*

to admire uhdmeerahr *admirar*

admission engtrahduh *entrada*

adult uhdooltoo/uh *adulto/a*

advantage vangtahzhãy
  vantagem (f)

advice kongselyoo *conselho*

aeroplane uhveeôw *avião*

to be afraid of ter medoo de *ter medo de*

after dpoyzh de *depois de*

again otruh vezh; de novoo *outra vez; de novo*

against kongtruh *contra*

age eedahd *idade* (f)

aggressive uhgreseevoo/uh *agressivo/a*

(a while) ago ah (bookahdoo) *há (bocado)*

to agree kongkoordahr *concordar*

agriculture uhgreekooltooru *agricultura*

ahead ah/ãy frengt *à/em frente*

aid (help) uhzhooduh *ajuda*

AIDS seeduh *SIDA*

air ahr *ar* (m)

air-conditioned ahrkongdeesiwnahdoo *ar condicionado* (m)

airmail veeuh uhehryuh *via aérea*

airport uhehrohportoo *aeroporto*

airport tax tahshuhdoo uhehroh portoo *taxa do aeroporto* (f)

alarm clock deshpertuhdor *despertador* (m)

all toodoo/todoo *tudo/todo*

allergy uhlerzheeuh *alergia*

to allow permeeteer *permitir*

almost kwaz *quase*

alone sohzeenyoo/uh *sozinho/a*

already zhah *já*

also tangbãy *também*

altitude ahlteetood *altitude* (f)

always sengpr *sempre*

ambassador engbaishuhdor/ engbaishuhtreesh *embaixador/embaixatriz*

among engtr *entre*

ancient angteegoo/uh *antigoa*

and ee *e*

angry zang-gahdoo/uh *zangado/a*

animals uhneemaish *animais* (m)

answer rreshpohshtuh *resposta*

ant foormeeguh *formiga*

antibiotics angteebeeohteekoo *antibiótico*

antiques angteegwidahdsh *antiguidades* (f)

antiseptic angtee-sehteekoo *anti-séptico*

any ahlgoong/ahlgoomuh *algum/alguma*

appointment engkongtroo *encontro*

archaeological uhrkiwlohzheekoo/uh *arqueológico/a*

architecture uhrkeetehtooruh *arquitectura*

to argue deeshkooteer *discutir*

arm brahsoo *braço*

to arrive shgahr *chegar*

arrival shgahduh *chegada*

art uhrt *arte* (f)

artist uhrteeshtuh *artista* (m/f)

artwork ohbruh de ahrt *obra de arte* (f)

ashtray singzayroo *cinzeiro*

to ask (for something) pdeer (oomuh koyzuh) *pedir (uma coisa)*

to ask (a question) pergoongtahr *perguntar*

aspirin uhshpeereenuh *aspirina*

asthmatic uhzhmahteekoo/uh *asmático/a*

aunt teeuh *tia*

automatic teller machine (ATM) moolteebangkoo *multibanco*

autumn (fall) otonoo *Outono*

avenue uhvneeduh *avenida*

B

baby behbeh *bebé* (m)

back (body) kohshtuhsh *costas* (f)

at the back (behind) uhtrahzh de *atrás de*

backpack moosheeluh *mochila*

bad mow/mah *mau/má*

bag mahluh *mala*

baggage buhgahzhǎy *bagagem* (f)

baggage claim rrkolyuh de buhgahzhǎysh *recolha de bagagens* (f)

bakery pahduhreeuh *padaria*

balcony vuhrangduh *varanda*

ball bohluh *bola*

band (music) bangduh de moozeekuh *banda de música*

bandage leeguhdooruh *ligadura*

bank bangkoo *banco*

banknotes nohtuhsh (de bangkoo) *notas (de banco)* (f)

a bar bahr *bar* (m)

basket seshtoo *cesto*

bath buhnyoo *banho*

bathing suit fahtoo de buhnyoo *fato de banho*

bathroom kahzuh de buhnyoo *casa de banho* (f)

battery buhtreeuh *bateria*

to be ser/shtahr *ser/estar*

beach praiuh *praia*

beautiful lingdoo/uh *lindo/a*

because poork *porque*

bed kuhmuh *cama*

bedroom kwartoo *quarto*

before angtesh *antes*

beggar pdingt *pedinte* (m/f)

begin koomsahr *começar*

behind uhtrahzh *atrás*

below ǎy baishoo *em baixo*

beside ow lahdoo de *ao lado de*

B

best mlyohr *melhor*

a bet uhpohshtuh *aposta*

between engtr *entre*

bicycle beeseeklehtuh *bicicleta*

big grangd *grande*

bill (account) kongtuh *conta*

biodegradable beeohdegruhdahvehl *biodegradável*

biography biwgruhfeeuh *biografia*

bird pahsuhroo *pássaro*

birth certificate serteedōw de nuhshseemengtoo *certidão de nascimento* (f)

birthday uhneeversahriw *aniversário*

bite (insect) peekahduh *picada*

black pretoo/uh *preto/a*

B&W (film) feelm uh pretoo ee brangkoo *filme a preto e branco* (m)

blanket koobertor *cobertor* (m)

blind sehgoo/uh *cego/a*

blood sang-g *sangue* (m)

blood group groopoo sang-gwiniw *grupo sanguíneo*

blood pressure tengsōw uhrtryahl *tensão arterial* (f)

blood test uhnahleez ow sang-g *análise ao sangue* (f)

blue uhzool *azul*

to board (ship, etc) engbuhrkahr *embarcar*

boarding pass kuhrtōw dengbahrk *cartão de embarque* (m)

boat bahrkoo *barco*

body korpoo *corpo*

book leevroo *livro*

to book (make a booking) rrzervahr (fuhzer oomuh rrzehrvuh) *reservar (fazer uma reserva)*

bookshop leevruhreeuh *livraria*

boots bohtuhsh *botas* (f)

border frongtayruh *fronteira*

boring uhboorrseedoo *aborrecido*

to borrow pdeer engpreshtahdoo *pedir emprestado*

both angboosh/uhs *ambos/as*

bottle guhrrahfuh *garrafa*

bottle opener sahkuh-rrolyuhsh *saca-rolhas* (m)

(at the) bottom (noo) foongdoo *(no) fundo*

box kaishuh *caixa*

boy rruhpahzh/meeoodoo/ mneenoo *rapaz/miúdo/menino*

boyfriend nuhmoorahdoo *namorado*

brain sehrebroo *cérebro*

brave vuhlengt *valente*

bread pōw *pão*

to break puhrteer *partir*

250

breakfast pkenoo-ahlmosoo *pequeno-almoço*

to breathe rreshpeerahr *respirar*

a bribe soobornoo *suborno*

to bribe sooboornahr *subornar*

bridge pongt *ponte* (f)

brilliant breelyangt *brilhante*

to bring truhzer *trazer*

broken puhrteedoo/uh *partido/a*

brother eermãw *irmão*

a bruise nohdwuh negruh *nódoa negra*

bucket bahld *balde* (m)

bug ingsehtoo *insecto*

to build kongshtrooeer *construir*

building prehdiw *prédio* (m)

bus (city) owtohkahrroo *autocarro*

bus (intercity) kahmiwnehtuh *camioneta*

bus station shtuhsõw de owtohkahrroosh *estação de autocarros* (m)

bus stop puhrahzhùày de owtohkahrroosh *paragem de autocarros*

business ngohsiwsh *negócios* (m)

busker uhrteeshtuh de rroouh *artista de rua* (m)

busy okoopahdoo/uh *ocupado/a*

but muhsh *mas*

buttons bootõysh *botões* (m)

to buy kongprahr *comprar*

C

camera kuhmuhruh; mahkeenuh footoograhfeekuh *câmara; máquina fotográfica*

camera shop lohzhuh de footoogruhfeeuhsh *loja de fotografias* (f)

can (aluminium) lahtuh *lata*

can opener ahbr lahtuhsh *abre-latas* (m)

to cancel kangslahr *cancelar*

candle vehluh *vela*

car kahrroo *carro*

car registration leevret *livrete* (m)

cards kahrtuhsh *cartas* (f)

caring bongdozoo/ bongdohzuh *bondoso/a*

to carry lvahr *levar*

cashier kaishuh *caixa*

cassette kahseht *cassete* (f)

castle kuhshtehloo *castelo*

cat gahtoo *gato*

cathedral kuhtdrahl *catedral* (f)

CD sede *CD* (m)

to celebrate feshtezhahr *festejar*

centimetre sengteemtroo *centímetro*

ceramic sruhmeekuh *cerâmica*

certificate serteefeekahdoo *certificado*

chair kuhdayruh *cadeira*

champagne shpoomangt/ shangpuhny *espumante* (m)/ *champanhe* (m)

chance sohrt *sorte* (f)

to change moodahr *mudar*

change (coins) trokoo *troco*

changing rooms veshteeahriwsh *vestiários* (m)

to chat up nuhmoorahr *namorar*

cheap buhrahtoo/uh *barato/a*

a cheat buhtootayroo/uh *batoteiro/a*

to check rrver/kongfeermahr *rever/confirmar*

check-in (desk) tshehk-een (bahlkõw) *check-in (balcão)* (m)

checkpoint poshtoo de kongtroloo *posto de controlo*

Cheers! ah toouh/vohsuh suhood! *À tua/vossa (sg/pl) saúde!*

cheese kayzhoo *queijo*

chemist fuhrmahsyuh *farmácia*

chess shuhdresh *xadrez* (m)

chest paytoo *peito*

chicken frang-goo *frango*

children kreeangsuhsh *crianças* (f)

chocolate shookoolaht *chocolate* (m)

to choose shkoolyer *escolher*

christian name nom de bahteezhmoo *nome de baptismo* (m)

Christmas Day deeuh de nuhtahl *Dia de Natal* (m)

church eegruhzhuh *igreja*

cigarette seegahrroo *cigarro*

cigarette papers puhpehl de seegahrroosh *papel de cigarros* (m)

cinema seenemuh *cinema* (m)

citizenship seeduhduhneeuh *cidadania*

city seedahd *cidade* (f)

city walls moorahlyuhsh *muralhas* (f)

classical art ahrt klahseekuh *arte clássica* (f)

clean lingpoo/uh *limpo/a*

cleaning serveesoo de lingpezuh *serviço de limpeza* (m)

cliff fuhlehzyuh *falésia*

to climb shkuhlahr/soobeer *escalar/subir*

cloak kahpuh *capa*

cloakroom gwarduhrropuh *guarda-roupa* (m)

clock rrelohzhiw *relógio*

to close fshahr *fechar*

closed fshahdoo/uh *fechado/a*

clothing rropuh *roupa*

clothes store lohzhuh de rropuh *loja de roupa*

cloud noováy *nuvem* (f)

cloudy nooblahdoo/uh *nublado/a*

coast koshtuh *costa*

coat kuhzahkoo *casaco*

cocaine kohkuheenuh *cocaína*

coins mwehdulush *moedas* (f)

a cold kongshteepuhsõw *constipação* (f)

cold (adj) freeõo/uh *frio/a*

colleague koolehguh *colega* (m/f)

college ooneeverseedahd *universidade* (f)

colour kor *cor* (f)

comb pengt *pente* (m)

to come veer/shgahr *vir/chegar*

comfortable kongfoortahvehl *confortável*

companion kongpuhnyayroo/uh *companheiro/a*

company kongpuhnyeeuh *companhia*

compass boosõoluh *bússola*

a concert kongsertoo *concerto*

to confirm (a booking) kongfeermahr (oomuh rrzehrvuh) *confirmar (uma reserva)*

Congratulations! puhruhbãysh! *Parabéns!*

constipation preezõw de vengtr *prisão de ventre*

to cook koozeenyahr *cozinhar*

Cool (coll) bshteeahl! *Bestial!*

corner shkeenuh *esquina*

interior kangtoo *canto*

exterior shkeenuh *esquina*

corrupt koorrooptoo/uh *corrupto/a*

cotton ahlgoodõw *algodão*

country puheesh *país* (m)

countryside kangpoo *campo*

a cough tohs *tosse* (f)

to count kongtahr *contar*

court (legal) treeboonahl *tribunal* (m)

court (tennis) kohrt de tehneesh *court de ténis* (m)

crafts uhrtzuhnahtoo *artesanato*

crazy muhlookoo/uh; lokoo/uh *maluco/a; louco/a*

credit card kuhrtõw de krehdeetoo *cartão de crédito*

creep (slang) uhnohrmahl! *anormal!*

cross (angry) zang-gahdoo/uh *zangado/a*

cross-country trail kuhmeenyoo *caminho*

a cuddle uhbrahsoo *abraço*

cup shahvnuh *chávena*

customs ahlfangdeguh *alfândega*

to cut koortahr *cortar*

D

dad puhpah *papá* (m)

daily deeahryuhmengt *diariamente*

to dance dangsahr *dançar*

dangerous preegozoo/
preegohzuh *perigoso/a*

dark shkooroo/uh *escuro/a*

date (appointment)
engkongtroo *encontro*

date (time) dahtuh *data*

to date (someone) suheer kong
ahlgáy *sair com alguém*

date of birth dahtuh de
nuhshseemengtoo *data de
nascimento* (f)

daughter feelyuh *filha*

dawn muhdroogahduh
madrugada

day deeuh *dia*

day after tomorrow
dpoyzh de ahmuhnyang
depois de amanhã

dead mortoo/mohrtuh *morto/a*

deaf soordoo/uh *surdo/a*

to deal (business) ngoosyahr
negociar

to deal (with people) leedahr
kong ahlgáy *lidar com
alguém*

to deal (cards) dahr (uhsh
kahrtuhsh) *dar (as cartas)*

death mohrt *morte* (f)

to decide dseedeer *decidir*

deep proofoongdoo/uh
profundo/a

deer veeahdoo *veado*

delay uhtrahzoo *atraso*

delicatessen shuhrkootuhreeuh
charcutaria

delirious dleerangt *delirante*

democracy dmookruhseeuh
democracia

dentist dengteeshtuh *dentista* (m)

to deny ngahr *negar*

deodorant dzodooreezangt
desodorizante (m)

to depart (leave) puhrteer *partir*

department stores grangdez
ahrmuhzáysh *grandes
armazéns* (m)

departure puhrteeduh *partida*

desert dzehrtoo *deserto*

destination dshteenoo *destino*

to destroy deshtrwir *destruir*

detail dtahly *detalhe* (m)

diabetic deeuhbehteekoo/uh
diabético/a

diary deeahriw *diário*

dice/die dahdoosh *dados* (m)

dictionary deesiwnahriw
dicionário

to die moorrer *morrer*

different deefrengt *diferente*

difficult deefeeseel *difícil*

dinner zhangtahr *jantar* (m)

direct deerehtoo/uh *directo/a*

director deerehtor/deerehtoruh
director/a

dirty soozhoo/uh *sujo/a*

disabled dfeesee-engt
deficiente (m/f)

disadvantage deshvangtahzhăy
desvantagem (f)

discount deshkongtoo desconto

to discover deshkoobreer
descobrir

disease dooengsuh doença

dismissal deshpdeemengtoo
despedimento

distributor deeshtreebwidor/uh
distribuidor/a

diving mergoolyoo mergulho

diving equipment
eekeepuhmengtoo de
mergoolyoo
equipamento de mergulho

dirty tongtôo/uh; kong
tongtooruhsh
tonto/a; com tonturas

to do fuhzer fazer

What are you doing?
oo ke eh ke shtah
uh fuhzer?
O que é que está a fazer?

doctor mehdeekoo/uh médico/a

documentary dookoomengtahriw
documentário

dog kŏw cão

dole soobseediw de
dzengpregoo subsídio de
desemprego

doll boonehkuh boneca

door pohrtuh porta

dope (drugs) drohguh droga

double dooploo/uh duplo/a

double bed kuhmuh de kuhzahl
cama de casal (f)

double room kwartoo dooploo
quarto duplo

a dozen oomuh doozyuh
uma dúzia

drama druhmuh drama (m)

dramatic druhmahteekoo/uh
dramático/a

to dream soonyahr sonhar

dress vshteadoo vestido

a drink beheeduh bebida

to drink beber beber

to drive kongdoozeer conduzir

driving licence kahrtuh de
kongdoosôw
carta de condução (f)

drug (medicine)
mdeekuhmengtoo/
rremehdiw medicamento/
remédio

drug (narcotic) drohguh droga

drug addiction tohkseekoh
dpengdengsyuh toxico-
dependência (f)

drug dealer puhsuhdor/
puhsuhdoruh passador/
passadora

drums buhtreeuh bateria

to be drunk shtahr bebuhdoo
estar bêbedo

to dry (clothes) skahr (rropuh)
secar (roupa)

dummy shooshuh chucha

E

each kuhduh *cada*

ear ooruhlyuh *orelha*

early sedoo *cedo*

to earn guhnyahr *ganhar*

earrings brinkoosh *brincos* (m)

ears (external) ooruhlyuhsh *orelhas* (f)

Earth tehrruh *Terra*

earth (soil) tehrruh *terra*

earthquake tremor de tehrruh *tremor de terra* (m)

east ehsht *Este* (m)

easy fahseel *fácil*

to eat koomer *comer*

editor eedeetor/eedeetoruh *editor/editora*

education eedookuhsŏw *educação* (f)

elections eelaysŏysh *eleições* (f)

electricity eelehtreeseedahd *electricidade* (f)

elevator eelvuhdor *elevador* (m)

embarassed engvergoonyahdoo/uh *envergonhado/a*

embarassment vergonyuh *vergonha*

embassy engbaishahduh *embaixada*

emergency eemerzhengsyuh *emergência*

employee engpregahdoo/uh *empregado/a*

employer puhtrŏw/puhtrouh *patrão/patroa*

empty vuhzeeoo/uh *vazio/a*

end fing *fim* (m)

to end uhkuhbahr *acabar*

endangered species shpehseeeesh ãy preegoo de shtingsŏw *espécies em perigo de extinção*

engagement kongproomeesoo *compromisso*

engine mootor *motor* (m)

English ing-glesh *inglês*

to enjoy (oneself) deeverteers *divertir-se*

enough soofeesee-engt *suficiente*

to enter engtrahr *entrar*

entertaining deeverteedoo *divertido*

envelope engvlohp *envelope* (m)

environment mayoo angbee-engt *meio-ambiente* (m)

epileptic eepeelehteekoo/uh *epiléptico/a*

equal opportunity eegwaldahd de opoortooneedahdesh *igualdade de oportunidades* (f)

equality eegwaldahd *igualdade* (f)

equipment eekeepuhmengtoo *equipamento*

European e-wroope-w/ e-wroopayuh *europeu/ europeia*

evening noyt *noite* (f)

every day todooz oozh deeuhsh *todos os dias*

example eezengploo *exemplo*

   For example, ...
   poor eezengploo, ...
   Por exemplo, ...

excellent shelengt; ohteemoo *excelente; óptimo*

exchange kangbiw de mweduh *câmbio de moeda*

to exchange kangbyahr mweduh *cambiar moeda*

exchange rate tahshuh de kangbiw *taxa de câmbio*

excluded shklooeedoo/uh *excluído/a*

   Excuse me.
   deshkoolp
   Desculpe.

to exhibit eezeebeer; shpor *exibir; expor*

exhibition shpoozeesõw *exposiçao (f)*

exit suheeduh *saída*

expensive kuhroo/uh *caro/a*

exploitation shplooruhsõw *exploração (f)*

express shprehsoo *expresso*

express mail koorrayoo uhzool *correio azul*

eye olyoo *olho*

F

face kahruh *cara*

factory fahbreekuh *fábrica*

factory worker oprahriw/yuh operário/a (m/f)

fall (autumn) otonoo *Outono*

family fuhmeelyuh *família*

famous fuhmozo/uh *famoso/a*

fan (hand-held) lehk *leque* (m)

fan (machine) vangtooeenyuh *ventoinha*

fans (of a team) uhdehptoosh/ uhsh *adeptos/as*

far longzh *longe*

farm kingtuh *quinta*

farmer uhgreekooltor/ uhgreekultoruh *agricultor/a*

fast (quickly) dprehsuh *depressa*

fat gordoo/uh *gordo/a*

father pai *pai* (m)

fault (someone's) koolpuh *culpa*

faulty dfaytwozo/dfaytwohzuh (obzhehktoosh) *defeituoso/a (objectos)*

fear medoo *medo*

to feel sengteer *sentir*

feelings sengteemengtoosh *sentimentos* (m)

fence serkuh *cerca*

festival feshteevahl *festival* (m)

fever fehbr *febre* (f)

few pokoosh *poucos*

fiancé/fiancée nuhmoorahdoo/ uh *namorado/a*

fiction feeksõw *ficção* (f)

fight lootuh *luta*

to fight lootahr *lutar*

figures noomroosh *números* (m)

to fill engsher *encher*

a film (negatives) feelm *filme* (m)

film (cinema) feelm *filme*

film (for camera) rroloo de footoogruhfeeuhsh *rolo de fotografias* (m)

film speed sengseebeeleedahd *sensibilidade* (f)

to find engkongtrahr *encontrar*

a fine mooltuh *multa*

finger dedoo *dedo*

fir uhbehtoo *abeto*

fire fogoo/ingsengdiw *fogo/ incêndio*

firewood luhnyuh *lenha*

first preemayroo/uh *primeiro/a*

first-aid kit shtozhoo de preemayroosh sookohrroosh *estojo de primeiros socorros* (m)

fish paysh *peixe* (m)

fish shop payshuhreeuh *peixaria*

flag bangdayruh *bandeira*

flat (land, etc) pluhnoo/uh *plano/a*

flea poolguh *pulga*

flashlight langtehrnuh *lanterna*

flight vo-oo *voo*

floor shōw *chão*

floor (storey) angdahr *andar* (m)

flour fuhreenyuh *farinha*

flower flor *flor* (f)

flower seller vengddor/ vengdedoruh de floresh *vendedor/vendedora de flores*

a fly moshkuh *mosca*

fog nvwayroo *nevoeiro*

to follow sgeer *seguir*

food koomeeduh *comida*

foot peh *pé* (m)

footpath kuhmeenyoo *caminho*

foreign shtranzhayroo/uh *estrangeiro/a*

forest floorehshtuh *floresta*

forever (puhruh) sengpr *(para) sempre*

to forget shkehsers *esquecer-se*

Forget about it!
nōw pengsezh maish neesoo!
Não penses mais nisso!

to forgive perdwar *perdoar*

fortnight doouhsh smuhnuhsh *duas semanas*

foyer veshteebooloo/ohl *vestíbulo/hall* (m)

free (not bound) leevr *livre*

free (of charge) grahteesh *grátis*

to freeze zhelahr/kongzhelahr *gelar/congelar*

friend uhmeegoo/uh *amigo/a*

frozen foods koomeeduh kongzhelahduh *comida congelada*

ENGLISH – PORTUGUESE

full shayoo/uh *cheio/a*

fun deeverteemengtoo
divertimento

for fun nuh bringkuhdayruh
na brincadeira

to have fun
deeverteers
divertir-se

funeral foonrahl *funeral* (m)

future footooroo *futuro*

G

game zhogoo *jogo*

garage guhrahzhãy/
ohfeeseenuh *garagem* (f)/
oficina

garbage leeshoo *lixo*

gardening zhuhrdeenahzhãy
jardinagem (f)

garden zhuhrding *jardim* (m)

gas cartridge kahrguh de gahsh
carga de gás (f)

gate poortõw *portão*

general zhenrahl *general* (m)

in general
ãy zherahl
em geral

Get lost!
peeruht!
Pira-te!

gift prengduh *prenda*

gig kongsertoo/
shpehtahkooloo *concerto*/
espectáculo

girl rruhpuhreeguh *rapariga*

girlfriend nuhmoorahduh
namorada

to give dahr *dar*

Could you give me ...?
duhvuhm ... ?
Dava-me ... ?

glass kohpoo/veedroo
copo/vidro

to go eer *ir*

Go straight ahead.
võw sengpr ãy frengt
Vão sempre em frente.

to go out with suheer kong
sair com

goal (aspiration) ohbzhehteevoo
objectivo

goat kahbruh *cabra*

God de-wsh *Deus*

of gold doroo *de ouro*

Good luck!
bouh sohrt
Boa sorte!

Goodbye.
uhde-wsh
Adeus.

government goovernoo *governo*

gram gruhmuh *grama*

grandchild nehtoo/uh *neto/a*

grandfather uhvo *avô*

grandmother uhvoh *avó* (f)

H

grapes oovuhsh *uvas* (f)

graphic art ahrtsh grahfeekush *artes gráficas* (f)

grass (garden) rehlvuh *relva*

grave spooltooruh *sepultura*

great grangd *grande*

  Great!
  beshtyahl!
  Bestial!

green verd *verde*

greengrocer koomerseeangt de ortuhleesuh *comerciante de hortaliça* (m/f)

to guess uhdeeveenyahr *adivinhar*

guide (person) geeuh *guia* (m/f)

guidebook geeuh *guia* (m)

guided trek shkoorsōw geeahduh *excursão guiada* (f)

guitar viohluh; geetahrruh poortoogezuh *viola; guitarra portuguesa*

H

hair kuhbeloo *cabelo*

hairbrush shkovuh de kuhbeloo *escova de cabelo* (f)

half mtahd *metade*

to hallucinate uhlooseenahr *alucinar*

ham przoongtoo *presunto*

hand mōw *mão* (f)

handbag kuhrtayruh; mahluh de snyoruh *carteira; mala de senhora*

handmade faytoo ah mōw *feito à mão*

handsome behloo/uh *belo/a*

happy fleesh *feliz*

harbour portoo *porto*

hard dooroo/uh *duro/a*

harrassment uhsehdiw *assédio*

hash ahsheesh *haxixe* (m)

to have ter *ter*

  Do you have ...?
  tāy ...?
  Tem ... ?

he el *ele*

head kuhbesuh *cabeça*

headache dor de kuhbesuh *dor de cabeça* (f)

health suhood *saúde* (f)

to hear oveer *ouvir*

heart kooruhsōw *coração*

heat kuhlor *calor* (m)

heater uhkehsdor *aquecedor* (m)

heavy pzahdoo/uh *pesado/a*

  Hello.
  olah
  Olá.

  Hello! (answering telephone)
  shtah lah?; shtah, sing?
  Está lá?; Está, sim?

260

helmet kuhpuhse capacete (m)

Help!
sookorroo!
Socorro!

to help uhzhoodahr ajudar

herbs ehrvuhsh ervas (f)

here uhkee aqui

heroin eerooeenuh heroína

high ahltoo/uh alto/a

to hike fuhzer
mongtuhnyeezhmoo fazer
montanhismo

hiking kuhmeenyahduh
caminhada

hill kooleenuh colina

to hire kongtruhtahr contratar

to hitchhike angdahr ah
boolayuh andar à boleia

HIV positive
sehrohpoozeeteevoo/uh
seropositivo/a

holiday fryahdoo feriado

holidays fehryuhsh férias (f)

homeless sãy uhbreegoo sem
abrigo (m)

honey mehl mel (m)

honeymoon lwuh de mehl
lua de mel (f)

horrible orreevehl horrível

horse kuhvahloo cavalo

horse riding angdahr uh
kuhvahloo andar a cavalo

hospital ohshpeetahl hospital

hot kengt quente

house kahzuh casa

housework
truhbahlyoo doomeshteekoo
trabalho doméstico

how komoo como

How do I get to …?
komoo eh ke shegoo uh …?
Como é que chego a … ?

hug uhbrahsoo abraço

human rights
deeraytooz oomuhnoosh
direitos humanos (m)

a hundred sãy cem

to be hungry ter fohm ter fome

husband muhreedoo marido

I

I e-w Eu

ice zheloo gelo

ice axe muhshahdoo
(puhruh oo zheloo)
machado (para o gelo)

ice cream zhelahdoo gelado

identification card beelyet
deedengteedahd
Bilhete de Identidade (m)

identification
eedengteefeekuhsõw
identificação (f)

idiot eedyohtuh idiota (m/f)

if se *se*

ill dooengt *doente* (m/f)

immigration eemeegruhsōw *imigração* (f)

important ingpoortangt *importante*

It's (not) important.
(nōw) eh ingpoortangt
(Não) é importante.

in a hurry kong/ah prehsuh *com/à pressa*

in front of diangt de *diante de*

included ingkloozeeveh *inclusive*

income tax ingposhtoo sobr osh rrengdeemengtoosh *imposto sobre os rendimentos* (m)

incomprehensible ingkongpree-engseevehl *incompreensível*

inequality dzeegwaldahd *desigualdade* (f)

to inject (self) ingzhehtahrs *injectar-se*

injury freeduh *ferida*

inside dengtroo *dentro*

insurance sgooroo *seguro*

intense ingtengsoo/uh *intenso/a*

interesting ingtresangt *interessante*

intermission ingtervahloo/powzuh *intervalo/pausa*

international ingternuhsiwnahl *internacional*

interview engtreveeshtuh *entrevista*

island eelyuh *ilha*

itch koomeeshōw; ter koomeeshōw comichão (f); ter comichão

itinerary eeteenerahriw *itinerário*

jail preezōw *prisão* (f)

jar zhahrroo *jarro*

jealous siwmengtoo/uh *ciumento/a*

jeans dzheens *jeans* (m)

jeep zheep *jeep*

jewellery zhwuhlyuhreeuh *joalharia*

job truhbahlyoo/engpregoo *trabalho/emprego*

joke uhndohtuh/pyahduh *anedota/piada*

to joke deezer oomuh pyaduh *dizer uma piada*

journalist zhoornuhleeshtuh *jornalista* (m/f)

journey vyazhāy *viagem* (f)

judge zhweesh/zhooeezuh *juiz/juiza*

juice soomoo *sumo*

to jump sahltahr *saltar*

jumper (sweater) kuhmeezohluh *camisola*

justice zhooshteesuh *justiça*

K

key shahv *chave* (f)

kick pongtuhpeh *pontapé* (m)

to kill muhtahr *matar*

kilogram keeloogruhmuh *quilograma* (m)

kilometre keelohmtroo *quilómetro*

kind (adj) uhmahvehl *amável*

kind (type) teepoo *tipo*

king rray *rei* (m)

kiss bayzhoo *beijo*

to kiss bayzhahr *beijar*

kitchen koozeenyuh *cozinha*

kitten guhteenyoo/uh *gatinho/a*

knee zhwuhlyoo *joelho*

knife fahkuh *faca*

to know (someone) koonyser *conhecer*

to know (something) suhber *saber*

I don't know.
(nôw) say
Não sei.

L

ake lahgoo *lago*

and tehrruh *terra*

anguage ling-gwuh *língua*

arge grangd *grande*

ast oolteemoo/uh *último/a*

last night ongtãy ah noyt *ontem à noite*

last week smuhnuh puhsahduh (nuh) *semana passada*

last year uhnoo puhsahdoo *ano passado*

late tahrd *tarde*

It's late.
shtah uhtruhzahdoo/uh
Está atrasado/a.

laugh guhrguhlyahduh *gargalhada*

launderette luhvangduhreeuh *lavandaria*

law lay *lei* (f)

lawyer uhdvooguhdoo/uh *advogado/a*

laxatives luhshangt *laxante* (m)

lazy pregeesozoo/ pregeesohzuh *preguiçoso/a*

loaded (petrol/gas) guhzooleenuh kong shoongboo *gasolina com chumbo* (f)

leader shehf *chefe* (m/f)

to learn uhprengder *aprender*

leather pehl/koroo *pele* (f)/ *couro*

ledge suhlee-engsyuh *saliência*

to be left (behind/over) feekahr uhtrahsh/soobrahr *ficar atrás/sobrar*

left (not right) shkerduh *esquerda*

L

D I C T I O N A R Y

left luggage dpohzeetoo de buhgahzhäysh *depósito de bagagens* (m)

leg pehrnuh *perna*

lens ohbzhehteevuh *objectiva*

lesbian lehzhbeekuh *lésbica*

less menoosh *menos*

letter kahrtuh *carta*

liar mengteerozoo/uh *mentiroso/a*

library beebliwtehkuh *biblioteca*

lice peeolyoosh *piolhos* (m)

to lie mengteer *mentir*

life veeduh *vida*

lift (elevator) eelvuhdor *elevador* (m)

light (n) loosh *luz* (f)

light (adj) lehv *leve*

light (clear) klahroo/uh *claro/a*

light bulb langpuhduh *lâmpada*

lighter eeshkayroo *isqueiro*

to like gooshtahr de *gostar de*

line leenyuh *linha*

lips lahbiwsh *lábios* (m)

to listen oveer *ouvir*

little (small) pkenoo/uh *pequeno/a*

little (amount) pokoo *pouco*

to live (somewhere) veever/moorahr *viver/morar*

local lookahl; dooz uhrrdohresh *local; dos arredores*

local bus owtohkahrroo *autocarro*

lock fshuhdooruh *fechadura*

to lock fshahr *fechar*

long kongpreedoo/uh *comprido/a*

long-distance bus kahmiwnehtuh ingtehrseedahdesh *camioneta inter-cidades* (f)

to lose perder *perder*

loss pehrduh *perda*

a lot mwingtoo/uh *muito/a*

loud ahltoo *alto* (adv)

to love uhmahr *amar*

lover uhmangt *amante* (m/f)

low baishoo/uh *baixo/a*

low/high blood pressure tengsõw baishuh/ahltuh *tensão baixa/alta*

loyal lyal *leal*

luck sohrt *sorte* (f)

lucky kong sohrt; soortoodoo/uh *com sorte; sortudo/a* (inf)

luggage buhgahzhäy *bagagem* (f)

luggage lockers kuhseefoozh de buhgahzhäy *cacifos de bagagem*

lump (external) ahltoo *alto*

lunch ahlmosoo *almoço*

lunchtime ohruh doo ahlmosoo *hora do almoço* (f)

luxury looshoo *luxo*

264

machine mahkeenuh *máquina*

mad doydoo/uh *doido/a*

made (of) faytoo (de) *feito (de)*

magazine rrveeshtuh *revista*

mail koorrayoo *correio*

mailbox kaishuh doo koorrayoo
caixa do correio (f)

main road
shtrahduh pringseepahl
estrada principal (f)

main square
lahrgoo pringseepahl
largo principal (m)

majority mayooreeuh; mayohr
pahrt *maioria; maior parte (f)*

to make fuhzer *fazer*

make-up muhkeelyahzhāy
maquilhagem (f)

man ohmãy *homem (m)*

manager shehf de sehksōw
chefe de secção(m/f)

many mwingtoosh/uhsh
muitos/as

map mahpuh *mapa (m)*

Can you show me on the map?
poodeeuh mooshtrahrm
noo mahpuh?
Podia mostrar-me no mapa?

marijuana muhreezhwuhnuh
marijuana

marital status shtahdoo seeveel
estado civil (m)

market merkahdoo *mercado*

to marry kuhzahr *casar*

marvellous muhruhveelyozo/uh
maravilhoso/a

massage muhsahzhāy
massagem (f)

match zhogoo *jogo*

matches fohshfooroosh *fósforos*

It doesn't matter.
nōw tāy ingpoortangsyuh
Não tem importância.

mattress koolshōw *colchão*

maybe tahlvesh *talvez*

mayor przeedengt duh
kuhmuhruh
presidente da câmara (m/f)

mechanic mkuhneekoo/uh
mecânico/a

medal mdahlyuh *medalha*

medicine mdeeseenuh/
rrmehdiw *medicina/remédio*

to meet engkongtrahrs
kong ahlgāy
encontrar-se com alguém

member mengbroo/uh
membro/a

menstruation mengshtrwuhsōw
menstruação (f)

menthol (cigarettes) de mengtohl
(seegahrroosh) *de mentol
(cigarros)*

menu eemengtuh *ementa*

message mengsahzhãy *mensagem* (f)

metal mtahl *metal* (m)

metre mehtroo *metro*

midnight mayuh-noyt *meia-noite* (f)

migraine engshuhkehkuh *enxaqueca*

milk layt *leite* (m)

millimetre meeleemtroo *milimetro*

million meelyõw *milhão*

mind mengt *mente* (f)

mineral water ahgwuh meenrahl *água mineral* (f)

a minute meenootoo *minuto*

Just a minute.
eh soh oong moomengtoo
É só um momento.

In (five) minutes.
duhkee a (singkoo) meenootoosh
Daqui a (cinco) minutos.

mirror shpuhlyoo *espelho*

to miss (feel absence) ter suhwdahdesh *ter saudades*

mistake eng-guhnoo *engano*

to mix meeshtoorahr *misturar*

mobile phone tehlehmohvehl *telemóvel* (m)

modem mohdehm *modem* (m)

moisturiser krehm eedruhtangt *creme hidratante* (m)

monastery mooshtayroo *mosteiro*

money deenyayroo *dinheiro*

monk mongzh *monge* (m)

monkey muhkahkoo *macaco*

month mesh *mês* (m)

monument moonoomengtoo *monumento*

moon loouh *lua*

more maish *mais*

morning muhnyang *manhã*

mosque meshkeetuh *mesquita*

mother mãy *mãe* (f)

mother-in-law sohgruh *sogra*

motorcycle mohtuh/ mohtohseeklehtuh *mota/motocicleta*

motorway (tollway) owtohshtrahduh *auto-estrada* (f)

mountain mongtuhnyuh *montanha*

mountain bike beeseeklehtuh de mongtuhnyuh *bicicleta de montanha*

mountain range sehrruh *serra*

mountaineering ahlpeeneezhmoo (fuhzer) *alpinismo (fazer)*

mouse rrahtoo *rato*

mouth bokuh *boca*

movie feelm *filme* (m)

ENGLISH – PORTUGUESE

Mum muhmang *Mamã*

muscle mooshkooloo *músculo*

museum mooze-w *museu* (m)

music moozeekuh *música*

musician moozeeakoo/uh *músico/a*

Muslim moosoolmuhnoo/uh *muçulmano/a*

mute moodoo/uh *mudo/a*

N

name nom *nome* (m)

nappy fruhlduh *fralda*

national park pahrk nuhsiwnahl *parque nacional* (m)

nationality nuhsiwnuhleedahd *nacionalidade* (f)

nature nuhtoorezuh *natureza*

nausea nowsyuh *náusea*

near pehrtoo *perto*

necessary nsesahriw/yuh *necessário/a*

necklace koolahr *colar* (m)

to need nseseetahr *necessitar*

needle (sewing) uhgoolyuh (de koozer) *agulha (de coser)* (f)

needle (syringe) uhgoolyuh (sering-guh) *agulha (seringa)* (f)

neither nãy; tangbãy nõw *nem; também não*

net rred *rede* (f)

never noongkuh *nunca*

new novoo/nohvuh *novo/a*

news nooteesyuhsh *notícias* (f)

newsagency uhzhengsyuh de nooteesyuhsh *agência de notícias* (f)

newspaper zhoornahl *jornal* (m)

New Year's Day deeuh duhnoo novoo *Dia do Ano Novo* (m)

New Year's Eve puhsahzhay duhnoo *Passagem de Ano* (f)

next prohseemoo/uh *próximo/a*

next to ow peh de *ao pé de*

next week smuhnuh ke vãy *semana que vem*

nice singpahteekoo/uh *simpático/a*

nickname ahlkoonyuh *alcunha*

night noyt *noite* (f)

no nõw *não*

noise buhroolyoo *barulho*

noisy buhroolyengtoo/uh *barulhento/a*

none nenyoong/nenyoomuh *nenhum/a*

noon mayoodeeuh *meio-dia* (m)

north nohrt *norte* (m)

N

D I C T I O N A R Y

nose nuhreesh *nariz* (m)

notebook kuhdehrnoo *caderno*

nothing nahduh *nada*

not yet uhingduh nõw *ainda não*

novel (book) rroomangs *romance* (m)

now uhgohruh *agora*

nurse engfermayruh *enfermeira*

O

obvious ohbviw/uh *óbvio/a*

ocean ohsyuhnoo *oceano*

offence ohfengsuh *ofensa*

office shkreetohriw/guhbeenet *escritória/gabinete* (m)

office work truhbahlyoo de shkreetohriw *trabalho de escritório*

office worker engpregahdoo de shkreetohriw *empregado de escritório*

often mwingtuhsh vezesh *muitas vezes*

oil (cooking) ohliw *óleo*

oil (crude) petrohliw *petróleo*

OK.
shtah bāy
Está bem.

old vehlyoo/uh *velho/a*

old city seedahd angteeguh *cidade antiga* (f)

olive oil uhzayt *azeite* (m)

olives uhzaytonuhsh *azeitonas* (f)

on āy/sobr *em/sobre*

on time uh tengpoo; uh ohruhsh *a tempo; a horas*

once oomuh vesh *uma vez*

one-way (ticket) (beelyet de) eeduh *(bilhete de) ida* (m)

only soh *só*

open uhbehrtoo/uh *aberto/a*

to open uhbreer *abrir*

opening uhbertooruh/ eenowgooruhsõw *abertura/ inauguração* (f)

opera ohpruh *ópera*

opera house tyahtroo de ohpruh *teatro de ópera* (m)

operation ohpruhsõw *operação* (f)

operator ohpruhdor/uh *operador/a*

opinion opeeneeõw *opinião* (f)

opposite āy frengt *em frente*

or o *ou*

oral orahl *oral*

orchestra ohrkehshtruh *orquestra*

order (in a restaurant) pdeedoo *pedido*

to order (in a restaurant) pdeer *pedir*

ordinary nohrmahl *normal*

organise ohrguhneezahr
organizar

orgasm ohrgahzhmoo orgasmo

original ohreezheenahl original

other otroo/uh outro/a

outgoing (personality)
uhbehrtoo/uh aberto/a

outside fohruh/shtreeor fora/
exterior

over sobr sobre

overcoat soobretoodoo/
kuhzahkoo sobretudo/casaco

to owe dver dever

owner donoo/uh dono/a

ozone layer kuhmahduh de
ozonoo camada de ozono (f)

P

pacifier shooshuh chucha

package engbroolyoo embrulho

packet (cigarettes)
mahsoo de tuhbahkoo/
seegahrroosh
maço de tabaco/cigarros (m)

padlock kuhdyahdoo cadeado

page pahzheenuh página

a pain dor dor (f)

painful dooloorozoo/
dooloorohzuh
doloroso/dolorosa

pain in the neck shahtoo/uh
chato/a (inf)

painkillers uhnahlzhehzeekoosh
analgésicos (m)

to paint pingtahr pintar

painter pingtor/pingtoruh
pintor/pintora

painting pingtooruh/kwadroo
pintura/quadro

pair (a couple) kuhzahl casal (m)

palace puhlahsiw palácio

paper puhpehl papel (m)

parcel engbroolyoo embrulho

parents paish pais (m)

park (garden) pahrk parque (m)

to park shtuhsiwnahr estacionar

parliament puhrluhmengtoo
parlamento

part pahrt parte (f)

party (celebration)
fehshtuh festa

party (politics) puhrteedoo
pooleeteekoo partido político

pass puhsahzhãy passagem (f)

passenger puhsuhzhayroo/uh
passageiro/a

passive puhseevoo/uh passivo/a

passport pahsuhpohrt
passaporte (m)

passport number noomroo doo
pahsuhpohrt número do
passaporte (m)

past puhsahdoo passado

path kuhmeenyoo caminho

patient (adj) dooengt
doente (m/f)

to pay puhgahr *pagar*

payment puhguhmengtoo
pagamento

peace pahsh *paz* (f)

peak ahltoo *alto*

pedestrian peeôw *peão*

pen (ballpoint)
shfehrohgrahfeekuh
esferográfica

pencil lahpeesh *lápis* (m)

penis pehneesh *pénis* (m)

penknife nuhvahlyuh *navalha*

pensioner pengsiwneeshtuh
pensionista (m)

people psouhsh *pessoas* (f)

pepper peemengtuh *pimenta*

percent poor sengtoo *por cento*

performance uhtoouhsôw
actuação (f)

performance ingterpretuhsôw
interpretação (f)

period pain dor mengshtrwahl
dor menstrual (f)

permanent permuhnengt
permanente

permission owtooreezuhsôw
autorização (f)

permit leesengsuh *licença*

person pesouh *pessoa*

personality persoonuhleedahd
personalidade (f)

to perspire trangshpeerahr
transpirar

petrol guhzooleenuh *gasolina* .

pharmacy fuhrmahsyuh
farmácia

phone book leeshtuh de tlefohn
lista de telefone (f)

phone box kahbeen (de tlefohn)
cabina (de telefone) (f)

phonecard kuhrtôw de tlefohn
cartão de telefone (m)

photo/photography
footoogruhfeeuh *fotografia*

photographer footohgruhfoo/
uh *fotógrafo/a*

to pick up rrkoolyer *recolher*

pie (savoury/sweet) engpahdduh/
tahrt *empada/tarte* (f)

piece bookahdoo *bocado*

pig porkoo *porco*

the Pill peelooluh *Pílula*

pillow ahlmoofahduh *almofada*

pillowcase fronyuh *fronha*

pine peenyayroo *pinheiro*

pink kor de rohzuh
cor-de-rosa (m)

place loogahr *lugar* (m)

place of birth loogahr de
nuhshseemengtoo *lugar de
nascimento* (m)

plain (geography) pluhneesee-e
planície (f)

ENGLISH – PORTUGUESE

plain (simple) singplesh *simples*

plane uhveeoŵ *avião*

planet pluhnetuh *planeta* (m)

plant plangtuh *planta*

to plant plangtahr *plantar*

plastic plahshteokoo *plástico*

plate prahtoo *prato*

plateau pluhnahltoo *planalto*

platform pluhtuhfohrmuh *plataforma*

play (theatre) pehsuh de tyahtroo *peça de teatro* (f)

to play (a game) zhoogahr *jogar*

to play (music) tookahr *tocar*

player (sports) zhooguhdorsh *jogadores*

playing cards zhogoo de kahrtuhsh *jogo de cartas* (m)

to play cards zhoogahr ahsh kahrtuhsh *jogar às cartas*

plug (bath) tangpuh *tampa*

plug (electricity) toomahduh *tomada*

pocket bolsoo *bolso*

poetry pwezeeuh *poesia*

to point uhpongtahr *apontar*

poker pohkehr *poker* (m)

police (officer) pooleesyuh *polícia* (m/f)

politics pooleeteekuh *política*

politicians pooleeteekoosh *políticos* (m)

pollen pohlāy *pólen* (m)

polls songdahzhāysh *sondagens* (f)

pollution poolwisoŵ *poluição* (f)

pool (swimming) peeshseenuh *piscina*

pool (game) beelyahr uhmreekuhnoo *bilhar americano* (m)

poor pohbr *pobre* (m/f)

popular poopoolahr *popular*

port portoo *porto*

port wine veenyoo doo portoo *vinho do Porto*

portrait sketcher dzenyuhdor de rretrahtoosh *desenhador de retratos* (m)

possible pooseevehl *possível*

It's (not) possible.
(nōw) eh pooseevehl
(Não) é possível.

postcard pooshtahl *postal* (m)

postcode kohdeegoo pooshtahl *código postal* (m)

postage frangkeeuh *franquia*

poster pohshtehr/kuhrtahsh *póster* (m)/*cartaz* (m)

post office koorrayoosh *correios* (m)

pot (ceramic) vahzoo *vaso*

pot (dope) muhreezhoouhnuh *marijuana*

271

D I C T I O N A R Y

pottery sruhmeekuh *cerâmica*

poverty poobrezuh *pobreza*

power pooder *poder* (m)

prayer ohruhsōw *oração* (f)

prayer book
leevroo dohruhsōysh
livro de orações (m)

to prefer prefreer *preferir*

pregnant grahveeduh *grávida*

pre-menstrual tension tengsōw
prehmengshtrwahl *tensão
pré-menstrual* (f)

to prepare prepuhrahr *preparar*

present (gift) prengduh *prenda*

present (time) prezengt
presente (m)

pressure prsōw *pressão* (f)

pretty booneetoo/uh *bonito/a*

prevention prvengsōw
prevenção (f)

to prevent ingpdeer *impedir*

price presoo *preço*

pride orgoolyoo *orgulho*

priest pahdr *padre* (m)

a print (artwork) sreegruhfeeuh
serigrafia

prison preezōw *prisão* (f)

prisoner prezoo/uh *preso/a*

private preevahdoo/uh
privado/a

private hospital ohshpeetahl
preevahdoo *hospital
privado* (m)

privatisation preevuhteezuhsōw
privatização (f)

to produce proodoozeer
produzir

producer proodootor/
proodootoruh *produtor/
produtora*

profession proofeesōw
profissão (f)

profit lookroo *lucro*

profitability rrengtuhbeeleedahd
rentabilidade (f)

program proogruhmuh
programa (m)

projector proozhehtor
projector (m)

promise proomehsuh *promessa*

to protect prootzher *proteger*

protected species
shpehsee-esh
prootezheeduhs
espécies protegidas (f)

protest prootehshtoo *protesto*

to protest prooteshtahr
protestar

public toilet
kahzuh de
buhnyoo poobleekuh
casa de banho pública (f)

to pull pooshahr *puxar*

pump bongbuh (de pooshahr)
bomba (de puxar) (f)

puncture (car) fooroo *furo*

to punish kuhshteegahr *castigar*

puppy kuhshorroo *cachorro*

pure pooroo/uh *puro/a*

to push engpoorrahr *empurrar*

to put por *pôr*

Q

qualifications lewuhleefeekuhsoys *qualificações* (f)

quality kwuhleedahd *qualidade* (f)

quarantine kwuhrengtenuh *quarentena*

quarrel deeshkoosow *discussão* (f)

quarter kwartoo *quarto*

question pergoongtuh *pergunta*

to question pergoongtahr *perguntar*

question (topic) keshtow *questão* (f)

queue feeluh *fila*

quickly deprehsuh *depressa*

quiet (adj) seelengsceozoo/uh *silencioso/a*

to quit dzeeshteer *desistir*

R

rabbit kwuhlyoo *coelho*

race (breed) rrahsuh *raça*

race (sport) koorreeduh *corrida*

racing bike beeseeklehtuh de koorreeduhsh *bicicleta de corridas* (f)

racism rrahseezhmoo *racismo*

racquet rrahkeht *raquete* (f)

radiator rrahdyuhdor *radiador* (m)

railroad leenyuh de kongboyoo *linha de comboios* (f)

railway station ehtuhsow de kongboyoosh *estação de comboios* (f)

rain shoovuh *chuva*

rape viwluhsow (sehkswal) *violação (sexual)* (f)

rare (meat) mahl puhsahdoo *mal passado*

a rash eerreetuhsow *irritação* (f)

rat rruhtuhzuhnuh *ratazana*

raw kroo/kroouh *cru/crua*

razor zheeleht *gilete* (f)

razor blades luhmeenuhzh duh zheeleht *lâminas da gilete* (f)

to read ler *ler*

ready prongtoo/uh *pronto/a*

to realise kongpree-engder *compreender*

reason rruhzow *razão* (f)

receipt rrseeboo *recibo*

to receive rrseber *receber*

recent rrsengt *recente*

recently rrsengtmengl *recentemente*

to recognise rrkoonyser *reconhecer*

to recommend rrkoomengdahr *recomendar*

recording gruhvuhsõw *gravação* (f)

recyclable rrseeklahvehl *reciclável*

refrigerator freegooreefeekoo *frigorífico*

refugee rrfoozhyahdoo/uh *refugiado/a*

refund rre-engbolsoo *reembolso*

to refund rre-engbolsahr *reembolsar*

to refuse rrkoozahr *recusar*

regional rrezhiwnahl *regional*

registered mail koorrayoo rrzheeshtahdoo *correio registado*

to regret luhmengtahr *lamentar*

relationship rrluhsõw *relação* (f)

to relax rrelahshahr *relaxar*

religion rrleezheeõw *religião* (f)

to remember lengbrahrs *lembrar-se*

remote rrmohtoo/uh *remoto/a*

rent rrengduh *renda*

to rent uhloogahr *alugar*

to repeat rrepteer *repetir*

republic rrehpoobleekuh *república*

reservation rrzehrvuh *reserva*

to reserve rrzervahr *reservar*

resignation dmeesõw *demissão* (f)

respect rreshpaytoo *respeito*

rest (relaxation) deshkangsoo *descanso*

rest (what's left) rehshtoo *resto*

to rest deshkangsahr *descansar*

restaurant rreshtowrangt *restaurante* (m)

resumé koorreekooloo *currículo*

retired rrfoormahdoo/uh *reformado/a*

to return voltahr *voltar*

return (ticket) beelyet de eeduh ee vohltuh *bilhete de ida e volta* (m)

review kreeteekuh *crítica*

rhythm rreetmoo *ritmo*

rich (wealthy) rreekoo/uh *rico/a*

to ride (a horse) mongtahr uh kuhvahloo *montar a cavalo*

right (correct) eezahtoo/uh; koorrehtoo/uh *exacto/a; correcto/a*

right (not left) deeraytuh *direita*

to be right ter rruhzõw *ter razão*

You're right. tãy rruhzõw *Tem razão.*

(civil) rights deeraytoosh seeveesh *direitos civis* (m)

right now uhgohruh mezhmoo *agora mesmo*

right-wing ahluh deeraytuh *ala direita*

ring (on finger) uhnehl *anel* (m)

ring (of phone; sound) tohk *toque* (m)

I'll give you (inf) a ring.
doly oomuh uhpeetuhdehluh
Dou lhe um apitadela.

rip-off ahldruhbees *aldrabice* (f)

risk reeshkoo *risco*

river reeoo *rio*

road (main) shtrahduh *estrada*

road map mahpuh de shtrahduhsh
mapa de estradas (m)

to rob uhsahltahr *assaltar*

rock rrohshuh *rocha*

rock climbing shkuhlahduh *escalada*

rock group groopoo de rrohk
grupo de rock (m)

room (number) (noomroo doo) kwartoo
(número do) quarto

rope kohrduh *corda*

round rrdongdoo/uh *redondo/a*

rubbish leeshoo *lixo*

rug tuhpet *tapete* (m)

ruins rrooeenuhsh *ruínas* (f)

rules rrehgruhsh *regras* (f)

to run koorrer *correr*

sad treesht *triste*

safe (adj) sgooroo/uh *seguro/a*

a safe kaishuh fohrt
caixa-forte (f)

safe sex sehksoo sgooroo
sexo seguro

salary suhlahriw *salário*

(for) sale vengduh (ah)
venda (à)

sale (bargains) sahldoosh
saldos (m)

sales department
dpuhrtuhmengtoo de vengduhsh
departamento de vendas (m)

salt sahl *sal* (m)

same mezhmoo/uh *mesmo/a*

sand uhrayuh *areia*

sanitary napkins pengsoosh eezhee-ehneekoosh
pensos higiénicos (m)

to say deezer *dizer*

school shkohluh *escola*

science see-engsyuhsh
ciências (f)

scientist see-engteeshtuh
cientista (m/f)

scissors tzoruh *tesoura*

to score muhrkahr *marcar*

script geeōw *guião*

sculpture shkooltooruh
escultura

S

sea mahr *mar* (m)

seasick engzhooahdoo/uh *enjoado/a*

seaside kohshtuh *costa*

seat loogahr/kuhdayruh *lugar* (m)/*cadeira*

seatbelt singtoo de sgoorangsuh *cinto de segurança* (m)

second (time) sgoongdoo *segundo*

to see ver *ver*

I see. (understand) shto uh ver *Estou a ver.*

selfish eegooeeshtuh *egoísta* (m/f)

to sell vengder *vender*

to send engvyahr *enviar*

sensible sengsahtoo/uh *sensato/a*

sentence (words) frahz *frase* (f)

sentence (prison) sengtengsuh *sentença*

to separate spuhrahr *separar*

series sehree-e *série* (f)

serious sehriw/sehryuh *sério/séria*

service (assistance) serveesoo *serviço*

several vahriwsh/vahryuhsh *vários/várias*

to sew koozer *coser*

sex sehksoo *sexo*

sexism muhsheezhmoo *machismo*

sexy sehksee *sexy*

shade songbruh *sombra*

shampoo shangpo *champô* (m)

shape fohrmuh *forma*

to share (with) puhrteelyahr *partilhar*

to share a dorm puhrteelyahr oong kwartoo *partilhar um quarto*

to shave fuhzer uh bahrbuh *fazer a barba*

she ehluh *ela*

sheep oovuhlyuh *ovelha*

sheet (bed) lengsohl *lençol* (m)

sheet (of paper) folyuh *folha*

shell kongshuh *concha*

shelves pruhtlayruhsh *prateleiras* (f)

ship bahrkoo *barco*

to ship mangdahr veeuh muhreeteemuh *mandar via marítima*

shirt kuhmeezuh *camisa*

shoe shop suhpuhtuhreeuh *sapataria*

shoes suhpahtoosh *sapatos* (m)

shop lohzhuh *loja*

to go shopping eer ahsh kongpruhsh *ir às compras*

276

short (length) koortoo/uh *curto/a*

short (height) baishoo/uh *baixo/a*

shortage shkuhsesh *escassez* (f)

shorts kuhlsoysh *calções* (m)

shoulders ongbroosh *ombros* (m)

to shout greetahr *gritar*

a show shpehtahkooloo *espectáculo*

to show mooshtrahr *mostrar*

shower doosh *duche* (m)

to shut fshahr *fechar*

shy teemeedoo/uh *tímido/a*

sick dooengt *doente* (m/f)

a sickness dooengsuh *doença*

side lahdoo *lado*

a sign seenahl *sinal* (m)

to sign uhseenahr *assinar*

signature uhseenuhtooruh *assinatura*

similar smelyangt *semelhante*

simple singplesh *simples*

sin pkahdoo *pecado*

since (May) dezhd (maioo) *desde (Maio)*

to sing kangtahr *cantar*

singer kangtor/uh *cantor/a*

single (person) soltayroo/uh *solteiro/a*

single (unique) ooneekoo/uh; soh *único/a; só*

single room kwartoo ingdeeveedwal *quarto individual* (m)

sister eermang *irmã* (f)

to sit sengtahrs *sentar-se*

size (of anything) tuhmuhnyoo *tamanho*

size (clothes) tuhmuhnyoo/noomroo *tamanho/número*

size (shoes) noomroo *número*

to ski skyahr *esquiar*

skin pehl *pele* (f)

sky sehoo *céu* (m)

to sleep doormeer *dormir*

sleeping bag sahkookuhmuh *saco-cama* (m)

sleeping car vuhgowkuhmuh *vagão-cama* (m)

sleeping pills kahlmangtesh puhruh doormeer *calmantes para dormir* (m)

sleepy kong sonoo *com sono*

slide (film) slaid/sdeeuhpoozeeteevoo *slide* (m)/*diapositivo*

slow/slowly lengtoo/uh; lengtuhmengt *lento/a; lentamente*

small pkenoo/uh *pequeno/a*

a smell shayroo *cheiro*

to smell shayrahr *cheirar*

to smile soorreer *sorrir*

to smoke foomahr *fumar*

soap suhboonet *sabonete* (m)

soccer footbohl *futebol* (m)

social sciences see-engsyuhsh soosyaish *ciências sociais* (f)

social welfare uhseeshtengsyuh soosyahl *assistência social* (f)

socialist sooseeuhleeshtuh *socialista* (m/f)

solid sohleedoo/uh *sólido/a*

some ahlgoong/ahlgoomuh *algum/alguma*

somebody/someone ahlgáy *alguém*

something ahlgoomuh koyzuh *alguma coisa*

sometimes ahzh vezesh *às vezes*

son feelyoo *filho*

song kangsõw *canção* (f)

soon sedoo *cedo*

I'm sorry.
deshkoolp
Desculpe.

sound song *som* (m)

south sool *sul* (m)

souvenir lengbrangsuh *lembrança*

souvenir shop lohzhuh de soovneersh *loja de souvenirs* (f)

space shpahsoo *espaço*

to speak fuhlahr *falar*

special shpesyahl *especial*

specialist shpesyuhleeshtuh *especialista*

speed vlooseedahd *velocidade* (f)

speed limit leemeet de vlooseedahd *limite de velocidade* (m)

spicy (hot) peekangt *picante*

sport deshportoo *desporto*

sportsperson deshpoorteeshtuh *desportista*

a sprain toorsdooruh *torcedura*

spring (season) preemuhvehruh *primavera*

square (adj) kwuhdrahdoo/uh *quadrado/a*

square (in town) prahsuh/lahrgoo *praça/largo*

stadium shtahdiw *estádio*

stage pahlkoo *palco*

stairway shkahduhsh *escadas* (f)

stamps seloosh *selos* (m)

standard (usual) stangdahrt/nohrmahl *standard/normal*

standard of living neevehl de veeduh *nível de vida* (m)

star shtreluh *estrela* (f)

to start koomsahr *começar*

station shtuhsõw *estação* (f)

stationers puhpluhreeuh *papelaria*

statue shtahtwuh *estátua*

to stay (remain) feekahr *ficar*

to steal rrobahr *roubar*

steep ingkleenahdoo/uh
inclinado/a

step dgrow degrau (m)

stomach shtomuhgoo estômago

stomachache
dor de shtomuhgoo
dor de estômago (f)

stone pehdruh pedra

stoned (drugged) droogahdoo,
uh kong oomuh pedrahduh
drogado; a com uma pedrada
(inf)

stop puhrahzhāy paragem (f)

to stop puhrahr parar

Stop!
pahr!
Pare!

stork sgonyuh cegonha

storm tengpeshtahd
tempestade (f)

story kongtoo conto

stove foogōw fogão

straight (direction) deeraytoo/uh
direito/a

strange shtruhnyoo/uh
estranho/a

stranger shtruhnyoo/uh
estranho/a

stream rreebayroo ribeiro

street rroouh rua

strength forsuh força

a strike grehv greve (f)

on strike grehv (shtahr áy)
greve (estar em)

string kohrduh corda

strong fohrt forte (m/f)

stubborn taymozoo/taymohzuh
teimoso/a

student shtoodangt
estudante

studio shtoodiw estúdio

stupid shtoopeedoo/uh
estúpido/a

style shteeloo estilo

subtitles lzhengduhsh legendas (f)

suburb sooboorbiw subúrbio

subway station shtuhsōw de
mehtroo estação de metro (f)

success sooseehsoo sucesso

to suffer soofrer sofrer

sugar uhsookahr açúcar (m)

suitcase mahluh mala

summer vrōw verão

sun sohl sol (m)

sunblock krehm prootehtor doo
sohl creme protector do sol (m)

sunburn kaymuhdooruh doo
sohl queimadura do sol (f)

sunglasses ohkooloozh de sohl
óculos de sol (m)

sunny shtahr sohl estar sol

sunrise uhmuhnyser
amanhecer (m)

sunset por doo sohl
pôr do sol (m)

Sure.
klahroo
Claro.

surfboard prangshuh de suhrf
prancha de surf (f)

surname uhpleedoo *apelido*

a surprise soorprezuh *surpresa*

to survive soobrveever
sobreviver

sweet dos *doce* (m)

to swim nuhdahr *nadar*

swimming nuhtuhsõw *natação* (f)

swimming pool peeshseenuh
piscina

swimsuit fahtoo de buhnyoo
fato de banho

sympathetic
kongpryengseevoo/uh
compreensivo/a

synthetic singtehteekoo/uh
sintético/a

syringe sring-guh *seringa*

T

table mezuh *mesa*

tail kowduh *cauda*

to take (away) lvahr *levar*

to take photographs teerahr
footoogruhfeeuhsh
tirar fotografias

to talk fuhlahr *falar*

tall ahltoo/uh *alto/a*

tampons tangpõysh *tampões* (m)

tasty suhboorozoo/
suhboorohzuh *saboroso/a*

tax ingposhtoo *imposto*

taxi stand prahsuh de
tahkseesh *praça de táxis* (f)

teacher proofsor/proofsoruh
professor/professora

teaching engseenoo *ensino*

team eekeepuh *equipa*

tear (crying) lahgreemuh
lágrima

to tear (rip) rruhzhgahr *rasgar*

technique tehkneekuh *técnica*

teeth dengtesh *dentes* (m)

telegram tlegruhmuh
telegrama (m)

telephone tlefohn *telefone* (m)

to telephone tlefoonahr *telefonar*

telescope tleshkohpiw
telescópio

television tleveezõw *televisão* (f)

to tell kongtahr *contar*

temperature (fever) fehbr *febre* (f)

temperature (weather)
tengpruhtooruh *temperatura*

temple tengploo *templo*

tennis tehneesh *ténis* (m)

tennis court kohrt de tehneesh
court de ténis (m)

tent tengduh *tenda*

terrible terreevehl *terrível*

to thank uhgruhdser *agradecer*

Thank you.
obreegahdoo/uh
Obrigado/a.

theatre lyuhtroo *teatro*

they elesh/ehluhsh *eles/elas*

thick grosoo/grohsuh *grosso/a*

thief luhdrôw *ladrão*

thin mahgroo/uh; feenoo/uh
magro/a; fino/a

to think pengsahr *pensar*

third tersayroo/uh *terceiro/a*

thirsty kong sed *com sede*

this (one) esht/ehshtuh *este/a*

thought pengsuhmengtoo
pensamento

throat guhrgangtuh *garganta*

ticket beelyet *bilhete* (m)

ticket collector rrveezor/uh
revisor/a

ticket machine mahkeenuh
doozh beelyetesh *máquina
dos bilhetes* (f)

ticket office beelytayruh
bilheteira

tide muhreh *maré* (f)

tight uhpertahdoo/uh
apertado/a

time tengpoo *tempo*

timetable orahriw *horário*

tin (can) lahtuh *lata*

tin opener ahbr-lahtuhsh
abre-latas (m)

tip (gratuity) goorzhetuh *gorjeta*

tired kangsahdoo/uh *cansado/a*

tissues lengsoozh de puhpehl
lenços de papel (m)

toad sahpoo *sapo*

toast toorrahduh *torrada*

tobacco tuhbahkoo *tabaco*

today oah *hoje*

together zhoongtoosh/uhsh
juntos/as

toilet paper puhpehl eezhee-
ohneekoo *papel higiénico* (m)

toilet kahzuh de buhnyoo *casa
de banho* (f)

tomorrow ahmuhnyang *amanhã*

tonight ehshtuh noyt *esta noite* (f)

too (as well) tangbay *também*

too much dmaish *demais*

tooth (front) dengt *dente* (m)

toothache dor de dengtesh
dor de dentes (f)

toothbrush shkuvuh de dengtesh
escova de dentes (f)

toothpaste pahshtuh de
dengtesh *pasta de dentes* (f)

torch (flashlight) langtehrnuh
lanterna

to touch tookahr *tocar*

tour shkoorsôw *excursão* (f)

tourist tooreeshtuh *turista* (m/f)

tourist information office
poshtoo de tooreezhmoo
posto de turismo

towards puhruh; ãy deerehsõw uh *para; em direcção a*

towel twalyuh *toalha*

tower torr *torre* (f)

toxic waste rrzeedwoosh tohkseekoosh *resíduos tóxicos* (m)

track (car-racing) peeshtuh de koorreeduhzh de kahrroosh; owtohdroomoo *pista de corridas de carros* (f); *autódromo*

track (footprints) pehgahduhsh *pegadas* (f)

track (sports) kangpoo; peeshtuh *campo; pista*

track (path) kuhmeenyoo *caminho*

traffic trahfgoo *tráfego*

traffic lights smahfooroosh *semáforos* (m)

trail (route) kuhmeenyoo *caminho*

train kongboyoo *comboio*

train station shtuhsõw de kongboyoosh *estação de comboios* (f)

tram eelehtreekoo *eléctrico*

transit lounge sahluh de shpehruh *sala de espera*

to translate truhdoozeer *traduzir*

to travel vyuhzhahr *viajar*

travel (agency) (uhzhengsyuhzh de) vyahzhãysh *(agência de) viagens* (f)

travel sickness engzhow *enjoo*

travel books leevroozh de vyazhãysh *livros de viagens* (m)

travellers cheques trahvlehrs shehkesh *traveller's cheques* (m)

tree ahrvoor *árvore* (f)

trek shkoorsõw *excursão* (f)

trendy (person) moodehrnoo/uh *moderno/a*

trip vyahzhãy *viagem* (f)

trousers kahlsuhsh *calças* (f)

truck kahmeeõw *camião*

trust kongfyangsuh *confiança*

to trust kongfyahr *confiar*

truth verdahd *verdade* (f)

to try proovahr *provar*

to try (to attempt) tengtahr *tentar*

T-shirt teeshuhrt *Tshirt* (f)

tune mloodeeuh *melodia*

Turn left/right.
veer ah shkerduh/deeraytuh *Vire à esquerda/direita.*

twice doouhsh vezesh *duas vezes* (f)

twin beds doouhsh kuhmuhsh *duas camas* (f)

to type shkrever ah mahkeenuh *escrever à máquina*

typical teepeekoo/uh *típico/a*

tyres pne-wsh *pneus* (m)

U

umbrella gwarduhshoovuh guarda-chuva (m)

to understand kongpryengder compreender

unemployment dzengpregou desemprego

unions singdeekahtoosh sindicatos (m)

universe ooneevehrsoo universo

university ooneeverseedahd universidade (f)

unleaded săy shoongboo sem chumbo

unsafe ingsegooroo/uh inseguro/a

until (June) uhteh (zhoonyoo) até (Junho)

unusual ingvoolgahr invulgar

up ăy seemuh; puhruh seemuh em cima; para cima

uphill engkohshtuh uhseemuh encosta acima

urgent oorzhengt urgente

useful ooteel útil

V

vacant vahgoo/uh; leevr vago/a; livre

vacation fehryuhsh férias (f)

vaccination vuhseenuh vacina

valley vahl vale (m)

valuable vuhleeozo/ vuhleeohzuh valioso/a

value (price) vuhlor valor (m)

vegetable lyoom/ohrtuhleesuh legume (m)/hortaliça

vegetarian vzhetuhreeuhnoo/ uh vegetariano/a

I'm vegetarian. so vzhetuhreeuhnoo/uh Sou vegetariano/a.

vein vayuh veia

venereal disease dwengsuh vnehryuh doença venérea

venue lookahl local (m)

very mwingtoo muito

video tape kahseht de veediw cassete de vídeo (f)

view (scenic) veeshtuh puhnooruhmeekuh vista panorâmica

village ahldayuh/poovoouhsŏw aldeia/povoação (f)

vine veedayruh videira

vineyard veenyuh vinha

virus veeroosh vírus (m)

visa veeshtoo visto

to visit veezeetahr visitar

voice vohsh voz (f)

volume vooloom volume (m)

to vote vootahr votar

W

Wait! shpehr *Espere!*

waiter engpregahdoo/uh de mezuh *empregado/a de mesa*

waiting room sahluh de shpehruh *sala de espera*

to walk angdahr/puhsyahr *andar/passear*

wall (inside) puhred *parede* (f)

wall (outside) mooroo *muro*

to want krer *querer*

war gehrruh *guerra*

wardrobe uhrmahriw/ gwarduhrropuh *armário* (m)/ *guarda-roupa* (m)

warm kengt *quente*

to warn uhveezahr *avisar*

to wash (something) luhvahr *lavar*

to wash (to bathe) toomahr buhnyoo *tomar banho*

washing machine mahkeenuh de luhvahr *máquina de lavar* (f)

watch rrlohzhiw *relógio*

to watch olyahr *olhar*

water ahgwuh *água*

water bottle guhrrahfuh de ahgwuh *garrafa de água*

waterfall kuhshkahtuh *cascata*

wave ongduh *onda*

way kuhmeenyoo *caminho*

Which way? ây ke deerehsõw? *Em que direcção?*

Way Out suheeduh *Saída*

we nohsh *nós*

weak frahkoo/uh *fraco/a*

wealthy rreekoo/uh *rico/a*

to wear veshteer *vestir*

weather tengpoo/kleemuh *tempo/clima* (m)

week smuhnuh *semana*

weekend fing de smuhnuh *fim de semana* (m)

to weigh pzahr *pesar*

weight pezoo *peso*

welcome bây-vingdoo/uh *bem-vindo/a*

welfare bây shtuhr *bem-estar* (m)

well bây *bem*

west ohehsht *oeste* (m)

wet moolyahdoo/uh *molhado/a*

what que ke

What time is it? ke ohruhsht sõw? *Que horas são?*

wheel rrohduh *roda*

when kwangdoo *quando*

ENGLISH – PORTUGUESE

When does it leave?
kwangdoo eh ke pahrt?
Quando é que parte?

where ongde *onde*

white brangkoo/uh *branco/a*

who käy *quem*

Who is it?
käy eh?
Quem é?

whole todoo *todo*

why poorke *porquê*

wide lahrgoo/uh *largo/a*

wife moolyehr *mulher* (f)

wild animal uhneemahl
sehlvahzhäy
animal selvagem (m)

to win guhnyahr *ganhar*

wind vengtoo *vento*

window zhuhnehluh *janela*

windscreen pahruhbreezuhsh
pára-brisas (m)

wine veenyoo *vinho*

winery uhdehguh *adega*

winter ingvehrnoo *Inverno*

to wish dzezhahr *desejar*

with kong *com*

within dengtroo *dentro*

without säy *sem*

woman moolyehr *mulher* (f)

wonderful muhruhveelyozoo/
muhruhveelyohzuh
maravilhoso/a

wood muhdayruh *madeira*

wool lang *lã*

word puhlahvruh *palavra*

work truhbahlyo *trabalho*

to work truhbuhlyahr *trabalhar*

work permit leesengsuh de
truhbahlyo
licença de trabalho (f)

world moongdoo *mundo*

worried preeohkoopahdoo/uh
preocupado/a

Don't worry!
nöw te preeohkoopsh!
Não te preocupes!

worth vuhlor *valor* (m)

wound freeduh *ferida*

to write shkrever *escrever*

writer shkreetor/shkreetoruh
escritor/escritora

wrong eerrahdoo/uh *errado/a*

Y

year uhnoo *ano*

yesterday ongtäy *ontem*

yet uhingduh *ainda*

you (pol) oo/uh snyor/snyoruh
o/a senhor/senhora

DICTIONARY

285

young zhohvǎy *jovem* (m/f)

youth (collective) zhoovengtood *juventude* (f)

youth hostel pozahduh duh zhoovengtood *pousada da juventude* (f)

zodiac zoodeeuhkoo *zodíaco*

zoo zhuhrding zwoolohzheekoo *jardim zoológico*

Generally, nouns ending in -o are masculine, while those ending in -a are feminine. In the dictionary that follows, the gender of nouns that don't follow this rule is indicated in parentheses after the noun.

For nouns that may be either masculine or feminine (as with nouns referring to people), the masculine then the feminine endings are given, as in:

adeptos/as uhdehptoosh/uhsh fans (of a team)

When a word changes according to whether it's masculine or feminine, both forms are given.

actor/actriz ahtor/ahtreezh actor

For adjectives, both masculine and feminine endings are given.

barulhento/a buhroolyengtoo/uh noisy

If the same ending is used for both masculine and feminine adjectives, this is indicated in parentheses.

alegre (m/f) uhlehgr happy

(See Grammar pages 25 and 26 for an explanation on gender.)

aberto/a uhbehrtoo/uh open

bordo uh bordoo aboard

borrecido/a uhboorrseedoo/ uh irritated

borto uhbortoo abortion

borto involuntário uhbortoo ingvooloongtahriw miscarriage

hraço uhbrahsoo a hug

bre-latas (m) ahbr-lahtuhsh tin opener

brir uhbreer to open

cabar uhkuhbahr to end

aceitar uhsaytahr to accept

acidente (m) uhseedengt accident

actor/actriz ahtor/ahtreezh actor

açúcar (m) uhsookahr sugar

adega uhdehguh wine cellar; lodge

adeptos/as uhdehptoosh/uhsh fans (of a team)

Adeus. uhde-wsh Goodbye.

287

adivinhar uhdeeveenyahr to guess

admirar uhdmeerahr to admire

advogado/a uhdvoogahdoo/uh lawyer

aeroporto uhehrohportoo airport

à frente ah frengt ahead

agência de notícias (f) uhzhengsyuh de nooteesyuhsh newsagency

agência de viagens (f) uhzhengsyuhzh de vyahzhāysh travel agency

agora (mesmo) uhgohruh (mezhmoo) (right) now

agradável uhgruhdahvehl friendly

agradecer uhgruhdser to thank

agressivo/a uhgreseevoo/uh aggressive

água (fria) ahgwuh (freeuh) (cold) water

agulha (de coser) (f) uhgoolyuh (de koozer) (sewing) needle

agulha (seringa) uhgoolyuh (sering-guh) needle (syringe)

ainda (não) uhingduh (nōw) (not) yet

ajuda uhzhooduh aid (help)

ajudar uhzhoodahr to help

ala direita ahluh deeraytuh right-wing

alcunha ahlkoonyuh nickname

aldeia ahldayuh village hamlet

aldrabice (f) ahldruhbees rip-off

alegre (m/f) uhlehgr happy

alergia uhlerzheeuh allergy

alergia ao pólen (f) uhlerzheeuh ow pohlāy hayfever

alfândega ahlfangdeguh customs

algum ahlgoong any/some

alguma coisa ahlgoomuh koyzuh something

almoço ahlmosoo lunch

almofada ahlmoofahduh pillow

alojamento uhloozhuhmengtoo accommodation

alto ahltoo loudly/peak/lump

alto/a ahltoo/uh high/tall

alucinar uhlooseenahr to hallucinate

alugar uhloogahr to rent

amador/a uhmuhdor/uh amateur

amanhã ahmuhnyang tomorrow

amanhecer (m) uhmuhnyser to dawn

amante (m/f) uhmangt lover

amar uhmahr to love

amável (m/f) uhmahvehl kind/affable

ambos/as angboosh/uhs both

amigo/a uhmeegoo/uh friend

A

analgésicos (m) uhnahlzhehzeekoosh painkillers

análise ao sangue (f) uhnahleez ow sang-g blood test

anarquista (m/f) uhnahrkeeshtuh anarchist

andar (m) angdahr storey

andar angdahr to walk

andar à boleia angdahr ah boolayuh to hitchhike

anedota uhndohtuh joke

anel (m) uhnehl ring (on linger); balcony/tier (theatre/stadium)

animal selvagem (m) uhneemahl sehlvahzhãy wild animal

aniversário uhneeversahriw birthday

ano uhnoo year

anteontem angteeongtãy day before yesterday

antes angtesh before; in the face of

antiguidades (f) angteegwidahdsh antiques

anúncio de emprego uhnoongsiw de engpregoo job advertisement

ao lado de ow lahdoo de beside

ao pé de ow peh de next to

apanhar uhpuhnyahr to take

apelido uhpleedoo surname

apertado/a uhpertahdoo/uh tight

apontar uhpongtahr to point

aposta uhpohshtuh a bet

aprender uhprengder to learn

apresentação (f) uhpresengtuhsõw presentation

aquecedor (m) uhkehsdor heater

aqui uhkee here

ar (m) ahr air

árbitro ahrbeetroo referee

ar condicionado (m) ahr kongdeesiwnahdoo air-conditioned

areia uhrayuh sand

armário uhrmahriw wardrobe

armazém de roupa (m) ahrmuhzãy de rropuh clothes store

arquitecto/a uhrkeetehtoo/uh architect

arquitectura uhrkeetehtooruh architecture

arte (f) ahrt art

artesanato uhrtzuhnahtoo crafts

artigos em pele (m) uhrteegooz ãy pehl leather goods

artista (m/f) uhrteeshtuh artist/musician/performer

artista de rua uhrteeshtuh de rroouh busker; street entertainer

árvore (f) ahrvoor tree

D
I
C
T
I
O
N
A
R
Y

às vezes ahzh vezesh sometimes

asas (f) ahzuhsh wings

asmático/a uhzhmahteekoo/uh asthmatic

assaltar uhsahltahr to rob

assédio uhsehdiw harrassment

assinar uhseenahr to sign

assinatura uhseenuhtooruh signature

até (Junho) uhteh (zhoonyoo) until (June)

a tempo uh tengpoo on time

atendedor de chamadas (m) uhtengdedor de shuhmahduhsh answering machine

atmosfera uhtmooshfehruh atmosphere

atrás uhtrahzh behind

atrás de uhtrahzh de at the back (behind)

atraso uhtrahzoo delay

através uhtruhvehsh across/through

aula owluh class (education)

autocarro owtohkahrroo local/city bus

auto-estrada (f) owtohshtrahduh motorway (tollway)

autorização (f) owtooreezuhsõw authorization/permission

avenida uhvneeduh avenue

avião uhveeõw aeroplane

avisar uhveezahr to warn

avó (f) uhvoh grandmother

avô (m) uhvo grandfather

azeite (m) uhzayt olive oil

azeitonas (f) uhzaytonuhsh olives

B

bagagem (f) buhgahzhãy luggage

baixo/a baishoo/uh low/short

(em) baixo ãy baishoo below

balde (m) bahld bucket

banco bangkoo bank

bandeira bangdayruh flag

banho buhnyoo bath

baptismo bahteezhmoo baptism

bar (m) bahr a bar

barato/a buhrahtoo/uh cheap

barco bahrkoo boat

barulhento/a buhroolyengtoo/uh noisy

barulho buhroolyoo noise

bastante buhshtangt enough

bateria buhtreeuh battery (car)

beber beber to drink

bebida bebeeduh a drink

beijar bayzhahr to kiss

beijo bayzhoo kiss

belo/a behloo/uh beautiful/
handsome

bem bãy well

bem-vindo bãy-vingdoo
welcome

Bestial!
bshteeahl
Great/Cool! (coll)

biblioteca beebliwtehkuh library

bicicleta beeseeklehtuh bicycle

bilhete (de ida)
bruelyet (de eeduh)
(one-way) ticket

bilhete de ida e volta (m)
beelyet de eeduh ee vohltuh
return ticket

Bilhete de Identidade (m)
beelyet deedengteeduhd
identification card

bilheteira
beelytayruh
ticket office

biodegradável
beeohdegruhdahvehl
biodegradable

Boa sorte!
bouh sohrt
Good luck!

Boa(s) tarde(s).
bouh(sh) tahrd(sh)
Good afternoon.

boca bokuh mouth

bocado bookahdoo piece

bola bohluh ball

bolso bolsoo pocket

bom bong good

Bom dia.
bong deeuh
Good morning.

bomba (de puxar) (f) bongbuh
(de pooshahr) pump

bondoso/a bongdozoo/
bongdohzuh kind/caring

bonito/u booneetoo/uh pretty

a bordo uh bordoo aboard

botas (f) bohtuhsh boots

botões (m) bootõysh buttons

braço brahsoo arm

branco/a brangkoo/uh white

brilhante breelyangt brilliant

bússola boosooluh compass

C

cabeça kuhbesuh head

(dor de) cabeça (f) (dor de)
kuhbesuh headache

cabelo kuhbeloo hair

cabina (de telefone) (f)
kahbeenuh (de tlefohn)
phone box

cabra kahbruh goat; bitch (slang)

cacifos de bagagem (m)
kuhseefoozh de buhgahzhãy
luggage lockers

cada kuhduh each

cadeado kuhdyahdoo padlock

cadeira kuhdayruh chair

caderno kuhdehrnoo notebook

caixa kaishuh box/carton/cashier

caixa do correio (f) kaishuh doo koorrayoo mailbox

caixa-forte (f) kaishuh fohrt safe (n)

calças (f) kahlsuhsh trousers

calções (m) kahlsōysh shorts

calmantes para dormir (m) kahlmangtesh puhruh doormeer sleeping pills

calor (m) kuhlor heat

cama kuhmuh bed

cama de casal (f) kuhmuh de kuhzahl double bed

camada de ozono (f) kuhmahduh de ozonoo ozone layer

câmara kuhmuhruh camera

cambiar moeda kangbyahr mweduh to exchange

câmbio de moeda (m) kangbiw de mweduh exchange

caminho kuhmeenyoo (foot)path

camioneta (inter-cidades) (f) kahmiwnehtuh (ingtehrseedahdesh) bus (intercity)

camisa kuhmeezuh shirt

camisola kuhmeezohluh jumper (sweater)

campeonatos (m) kangpiwnahtoosh championships

campo kangpoo countryside

canção (f) kangsōw song

cancelar kangslahr to cancel

cansado/a kangsahdoo/uh tired

cantor/cantora kangtor/ kangtoruh singer

cão kōw dog

cara kahruh face

caro/a kahroo/uh expensive

carro kahrroo car

carta kahrtuh letter

carta de condução (f) kahrtuh de kongdoosōw driving licence

cartão de crédito kuhrtōw de krehdeetoo credit card

cartão de embarque (m) kuhrtōw dengbahrk boarding pass

cartão de telefone (m) kuhrtōw de tlefohn phonecard

cartas (f) kahrtuhsh cards

carteirade de senhora (f) kuhrtayruh de snyoruh handbag

casa kahzuh house

casa de banho (f) kahzuh de buhnyoo bathroom/toilets

casaco kuhzahkoo coat

casal (m) kuhzahl pair (a couple)

casamento kuhzuhmengtoo
marriage

cascata kuhshkahtuh waterfall

castelo kuhshtehloo castle

castigar kuhshteegahr to punish

catedral (f) kuhtdrahl cathedral

cauda kowduh tail

cedo sedoo early/soon

cego/a sehgoo/uh blind

cem say a hundred

centímetro sengteemtroo
centimetre

central do telefone (f) sengtrahl
doo tlefohn telephone office

centro de emprego sengtroo
dengpregoo job centre

cerâmica sruhmeekuh pottery

cerca serkuh fence

certidão de nascimento (f)
serteedõw de
nuhshseemengtoo birth
certificate

cesto seshtoo basket

céu (m) sehoo sky

*chamada interurbana/
internacional* (f) shuhmahduh
ingtehroorbuhnuh/
ingternuhsiwnahl
long distance call

champô shangpo shumpoo

chão shõw floor

charcutaria shuhrkootuhreeuh
delicatessen

chave (f) shahv key

chávena shahvnuh cup

Já chega!
zhah sheguh!
Enough!

chefe (m/f) shehf
leader/boss/chief

chefe de secção (m/f)
shehf de sehksõw
manager

chegadas (f) shgahduhsh
arrivals

chegar shgahr to arrive

cheio/a shayoo/uh full *cheirar*
shayrahr to smell

cheiro shayroo a smell

chucha shooshuh dummy/
pacifier

chuva shoovuh rain

cidadania seeduhduhneeuh
citizenship

cidade (f) seedahd city

cidade antiga (f) seedahd
angteeguh old city

ciências (f) see-engsyuhsh
science

cientista (m/f) see-engteeshtuh
scientist

cigarro seegahrroo cigarette

(em) cima ãy seemuh above

cinto de segurança (m) singtoo
de sgoorangsuh seatbelt

cinzeiro singzayroo ashtray

cinzento singzengtoo grey

ciumento/a
siwmengtoo/uh jealous

Claro.
klahroo
Sure.

claro/a klahroo/uh light (clear)

classe social (f) klahs soosyahl
class (social)

clima (m) kleemuh weather

cobertor (m) koobertor blanket

cocaína kohkuheenuh cocaine

código postal (m) kohdeegoo
pooshtahl postcode

coelho kwuhlyoo rabbit

colar (m) koolahr necklace

colchão koolshōw mattress

colega (m/f) koolehguh colleague

colina kooleenuh hill

com kong with

começar koomsahr begin

comer koomer to eat

comerciante (m/f)
koomerseeangt shop owner

comerciante de hortaliça (m/f)
koomerseeangt de
ortuhleesuh greengrocer

comichão (f) koomeeshōw itch

(ter) comichão (ter)
koomeeshōw to itch

comida koomeeduh food

como komoo how

companheiro/a
kongpuhnyayroo/uh
companion

companhia kongpuhnyeeuh
company

comprar kongprahr to buy

compreender kongpree-engder
to realise/understand

compreensivo/a
kongpryengseevoo/uh
sympathetic

comprido/a
kongpreedoo/uh long

comprimido
kongpreemeedoo pill

concentração (f)
kongsengtruhsōw
rally/concentration

concerto kongsertoo concert/gig

concordar kongkoordahr to
agree

Não) concordo.
(nōw) kongkohrdoo
I (don't) agree.

conduzir kongdoozeer to drive

confiança kongfyangsuh trust/
confidence

confiar kongfyahr to trust

confirmar (uma reserva)
kongfeermahr
(oomuh rrzehrvuh)
to confirm (a booking)

PORTUGUESE – ENGLISH

confortável kongfoortahvehl comfortable

conhecer koonyser to know (someone)

conselho kongselyoo advice

constipação (f) kongshteepuhsöw cold

construir kongshtrooer to build

conta kongtuh bill (account)

contar kongtahr to count/tell

conto kongtoo story

contos (m) kongtoosh short stories

contra kongtruh against

conhtratar köngtruhtahr to hire

copo kohpoo glass

cor (f) kor colour

coração kooruhsöw heart

corda kohrduh rope/string

corpo korpoo body

correio (azul) (m) koorrayoo (uhzool) (express) mail

correio registado koorrayoo rrezheeshtahdoo registered mail

correios (m) koorrayoosh post office

correr koorrer to run

cortar koortahr to cut

coser koozer to sew

costa kohshtuh seaside

costas (f) kohshtuhsh back (body)

cozinha koozeenyuh kitchen

cozinhar koozeenyahr to cook

creme protector do sol (m) krehm prootehtor doo sohl sunblock

criança kreeansuh child

crianças (f) kreeangsuhsh children

crítica kreeteekuh review/ criticism

cru/crua kroo/kroouh raw

cruz (f) kroosh cross (religious)

culpa koolpuh fault (someone's)

cupão koopow coupon

currículo koorreekooloo resumé

curto/a koortoo/uh short (length)

D

dados (m) dahdoosh dice/die/data

dança dangsuh dancing

dançar dangsahr to dance

daqui a duhkee uh within

dar dahr to give

dar-se conta dahrs kongtuh to realise

data dahtuh date (time)

data de nascimento (f) dahtuh de nuhshseemengtoo date of birth

295

decidir dseedeer to decide

décimo/a dehseemoo/uh tenth

dedo dedoo finger

deficiente (m/f) dfeesee-engt disabled

degrau (m) dgrow step

delirante dleerangt delirious

demais dmaish too much

demonstração (f) dmongshtruhsōw demonstration

dentes (m) dengtesh teeth

dentista (m/f) dengteeshtuh dentist

dentro dengtroo inside

dentro de (uma hora) dengtroo de (oomuh ohruh) within (an hour)

departamento de vendas (m) dpuhrtuhmengtoo de vengduhsh sales department

depois de dpoyzh de after

depois de amanhã dpoyzh de ahmuhnyang day after tomorrow

depósito de bagagens (m) dpohzeetoo de buhgahzhãysh left luggage

depressa deprehsuh fast/quickly

descansar deshkangsahr to rest

descanso deshkangsoo rest (relaxation)

descendente deshsengdengt descendent

descobrir deshkoobreer to discover

desconto deshkongtoo discount

descrição do trabalho (f) deshkreesōw doo truhbahlyoo job description

Desculpe. deshkoolp Excuse me; I'm sorry.

desde (Maio) dezhd (maioo) since (May)

desemprego dzengpregoo unemployment

desenho dzuhnyoo design

desigualdade (f) dzeegwaldahd inequality

desistir dzeeshteer to quit

desodorizante (m) dzodooreezangt deodorant

despedimento deshpdeemengtoo dismissal

despertador deshpertuhdor alarm clock

desporto deshportoo sport

destino dshteenoo destination/destiny/fate

destruir deshtrwir to destroy

desvantagem (f) deshvangtahzhãy disadvantage

detalhe (m) dtahly detail

PORTUGUESE – ENGLISH

Deus de-wsh God

dever dver to owe; must; duty

dia (m) deeuh day

dia de anos (m) deeuh duhnoosh birthday

diante de diangt de in front of

diariamente deeahryuhmengt daily

diário deeuliriw diary

dicionário deesiwnahriw dictionary

diferente doefrengt different

difícil deefeeseel difficult

dinheiro deenyayroo money

directo/a deerehtoo/uh direct

director/directora Jeerehtor/ deerehtoruh director/manager

direita deeraytuh right (not left)

direito/a deeraytoo/uh straight (direction)

direitos civis (m) deeraytoosh seeveesh civil rights

direitos humanos (m) deeraytooz oomuhnoosh human rights

discriminação (f) deeshkreemeenuhsõw discrimination

discussão (f) deeshkoosõw quarrel/discussion

discutir deeshkooteer to argue/to discuss

disparar deeshpuhrahr to shoot

distribuidor/distribuidora deeshtreebwidor/ deeshtreebwidoruh distributor

divertido/a deevertecdoo/uh entertaining/fun

divertimento deeverteemengtoo entertainment

divertir-se deeverteers to have fun; enjoy oneself

dizer deezer to say

doce dos sweet

doença dooengsuh disease/illness

doença venérea dwengsuh vnehryuh venereal disease

doente dooengt ill; patient (adj)

doido/a doydoo/uh mad

doloroso/a dooloorozoo/uh painful

domingo dooming-goo Sunday

dono/a donoo/uh owner

dor (f) dor a pain

dor de dentes (f) dor de dengtesh toothache

dor de estômago (f) dor de shtomuhgoo stomachache

dormir doormeer to sleep

dramático/a druhmahteekoo/uh dramatic

droga drohguh dope (drugs)

drogado/a droogahdoo/uh stoned (drugged)

duas camas (f) doouhsh kuhmuhsh twin beds

duas semanas (f) doouhsh smuhnuhsh fortnight

duas vezes (f) doouhsh vezesh twice

duche (m) doosh shower

duplo dooploo double

duro/a dooroo/uh hard

E

e ee and

ecrã (m) ekrang screen

educação (f) eedookuhsõw education

egoísta (m/f) eegooeeshtuh selfish

ela ehluh she

ele el he

eléctrico eelehtreekoo tram

eleições (f) eelaysõysh elections

elas/eles ehluhsh/elesh they

elevador (m) eelvuhdor lift (elevator)

em ãy on

embaixada engbaishahduh embassy

embarcar engbuhrkahr to board (ship, etc)

embrulho engbroolyoo package

ementa eemengtuh menu

emergência eemerzhengsyuh emergency

empada engpahduh pie

empregado/a engpregahdoo/uh employee

empregado/a de mesa engpregahdoo/uh de mezuh waiter

empurrar engpoorrahr to push

encantador/encantadora engkangtuhdor/ engkangtuhdoruh charming

encher engsher to fill

encontrar engkongtrahr to find

encontrar-se com alguém engkongtrahrs kong ahlgãy to meet someone

encontro engkongtroo date (appointment)

encosta acima engkohshtuh uhseemuh uphill

endereço engdresoo address

enfermeira engfermayruh nurse

engano eng-guhnoo mistake

enjoado/a engzhooahdoo/uh seasick

enjoo engzhow travel sickness

ensino engseenoo teaching

entrada engtrahduh admission

entrar engtrahr to enter

entre engtr among/between

entrevista engtreveeshtuh interview

envelope (m) engvlohp envelope

envergonhado/a
engvergoonyahdoo/uh
embarassed

enviar engvyahr to send

enxaqueca engshuhkehkuh
migraine

epiléptico/a
eepeelehteekoo/uh epileptic

equipa eekeepuh team

equipamento eekeepuhmengtoo
equipment

errado/a eerrahdoo/uh wrong

ervas (f) ehrvuhsh herbs

escadas (f) shkahduhsh stairway

escalar shkuhlahr to climb

escassez (f) shkuhsesh shortage

escola shkohluh school

escola pré-primária shkohluh
prehpreemahryuh
kindergarten

escolher shkoolyer to choose

escova (de cabelo) (f) shkovuh
(de kuhbeloo) (hair)brush

escova de dentes (f) shkovuh de
dengtesh toothbrush

escrever shkrever to write

escrever à máquina shkrever ah
mahkeenuh to type

escritor/escritora shkreetor/
shkreetoruh writer

escritório shkreetohriw office

escultura shkooltooruh sculpture

escuro/a shkooroo/uh dark

esferográfica
shfehrohgrahfeekuh
pen (ballpoint)

esfregaço shfregahsoo pap
smear

espaço shpahsoo space

especial shpesyahl special

especialista (m/f)
shpesyuhleeshtuh specialist

espécies em perigo de extinção (f)
shpehsee-esh áy preegoo
de shtingsőw
endangered species

espectáculo
shpehtahkooloo
a show

espelho shpuhlyoo mirror

esperar shpehruh to wait/hope

Espere!
shpehr!
Wait!

espumante (m) shpoomangt
champagne

esquecer-se shkehsers to forget

esquerda shkerduh left (not right)

(de) esquerda de shkerduh
left-wing

esqui (m) skee skiing

esquiar skyahr to ski

esquina shkeenuh corner

F

Está bem.
shtah bãy
OK.

Está lá/sim?
shtah lah/sing?
Hello! (answering telephone)

estação (f) shtuhsõw station

estação de autocarros (f)
shtuhsõw de
owtohkahrroosh bus station

estacionar shtuhsiwnahr to park

estádio shtahdiw stadium

estado civil (m) shtahdoo
seeveel marital status

esta noite (f) ehshtuh noyt
tonight

estar bêbedo shtahr bebuhdoo
to be drunk

estar sol shtahr sohl sunny

esta semana ehshtuh smuhnuh
this week

estátua shtahtwuh statue

este (m) ehsht east

este/a esht/ehshtuh this (one)

esteira shtayruh mat

estilo shteeloo style

estojo de primeiros socorros (m)
shtozhoo de preemayroosh
sookohrroosh first-aid kit

estômago shtomuhgoo stomach

estrada (principal) shtrahduh
(pringseepahl) (main) road

estrangeiro/a
shtranzhayroo/uh
foreign

estranho/a shtruhnyoo/uh
strange/stranger

estrelas (f) shtreluhsh stars

estudante (m/f) shtoodangt
student

estúdio shtoodiw studio

estúpido/a shtoopeedoo/uh
stupid

eutanásia e-wtuhnahzyuh
euthanasia

exacto/a eezahtoo/uh right
(correct)

excursão (guiada) shkoorsõw
(geeahduh) (guided) trek/tour

exemplo eezengploo example

exibir eezeebeer to exhibit

exploração (f) shplooruhsõw
exploitation

exposição (f) shpoozeesõw
exhibition

expresso shprehsoo express

F

fábrica fahbreekuh factory

faca fahkuh knife

fácil fahseel easy

falar fuhlahr to speak/talk

falésia fuhlehzyuh cliff

família fuhmeelyuh family

farmácia fuhrmahsyuh chemist (pharmacy)

fato de banho fahtoo de buhnyoo swimsuit

fazer fuhzer to make

fazer a barba fuhzer uh bahrbuh to shave

fazer uma chamada fuhzer oomuh shuhmahduh to telephone

febre (f) fehbr fever/temperature

fechado/a fshahdoo/uh closed

fechadura fshuhdooruh lock

fechar fshahr to close/lock

feito (de) faytoo (de) made (of)

feito à mão faytoo ah mōw handmade

feliz fleesh happy

feriado fryahdoo holiday

férias (f) fehryuhsh holidays

ferida freeduh injury

festa fehshtuh party (celebration)

festejar feshtezhahr to celebrate

ficar feekahr to stay (remain)

ficar atrás feekahr uhtrahsh to be left (behind/over)

fila feeluh queue

filho/a feelyoo/uh son/daughter

filme feelm film (movie)

filme (a preto e branco) (m) feelm (uh pretoo ee brangkoo) (B&W) film

(com) filtro kong feeltroo filtered

fim fing end

fim de semana (m) fing de smuhnuh weekend

fio dental (m) feeoo dengtahl dental floss

flor (f) flor flower

floresta (protegidu) floorehshtuh (prootezheeduh) (protected forest)

fogão foogōw stove

fogo fogoo fire

folha folyuh sheet (of paper)

fora fohruh outside/abroad

força forsuh strength

forma fohrmuh shape

formiga foormeeguh ant

forte (m/f) fohrt strong

fósforos (m) fohshfooroosh matches

fotografia footoogruhfeeuh photo/photography

fraco/a frahkoo/uh weak

fralda frahlduh nappy (diaper)

frango frang-goo chicken

franquia frangkeeuh postage

frase (f) frahz sentence (words)

à frente ah frengt ahead

(em) frente āy frengt opposite (space)

frigorífico freegooreefeekoo refrigerator

fronha fronyuh pillowcase

fronteira frongtayruh border

fundo foongdoo bottom (place)

furgoneta foorgoonehtuh van

furo fooroo puncture (car)

futuro footooroo future

G

ganhar guhnyahr to earn

gargalhada guhrguhlyahduh laugh

garganta guhrgangtuh throat

garrafa guhrrahfuh bottle

gasolina guhzooleenuh petrol

gasolina com chumbo (f) guhzooleenuh kong shoongboo leaded petrol (gas)

gato gahtoo cat

gelado zhelahdoo icecream

gelar zhelahr to freeze

gelo zheloo ice

gémeos (m) zhehmiwsh twins

gentes (f) zhengtesh people

geral zherahl general

gerente (m/f) zherengt manager

gilete (f) zheeleht razor

gordo/a gordoo/uh fat

gorjeta goorzhetuh tip (gratuity)

gostar de gooshtahr de to like

governo goovernoo government

grama gruhmuh gram

grande grangd big

grandes armazéns (m) grangdez ahrmuhzäysh department stores

gravação (f) gruhvuhsöw recording

grávida grahveeduh pregnant

greve (f) grehv a strike

gritar greetahr to shout

grosso/a grosoo/uh thick

grupo sanguíneo groopoo sang-gwiniw blood group

guarda-chuva (m) gwarduhshoovuh umbrella

guarda-roupa (m) gwarduhrropuh closet/ cloakroom

guerra gehrruh war

guia geeuh guidebook

guia (m/f) geeuh guide (person)

guia audio (m) geeuh owdiw guide (audio)

guião geeöw script

H

há (bocado) ah (bookahdoo) (a while) ago

haxixe (m) ahsheesh hash

302

PORTUGUESE – ENGLISH

hoje ozh today

homem (m) ohmãy man

hora do almoço (f) ohruh doo ahlmosoo lunchtime

horário orahriw timetable

horrível (m/f) orreevehl horrible

hospital (m) ohshpeetahl hospital

I

idade (f) eedahd age

identificação (f) eedengteefeekuhsõw identification

igreja eegruhzhuh church

igualdade (f) eegwaldahd equality

ilha eelyuh island

imigração (f) eemeegruhsõw immigration

impedir ingpdeer to prevent

imposto (sobre os rendimentos) (m) ingposhtoo (sobr osh rrengdeemengtoosh) (income) tax

inclusive ingkloozeeveh included

incompreensível ingkongpree-engseevehl incomprehensible

indigestão (f) ingdeezheshtõw indigestion

inglês ing-glesh English

injecçao (t) ingzhehsõw injection

injectar-se ingzhehtahrs to inject (yourself)

insecto ingsehtoo bug

inseguro/a ingsegooroo/uh unsafe

instrutor/instrutora ingshtrootor/ ingshtrootoruh instructor

interessante ingtresangt interesting

Inverno ingvahrnoo winter

invulgar ingvoolgahr unusual

ir eer to go

ir às compras eer ahs kongpruhsh to go shopping

irmã eermang sister

irmão eermõw brother

irritação (f) eerreetuhsõw rash/irritation

isqueiro eeshkayroo lighter

itinerário eeteenerahriw itinerary

J

já zhah already

janela zhuhnehluh window

jantar (m) zhangtahr dinner

jardim de infância (m) zhuhrding de ingfangsyuh childminding

jardim zoológico (m) zhuhrding zwoolohzheekoo zoo

jardin (m) zhuhrding garden

jardinagem (f) zhuhrdeenahzhãy gardening

jarro zhahrroo jar

joalharia zhwuhlyuhreeuh jewellery

joelho zhwuhlyoo knee

jogadores zhooguhdorsh players (sports)

jogar zhoogahr to play (a game)

jogo zhogoo game (boardgame or sport)

jornais (m) zhoornaish newspapers

jornal (m) zhoornahl newspaper

jornalista (m/f) zhoornuhleeshtuh journalist

jovem (m/f) zhohváy young

juiz/juíza zhweesh/zhooeezuh judge

juntos/as zhoongtoosh/uhsh together

justiça zhooshteesuh justice

juventude (f) zhoovengtood youth (collective)

L

lã lang wool

lábios (m) lahbiwsh lips

lado lahdoo side

ladrão/ladra luhdrôw/lahdruh thief

lago lahgoo lake

lágrima lahgreemuh tear (crying)

lama luhmuh mud

lamentar luhmengtahr to regret

lâminas da gilete (f) luhmeenuhzh duh zheeleht razor blades

lâmpada langpuhduh light bulb

lanterna langtehrnuh torch (flashlight)

lápis (m) lahpeesh pencil

largo (*principal*) lahrgoo (pringseepahl) (main) square (in town)

largo/a lahrgoo/uh wide

lata lahtuh tin (can)

lavandaria luhvangduhreeuh launderette

lavar luhvahr to wash (something)

laxante (m) luhshangt laxatives

leal (m/f) lyal loyal

legendas (f) lzhengduhsh subtitles

legume (m) lgoom vegetable

lei (f) lay law

leite (m) layt milk

lembrança lengbrangsuh souvenir

lembrar-se lengbrahrs to remember

lençol (m) lengsohl sheet (bed)

lenços de papel (m) lengsoozh de puhpehl tissues

lenha luhnyuh firewood

L

lentamente lengtuhmengt slowly

lento/a lengtoo/uh slow

leque (m) lehk fan (hand-held)

ler ler to read

lésbica lehzhbeekuh lesbian

levar lvahr to carry/take

leve lehv light (adj)

licença leesengsuh permit

licença de trabalho (f) leesengsuh de truhbahlyo work permit

liceu (m) leese-w high school

lidar com alguém leedahr kong ahlgãy to deal (with people)

ligadura leeguhdooruh bandage

lilás leelahsh purple

limite de velocidade (m) leemeet de vlooseedahd speed limit

limpo/a lingpoo/uh clean

lindo/a lingdoo/uh beautiful

língua (f) ling-gwuh language

linha leenyuh line

linha de comboio (f) leenyuh de kongboiw railroad

lista de telefone (f) leeshtuh de tlefohn phone book

livraria leevruhreeuh bookshop

livre leevr free (not bound)

livrete (m) leevret car registration

livro leevroo book

livros de viagens (m) leevroozh de vyazhũysh travel (books)

lixo leeshoo rubbish

local (m) lookahl venue; local (adj)

localização (f) lookuhleezuhsõw location

loja lohzhuh shop

loja de artigos regionais (f) lohzhuh de uhrteegoosh rrezhiwnaish souvenir shop

loja de fotografias (f) lohzhuh de footoogruhfeeuhsh camera shop

loja de roupa lohzhuh de rropuh clothes store

lombriga (f) longbreeguh worm

longe longzh far

louco/a lokoo/uh crazy

lua loouh moon

lugar (m) loogahr seat/place

lugar de nascimento (m) loogahr de nuhshseemengtoo place of birth

luta lootuh fight

lutar lootahr to fight

luxo looshoo luxury

luz (f) loosh light

M

macaco muhkahkoo monkey

machismo muhsheezhmoo sexism

maço de tabaco/cigarros (m) mahsoo de tuhbahkoo/ seegahrroosh packet (of cigarettes)

madeira muhdayruh wood

madrugada muhdroogahduh dawn

mãe (f) mãy mother

maioria mayooreeuh majority

maior parte (f) mayohr pahrt majority

mais maish more

mal mahl wrong

Fiz mal.
feesh mahl
I'm wrong. (my fault)

mal passado mahl puhsahdoo rare (meat)

mala mahluh bag/suitcase

maluco/a muhlookoo/uh crazy

Mamã muhmang Mum

mandar via marítima mangdahr veeuh muhreeteemuh to ship

mandato mangdahtoo term of office

manhã muhnyang morning

mão (f) mõw hand

mapa (de estradas) (m) mahpuh (de shtrahduhsh) (road) map

maquilhagem (f) muhkeelyahzhãy make-up

máquina mahkeenuh machine

máquina de lavar (f) mahkeenuh de luhvahr washing machine

máquina dos bilhetes (f) mahkeenuh doozh beelyetesh ticket machine

mar (m) mahr sea

maré (f) muhreh tide

marido muhreedoo husband

mas muhsh but

matar muhtahr to kill

mau/má mow/mah bad

medicamento mdeekuhmengtoo drug (medicine)

medicina mdeeseenuh medicine

médico/a mehdeekoo/uh doctor

meditação (f) mdeetuhsõw meditation

medo medoo fear

meia-noite (f) mayuh-noyt midnight

meio-ambiente (m) mayoo angbee-engt environment

meio-dia (m) mayoodeeuh noon

mel (m) mehl honey

melhor mlyohr best

melodia mloodeeuh tune

membro/a mengbroo/uh member

menos menoosh less

mensagem (f) mengsahzhãy message

menstruação (f) mengshtrwuhsõw menstruation

mente (f) mengt mind

mentir mengteer to lie

mentiroso/a mengteerozoo/uh liar

(de) mentol (cigarros) de mengtohl (seegahrroosh) menthol (cigarettes)

mercado merkahdoo market

mergulho mergoolyoo diving

mês (m) mesh month

mesa mezuh table

mesmo/a mezhmoo/uh same

mesquita meshkeetuh mosque

metade (f) mtahd half

meteorito mtiwreetoo meteor

metro mehtroo metre

milhão meelyõw million

milímetro meeleemtroo millimetre

minuto meenootoo a minute

miúdo meeoodoo boy

mochila moosheeluh backpack

moderno/a moodehrnoo/uh trendy (person); modern

moedas (f) mwehduhsh coins

mola mohluh spring (coil)

molhado/a moolyahdoo/uh wet

monge (m) mongzh monk

montanha mongtuhnyuh mountain

monumento moonoomengtoo monument

morada moorahduh address

morar moorahr to live (somewhere)

mordedura moordedooruh bite

morrer moorrer to die

morte (f) mohrt death

morto/a mortoo/uh dead

mosca moshkuh fly

mostrar mooshtrahr to show

mota mohtuh motorcycle

motor (m) mootoor engine

mudar moodahr to change

mudo/a moodoo/uh mute

muitas vezes mwingtuhsh vezesh often

muito mwingtoo very

muito/a mwingtoo/uh a lot

muitos/as mwingtoosh/uhsh many

mulher (f) moolyehr woman/wife

multa mooltuh a fine

multibanco moolteebungkoo automatic teller machine (ATM)

mundo moongdoo world

muralhas (f) moorahlyuhsh city walls

muro mooroo wall (outside)

músculo mooshkooloo muscle

museu (m) mooze-w museum

música moozeekuh music

músico/a moozeekoo/uh musician

N

nada nahduh nothing

nadar nuhdahr to swim

namorado/a nuhmoorahdoo/uh boyfriend/girlfriend

namorar nuhmoorahr to chat up

não nõw no

nariz (m) nuhreesh nose

natação (f) nuhtuhsõw swimming

natureza nuhtoorezuh nature

navalha nuhvahlyuh penknife

necessário/a nsesahriw/yuh necessary

necessitar nseseetahr to need

negar ngahr to deny

negociar ngoosyahr to deal (business)

negócios (m) ngohsiwsh business

nem nãy neither

nenhum/nenhuma nenyoong/nenyoomuh none

neto/a nehtoo/uh grandchild

nevoeiro nvwayroo fog

noite (f) noyt evening/night

noivo/a noyvoo/uh fiancé/fiancée

nome (m) nom name

nome de baptismo (m) nom de bahteezhmoo Christian name

normal nohrmahl ordinary

norte (m) nohrt north

nós nohsh we

notas (de banco) (f) nohtuhsh (de bangkoo) (bank)notes

noticiário nooteeseeahriw current affairs

notícias (f) nooteesyuhsh news

novo/a novoo/nohvuh new

nublado/a nooblahdoo/uh cloudy

número noomroo size (clothes/shoes)

número do passaporte (m) noomroo doo pahsuhpohrt passport number

número do quarto noomroo doo kwartoo room number

números (m) noomroosh figures

nunca noongkuh never

nuvem (f) noovãy cloud

O

objectiva ohbzhehteevuh lens

Obrigado/a.
obreegahdoo/uh
Thank you.

óbvio/a ohbviw/uh obvious

óculos de sol (m) ohkooloozh de sohl sunglasses

ocupado/a ohkoopahdoo/uh busy

oeste (m) ohehsht west

Olá.
olah
Hello.

óleo ohliw oil (cooking)

olhar olyahr to look/watch

olho olyoo eye

ombros (m) ongbroosh shoulders

onde ongde where

ontem ongtãy yesterday

operação (f) ohpruhsõw operation

operador/operadora ohpruhdor/ ohpruhdoruh operator

opinião (f) opeeneeõw opinion

oportunidade (f) ohpoortooneedahd chance

óptimo ohteemoo excellent

orelhas (f) ooruhlyuhsh ears

ou o or

(de) ouro doroo of gold

Outono otonoo autumn (fall)

outra vez otruh vezh again

outro/a otroo/uh other

ouvir oveer to hear/listen

P

padaria pahduhreeuh bakery

padre (m) pahdr priest

pagamento puhguhmengtoo payment

pagar puhgahr to pay

página pahzheenuh page

pai (m) pai father

pais (m) paish parents

país (m) puheesh country

palácio puhlahsiw palace

palavra puhlahvruh word

pão põw bread

papá (m) puhpah dad

papel (m) puhpehl paper

papelaria puhpluhreeuh stationers

papel de cigarros (m) puhpehl de seegahrroosh cigarette papers

papel higiénico (m) puhpehl eezhee-ehneekoo toilet paper

para puhruh towards/for

Parabéns!
puhruhbãysh!
Congratulations!; Happy birthday!

paragem (f) puhrahzhäy stop

paragem de autocarros (f) puhrahzhäy de owtohkahrroosh bus stop

parar puhrahr to stop

Pare!
pahr!
Stop!

parede (f) puhred wall (inside)

parlamento puhrluhmengtoo parliament

parque (m) pahrk park (garden)

parque de estacionamento (m) pahrk de shtuhsiwnuhmengtoo park (car park)

parque nacional (m) pahrk nuhsiwnahl national park

parte (f) pahrt part

partida puhrteeduh departure

partido político puhrteedoo pooleeteekoo party (politics)

partido/a puhrteedoo/uh broken

partilhar puhrteelyahr to share (with)

partilhar um quarto puhrteelyahr oong kwartoo to share a dorm

partir puhrteer to break/depart

Páscoa pahshkwuh Easter

passado puhsahdoo past

passageiro/a puhsuhzhayroo/ uh passenger

passagem (f) puhsahzhäy pass

Passagem de Ano (f) puhsahzhäy duhnoo New Year's Eve

pássaro pahsuhroo bird

passeio puhsayoo a stroll/walk

passivo/a puhseevoo/uh passive

pasta de dentes (f) pahshtuh de dengtesh toothpaste

patrão/patroo puhtrõw/ puhtrouh employer

paz (f) pahsh peace

PBX (m) pebesheehs telephone office

pé (m) peh foot

peão peeõw pedestrian

peça de teatro (f) pehsuh de tyahtroo play (theatre)

pecado pkahdoo sin

pedido pdeedoo order (in a restaurant)

pedinte (m/f) pdingt beggar

pedir pdeer to order (in a restaurant)

pedir emprestado pdeer engpreshtahdoo to borrow

pedir (uma coisa) pdeer (oomuh koyzuh) to ask (for something)

pedra pehdruh stone

pegadas (f) pehgahduhsh track (footprints)

peito paytoo chest

PORTUGUESE – ENGLISH

peixaria payshuhreeuh
fish shop

peixe (m) paysh
fish (alive or as food)

pele (f) pehl skin

pensamento pengsuhmengtoo
thought

pensar pengsahr to think

pensionista (m/f)
pengsiwneeshtuh
pensioner

pensos higiénicos (m)
pengsoosh eezheen-
ehneekoosh
sanitary napkins

pente (m) pengt comb

pequeno-almoço (m)
pkenoo-ahlmosoo breakfast

pequeno/a pkenoo/uh
little (small)

perda pehrduh loss

perder perder to lose

perdoar perdwar to forgive

pergunta pergoongtuh question

perigoso/a preegozoo/
preegohzuh dangerous

período preeoodoo menstruation

permitir permeeteer to allow

perna pehrnuh leg

perto pehrtoo near

pesado/a pzahdoo/uh heavy

pesar pzahr to weigh

peso pezoo weight

pessoa pesouh person

petróleo petrohliw oil (crude)

picada peekahduh bite (insect)

picante peekangt spicy (hot)

Pílula peelooluh the Pill

pimenta peemengtuh pepper

pintar pingtahr to paint

pintor/pintora pingtor/
pingtoruh painter

pintura pingtooruh
painting (the art)

Pira-te!
peerultl!
Get lost!

piscina peeshseenuh
pool (swimming)

pneus (m) pne-wsh tyres

pobre (m/f) pohbr poor

poder (m)
pooder
power; to be able; can

poesia pwezeeuh poetry

pólen (m) pohläy pollen

polícia (m/f) pooleesyuh
police (officer)

política pooleeteekuh politics

poluição (f) poolwisõw pollution

pontapé (m) pongtuhpeh kick

ponte (f) pongt bridge

pôr por to put

por cento poor sengtoo per cent

pôr do sol (m) por doo sohl
sunset

porque poork because

porquê poorke why

porta pohrtuh door

portão poortõw gate

porto portoo port/harbour

possível pooseevehl possible

postal (m) pooshtahl postcard

posto de controlo poshtoo de
kongtroloo checkpoint

posto de turismo poshtoo de
tooreezhmoo tourist information office

pouco pokoo a little (amount)

pousada da juventude (f)
pozahduh duh zhoovengtood
youth hostel

povo povoo people

praça prahsuh square (in town)

praça de táxis (f) prahsuh de
tahkseesh taxi stand

praia praiuh beach

prata (de) prahtuh (de) of silver

prateleiras (f) pruhtlayruhsh
shelves

prato prahtoo plate

preço presoo price

prédio prehdiw building

preferir prefreer to prefer

prenda prengduh gift

preocupado/a
preeohkoopahdoo/uh
worried

preparar prepuhrahr to prepare

presente (m) prezengt present
(time/gift)

presidente (m/f) przeedengt
president

presidente da câmara (m/f)
przeedengt duh kuhmuhruh
mayor

preso (m/f) prezoo prisoner

pressão (f) prsõw pressure

presunto przoongtoo ham

preto/a pretoo/uh black

prevenção (f) prvengsõw prevention

primavera preemuhvehruh
spring (season)

primeiro/a preemayroo/uh first

prisão (f) preezõw jail

prisão de ventre (f) preezõw de
vengtr constipation

privado/a preevahdoo/uh
private

procurar prokoorahr to look for

produzir proodoozeer to produce

professor/professora proofsor/
proofsoruh teacher

profissão (f) proofeesõw profession

profundo/a proofoongdoo/uh
deep

PORTUGUESE – ENGLISH

promessa proomehsuh promise

pronto/a prongtoo/uh ready

proteger prootzher protect

provar proovahr to try

próximo/a prohseemoo/uh next

pulga poolguh flea

puro/a pooroo/uh pure

puxar pooshahr to pull

Q

quadrado/a kwuhdrahdoo/uh
square (adj)

quadro kwadroo painting

qualidade (f) kwuhleedahde
quality

qualificações (f)
kwuhleefeekuhsõys
qualifications

quando kwangdoo when

quarentena kwuhrengtenuh
quarantine

quarta-feira kwartuh fayruh
Wednesday

quarto kwartoo (bed)room/
quarter

quarto duplo kwartoo dooploo
double room

quarto individual (m) kwartoo
ingdeeveedwal single room

quase kwaz almost

que ke what

queijo kayzhoo cheese

queimadura do sol (f)
kaymuhdooruh doo sohl
sunburn

quem kãy who

quente kengt hot/warm

querer krer to want

questão (f) keshtow
question (topic)

questionar keshtiwnahr to
question

quilo(grama) (m)
keeloo(gruhmuh) kilogram

quilómetro keelohmtroo
kilometre

quinta kingtuh farm

quinta-feira kingtuh fayruh
Thursday

R

ramo rruhmoo branch

rapariga rruhpuhreeguh girl

rapaz (m) rruhpahzh boy

rasgar rruhzhgahr to tear (rip)

ratazana rruhtuhzuhnuh rat

razão (f) rruhzõw reason

receber rrseber to receive

recente(mente) rrsengt(mengt)
recent(ly)

recibo rrseeboo receipt

reciclável rrseeklahvehl
recyclable

D
I
C
T
I
O
N
A
R
Y

313

recolha de bagagens (f)
rrkolyuh de buhgahzhãysh
baggage claim

recolher rrkoolyer to pick up

recomendar rrkoomengdahr
to recommend

reconhecer rrkoonyser
to recognise

recusar rrkoozahr to refuse

redondo/a rrdongdoo/uh round

reembolsar rre-engbolsahr to
refund

reembolso rre-engbolsoo refund

refugiado/a rrfoozhyahdoo/uh
refugee

regional rrezhiwnahl regional

regras (f) rehgruhsh rules

relação (f) rrluhsõw relationship

relaxar rrelahshahr to relax

religião (f) rrleezheeõw religion

relógio rrelohzhiw clock/watch

relva rehlvuh grass (garden)

remar rrmahr rowing

remédio rremehdiw
drug (medicine)

renda rrengduh rent

rentabilidade (f)
rrengtuhbeeleedahd
profitability

repetir rrepteer to repeat

reserva rrzehrvuh reservation

reservar rrzervahr
to reserve/book

respeito rreshpaytoo respect

respirar rreshpeerahr to breathe

resposta rreshpohshtuh answer

restaurante (m)
rreshtowrangt
restaurant

resto rehshtoo rest (what's left)

rever rrver to check

revisor/revisora
rrveezor/rrveezoruh
ticket collector

revista rrveeshtuh magazine

rico/a rreekoo/uh rich/wealthy

rio reeoo river

risco rreeshkoo risk/scratch

ritmo rreetmoo rhythm

rocha rrohshuh rock

roda rrohduh wheel

rolo de fotografias (m)
rroloo de footoogruhfeeuhsh
film (for camera)

romance (m)
rroomangs
novel (n)

rotunda rrootoongduh
roundabout

roubar rrobahr to steal

roupa rropuh clothing

rua rroouh street

ruínas (f) rrooeenuhsh ruins

PORTUGUESE – ENGLISH

S

sábado sahbuhdoo Saturday

saber suhber to know

sabonete (m) suhboonet soap

saboroso/a suhboorozoo/ suhboorohzuh tasty

saca-rolhas (m) sahkuh-rrolyuhsh bottle opener

saco-cama (m) sahkookuhmuh sleeping bag

Saída. suheeduh Way Out.

sair com suheer kong to go out with

sal (m) sahl salt

sala de espera sahluh de shpehruh waiting room; transit lounge

salário suhlahriw salary

saldos sahldoosh sale (bargains)

saliência suhlee-engsyuh ledge

saltar sahltahr to jump

salvar sahlvahr to save (rescue)

sangue (m) sang-g blood

santo/a sangtoo/uh saint

sapataria suhpuhtuhreeuh shoe shop

sapatos (m) suhpahtoosh shoes

(ter) saudades ter suhwdahdesh to miss (feel absence)

saúde (f) suhood health

se se if

secar (roupa) skahr (rropuh) to dry (clothes)

(com) sede kong sed thirsty

seguinte sgingt next

seguir sgeer to follow

segunda-feira sgoongduh fayruh Monday

segundo sgoongdoo second (time)

seguro sgooroo insurance

seguro/a sgooroo/uh safe (adj)

selos (m) seloosh stamps

sem say without

semáforos (m) smahfooroosh traffic lights

semana (passada) smuhnuh (puhsahduh) (last) week

semana que vem (f) smuhnuh ke vay next week

sem chumbo say shoongboo unleaded

semelhante smelyangt similar

sempre sengpr always

sensato/a sengsahtoo/uh sensible/wise

sensibilidade (f) sengseebeeleedahd film speed

sentar-se sengtahrs to sit

sentença sengtengsuh sentence (prison)

sentimentos (m) sengteemengtoosh feelings

sentir sengteer to feel

separar spuhrahr to separate

ser ser to be

série (f) sehree-e series

seropositivo/a sehrohpoozeeteevoo/uh HIV positive

serra sehrruh mountain range

serviço serveesoo service (assistence)

serviço de limpeza (m) serveesoo de lingpezuh cleaning service

sexo (seguro) sehksoo (sgooroo) (safe) sex

sexta-feira suhshtuh-fayruh Friday

SIDA (m) seeduh AIDS

silencioso/a seelengseeozoo/ seelengseeohzuh quiet (adj)

simpático/a singpahteekoo/uh nice/friendly

simples (m/f) singplesh plain (simple)

sinal (m) seenahl a sign

sintético/a singtehteekoo/uh synthetic

só soh only

sobre sobr over/on

sobretudo soobretoodoo overcoat

sobreviver soobreveever to survive

sócio/a sohsiw/yuh member

Socorro! sookorroo! Help!

sofrer soofrer to suffer

sogro/a sogroo/sohgruh father/mother-in-law

sol (m) sohl sun

sólido/a sohleedoo/uh solid

solteiro/a soltayroo/uh single (person)

som (m) song sound

sombra songbruh shade/shadow

sondagens (f) songdahzhäysh polls

sonhar soonyahr to dream

(com) sono kong sonoo sleepy

sorrir soorreer to smile

sorte (f) sohrt luck/chance

sozinho/a sohzeenyoo/uh alone

standard stangdahrt standard (usual)

subir soobeer to climb

suborno soobornoo a bribe

subsídio de desemprego soobseediw de dzengpregoo unemployment benefit

subúrbio sooboorbiw suburb

subúrbios de (m) sooboorbiwzh de suburbs of

PORTUGUESE – ENGLISH

sucesso soosehsoo success

suficiente soofeesee-engt enough

sujo/a soozhoo/uh dirty

sul (m) sool south

sumo soomoo juice

surdo/a soordoo/uh deaf

surpresa soorprezuh a surprise

T

tabacaria tuhbuhkuhreeuh
tobacco kiosk

Taça do Mundo (f) tahsuh doo
moongdoo World Cup

tacho tahshoo pan

talvez tahlvesh maybe

tamanho tuhmuhnyoo size (of
anything)

também tangbáy also/too

também não tangbáy nõw
neither

tampa tangpuh plug (bath)

tampões tangpõysh tampons

tapete (m) tuhpet rug

tarde tahrd afternoon/late

taxa de câmbio (f) tuhshuh de
kangbiw exchange rate

taxa do aeroporto (f)
tahshuh doo uhehrohportoo
airport tax

teatro tyahtroo theatre

teatro clássico tyatroo
klahseekoo classical theatre

teatro de ópera (m)
tyahtroo de ohpruh
opera house

teclado tehklahdoo keyboard

técnica tehkneekuh technique

telemóvel (m) tehlehmohvehl
mobile phone

telenovela tehlehnoovehluh
soap opera

televisão (f) tleveezõw television

temperatura lengpruhtooruh
temperature (weather)

tempestade (f) tengpeshtahd
storm

templo tengploo temple

tempo tengpoo time/weather

a tempo uh tengpoo on time

tenda tengduh tent

tensão arterial (f)
tengsow uhrtryahl
blood pressure

tensão baixa/alta (f)
tengsõw baishuh/ahltuh
low/high blood pressure

tensão pré-menstrual (f)
tengsõw prehmengshtrwahl
pre-menstrual tension

tentar tengtahr to try/attempt

ter ter to have

ter saudades
ter suhwdahdesh
to miss (feel absence)

terça-feira tersuh fayruh Tuesday

terceiro/a tersayroo/uh third

terra tehrruh Earth/soil/land

terrível (m/f) terreevehl terrible

tesoura tzoruh scissors

teste (m) tehsht test

testes nucleares tehshtesh nookliarsh nuclear testing

tímido/a teemeedoo/uh shy

tio/a teeoo/uh uncle/aunt

típico/a teepeekoo/uh typical

tipo teepoo kind (type)

tirar fotografias teerahr footoogruhfeeuhsh to take photographs

toalha twalyuh towel

tocar tookahr to touch; to play (music)

todo todoo whole

todos os dias todoosh oozh deeuhsh every day

tomada toomahduh plug (electricity)

tomar banho toomahr buhnyoo to wash (to bathe)

tomar conta de toomahr kongtuh de to look after

toque (do telefone) (m) tohk (doo tlefohn) ring (of phone)

torrada toorrahduh toast

torre (f) torr tower

tosse (f) tohs a cough

trabalhar truhbuhlyahr to work

trabalho truhbahlyo work

traduzir truhdoozeer to translate

tráfego trahfgoo traffic

transpirar trangshpeerahr to perspire

trazer truhzer to bring

tribunal (m) treeboonahl court (legal)

triste treesht sad

troco trokoo change (coins)

tudo toodoo all

turista (m/f) tooreeshtuh tourist

U

último/a oolteemoo/uh last

uma dúzia oomuh doozyuh a dozen

uma vez oomuh vesh once; one time

único/a ooneekoo/uh single (unique)

útil ooteel useful

uvas (f) oovuhsh grapes

V

vaca vahkuh cow

vacina vuhseenuh vaccination

vagão-cama (m) vuhgõwkuhmuh sleeping car

318

vagão-restaurante (m) vuhgõw rreshtowrangt dining car

vago/a vahgoo/uh vacant

valioso/a vuhleeozoo/vuhleeohzuh valuable

valor (m) vuhlor value/worth

Vamos. vuhmoosh Let's go.

vários/várias vahriwsh/ vahriyuhsh several

vaso vahzoo pot (ceramic)

vazio/a vuhzeeoo/uh empty

vegetação (f) vzhetuhsõw vegetation

vegetariano/a vzhetuhreeuhnoo/uh vegetarian

vela vehluh candle

velho/a vehlyoo/uh old

velocidade (f) vlooseedahd speed

vencedor/vencedora (m) vengsdor/vengsdoruh winner

(à) venda (ah) vengduh (for) sale

vender vengdar to sell

veneração (f) vneruhsõw worship

ventilador (m) vengteeluhdor · fan (machine)

vento vengtoo wind

ventoinha vengtooeenyuh fan (machine)

ver ver to see

verão vrõw summer

verdade (f) verdahd truth

vergonha vergonyuh embarassment

vestiários (m) veshteeahriwsh changing rooms

vestíbulo veshteebooloo foyer

vestido vshteedoo dress (n)

vestir veshteer to wear

via aérea veeuh uhehryuh air mail

viagem (f) vyazhãy journey

viajar vyuhzhahr to travel

vida veeduh life

vinha veenyuh vineyard

vinho (do Porto) veenyoo (doo portoo) (port) wine

viola viohluh guitar

violação (sexual) (f) viwluhsõw (sehkswal) rape

vir veer to come

visitar veezeetahr to visit

vista panorâmica veeshtuh puhnooruhmeekuh view (scenic)

visto veeshtoo visa

viver veever
  to live (somewhere)

voltar voltahr to return

voo vo-oo flight

votar vootahr to vote

voz (f) vohsh voice

X

xadrez (m) shuhdresh chess

Z

zangado/a zang-gahdoo/uh
  angry

zodíaco zoodeeuhkoo zodiac

PORTUGUESE FINDER

F
I
N
D
E
R

F
I
N
D
E
R

Phrasebooks

L onely Planet phrasebooks are packed with essential words and phrases to help travellers communicate with the locals. With colour tabs for quick reference, an extensive vocabulary and use of script, these handy pocket-sized language guides cover day to day travel situations.

- handy pocket-sized books
- easy to understand Pronunciation chapter
- clear & comprehensive Grammar chapter
- romanisation alongside script to allow ease of pronunciation
- script throughout so users can point to phrases for every situation
- full of cultural information and tips for the traveller

'... vital for a real DIY spirit and attitude in language learning'

– Backpacker

'The phrasebooks have good cultural backgrounders and offer solid advice for challenging situations in remote locations'

– San Francisco Examiner

Australian (Australian English, Aboriginal & Torres Strait languages) • Baltic (Estonian, Latvian, Lithuanian) • Bengali • Brazilian • British (English, dialects, Scottish Gaelic, Welsh) • Burmese • Cantonese • Central Asia (Kazakh, Kyrgyz, Pashto, Tajik, Tashkorghani, Turkmen, Uyghur, Uzbek & others) • Central Europe (Czech, German, Hungarian, Polish, Slovak, Slovene) • Costa Rica Spanish • Czech • Eastern Europe (Albanian, Bulgarian, Croatian, Czech, Hungarian, Macedonian, Polish, Romanian, Serbian, Slovak, Slovene) • East Timor (Tetun, Portuguese) • Egyptian Arabic • Ethiopian (Amharic) • Europe (Basque, Catalan, Dutch, French, German, Greek, Irish, Italian, Maltese, Portuguese, Scottish Gaelic, Spanish, Turkish, Welsh) • Farsi (Persian) • Fijian • French • German • Greek • Hebrew • Hill Tribes (Lahu, Akha, Lisu, Mong, Mien & others) • Hindi & Urdu • Indonesian • Italian • Japanese • Korean • Lao • Latin American Spanish • Malay • Mandarin • Mongolian • Moroccan Arabic • Nepali • Pidgin • Pilipino (Tagalog) • Polish • Portuguese • Quechua • Russian • Scandinavian (Danish, Faroese, Finnish, Icelandic, Norwegian, Swedish) • South-East Asia (Burmese, Indonesian, Khmer, Lao, Malay, Pilipino (Tagalog), Thai, Vietnamese) • South Pacific (Fijian, Hawaiian, Kanak languages, Maori, Niuean, Rapanui, Rarotongan Maori, Samoan, Tahitian, Tongan & others) • Spanish (Castilian, also includes Catalan, Galician & Basque) • Sinhala • Swahili • Thai • Tibetan • Turkish • Ukrainian • USA (US English, vernacular, Native American, Hawaiian) • Vietnamese

AFRICA Africa on a shoestring • Cairo • Cape Town • East Africa • Egypt • Ethiopia, Eritrea & Djibouti • The Gambia & Senegal • Healthy Travel Africa • Kenya • Malawi • Morocco • Mozambique • Read This First: Africa • South Africa, Lesotho & Swaziland • Southern Africa • Southern Africa Road Atlas • Tanzania, Zanzibar & Pemba • Trekking in East Africa • Tunisia • Watching Wildlife East Africa • Watching Wildlife Southern Africa • West Africa • World Food Morocco • Zimbabwe, Botswana & Namibia

AUSTRALIA & THE PACIFIC Aboriginal Australia & the Torres Strait Islands • Auckland • Australia • Australia Road Atlas • Bushwalking in Australia • Cycling Australia • Cycling New Zealand • Fiji • Healthy Travel Australia, NZ and the Pacific • Islands of Australia's Great Barrier Reef • Melbourne • Micronesia • New Caledonia • New South Wales & the ACT • New Zealand • Northern Territory • Outback Australia • Out to Eat – Melbourne • Out to Eat – Sydney • Papua New Guinea • Queensland • Rarotonga & the Cook Islands • Samoa • Solomon Islands • South Australia • South Pacific • Sydney • Sydney Condensed • Tahiti & French Polynesia • Tasmania • Tonga • Tramping in New Zealand • Vanuatu • Victoria • Walking in Australia • Watching Wildlife Australia • Western Australia

CENTRAL AMERICA & THE CARIBBEAN Bahamas, Turks & Caicos • Baja California • Bermuda • Central America on a shoestring • Costa Rica • Cuba • Dominican Republic & Haiti • Eastern Caribbean • Guatemala • Guatemala, Belize & Yucatán: La Ruta Maya • Havana • Healthy Travel Central & South America • Jamaica • Mexico • Mexico City • Panama • Puerto Rico • Read This First: Central & South America • World Food Mexico • Yucatán

EUROPE Amsterdam • Amsterdam Condensed • Andalucía • Austria • Barcelona • Belgium & Luxembourg • Berlin • Britain • Brussels, Bruges & Antwerp • Budapest • Canary Islands • Central Europe • Copenhagen • Corfu & the Ionians • Corsica • Crete • Crete Condensed • Croatia • Cycling Britain • Cycling France • Cyprus • Czech & Slovak Republics • Denmark • Dublin • Eastern Europe • Edinburgh • England • Estonia, Latvia & Lithuania • Europe on a shoestring • Finland • Florence • France • Frankfurt Condensed • Georgia, Armenia & Azerbaijan • Germany • Greece • Greek Islands • Hungary • Iceland, Greenland & the Faroe Islands • Ireland • Istanbul • Italy • Krakow • Lisbon • The Loire • London • London Condensed • Madrid • Malta • Mediterranean Europe • Milan, Turin & Genoa • Moscow • Mozambique • Munich • The Netherlands • Normandy • Norway • Out to Eat – London • Paris • Paris Condensed • Poland • Portugal • Prague • Provence & the Côte d'Azur • Read This First: Europe • Rhodes & the Dodecanese • Romania & Moldova • Rome • Rome Condensed • Russia, Ukraine & Belarus • Scandinavian & Baltic Europe • Scotland • Sicily • Slovenia • South-West France • Spain • St Petersburg • Sweden • Switzerland • Trekking in Spain • Tuscany • Venice • Vienna • Walking in Britain • Walking in France • Walking in Ireland • Walking in Italy • Walking in Spain • Walking in Switzerland • Western Europe • World Food France • World Food Ireland • World Food Italy • World Food Spain